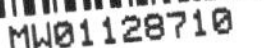
MW01128710

CITY
DHARMA

UNCORRECTED PROOF

CITY DHARMA

KEEPING YOUR COOL IN THE CHAOS

ARTHUR JEON

HARMONY BOOKS NEW YORK

Published by Harmony Books, New York, New York. Member of the Crown Publishing Group, a division of Random House, Inc.
www.crownpublishing.com

Printed in the United States of America

Design by Karen Minster

Library of Congress Cataloging-in-Publication Data
Jeon, Arthur.
City dharma: keeping your cool in the chaos/Arthur Jeon.
1. Buddhism—Psychology. 2. Emotions—Religious aspects—Buddhism. 3. Spiritual life—Buddhism. I. Title.
BQ4570.P76J46 2004
294.3'444—dc22
2003019823

ISBN 1-4000-4908-3

10 9 8 7 6 5 4 3 2 1

First Edition

For

CATHERINE INGRAM,

my cherished teacher

For

HELENA KRIEL,

my favorite dharma buddy

For all my other teachers,
intentional and otherwise

CONTENTS

ACKNOWLEDGMENTS

Writing a book doesn't happen in a vacuum. It requires support in the way of feedback, guidance, and creating the space to write. This book couldn't have been written without substantial help in different areas from many people.

Catherine Ingram, my teacher who introduced me to the dharma, is the reason this book got written. Catherine, I hope to travel down the path into old age with you as my dear friend.

Helena Kriel, what can I say to the sister I never had? You have been instrumental in your editing and support, as well as my favorite person with whom to have insane spiritual discussions. May we be on the porch with all our friends, flapping our gums about the dharma, when we're all ninety years old!

The generous and ever youthful Maja Kriel was crucial in providing me three months of sublime freedom in Johannesburg, South Africa, in which to write the first draft of this book, free from the worries of quotidian life. I will never forget this gift, the stimulating discussions, and all the beautiful food! May your kitchen be crumb-free forever! The rest of the Kriel family, David Zeffert, Ross and Lexi Kriel, and of course Drumie, provided valuable sounding boards and support at crucial moments, as well as tolerating my home invasion with good cheer. Much gratitude to you all.

Mom and Dad, you have supported me through the years and the tears and the many different and challenging roads I've chosen. I wouldn't be who I am without you, and I love you both. To Evan and the rest of my family, thank you for your continued encouragement.

Lea Russo literally picked me up off the floor after my computer was stolen, bought a scanner, and helped scan in the hard copy of the manuscript, not to mention editing the book after it was written. Lea, you have been irreplaceable in getting this book done.

Andy Stern and Damon Lindelof, you both provided crucial support at critical times without even a moment's hesitation or question—generosity in action. Thank you from the bottom of my heart.

Eileen Cope, you saw the potential in this book where others didn't and then went out and got me a two-book deal, all the while making it seem easy. Not only are you responsive, competent, and fun, but I feel completely secure with you at the helm.

Teryn Johnson, you are a brilliant, diligent editor and a joy to work with. You honed the book into its final form. I look forward to the next book just so we can spend more time together!

Special thanks to Linda Loewenthal, who first brought the book into Harmony, and Shaye Areheart, who has so competently taken over the helm. For the rest of the team at Harmony, including my publicists, Darlene Faster and Katherine Beitner, thank you for your care and competence.

To all my other friends who gave me support and feedback and love during this journey, you are family. Thank you.

Finally, acknowledgment must be paid to the teachers Dr. Finklestein, Ph.D., D.O.G., and Dr. Omar Omario, M.D., Ph.D., K.A.T. as well as Sri Sri Bushilinka, spiritual avatar. You all continue to teach me the meaning of the words "playful presence."

CITY
DHARMA

INTRODUCTION

> The real voyage of discovery consists not in seeing new landscapes, but in having new eyes.
>
> —MARCEL PROUST

I walk toward my apartment on a hot spring night. Santa Ana winds bend the slender palm trees on my street, shaking loose the brown fronds clustered at the top. They twirl down like scythes, beautiful and from the wrong angle dangerous, making a crunching sound as they hit the ground.

It's one of those nights in Los Angeles when the air is so dry and breathless, it feels as though an earthquake or a serial killer could be the nightcap for the evening. I smile at the thought: the mind is such a trip, and I'm happy to just observe it.

I've spent a year working on *City Dharma*, and I'm halfway through the first rewrite, a month away from handing it in to my publisher. The book is still a work in progress, but the proverbial light at the end of the tunnel, a tiny pinprick in what was total darkness, has appeared. It's the end of an internal and external journey that included lots of travel, reading, and reflection. I lived for a couple of months in Johannesburg, South Africa, adding research from what is considered to be one of the most dangerous cities on the planet.

I climb the stairs to my apartment, back from a birthday party that ran late, and unlock my front door. My cat greets me with a customary *yeeeeoooow*. Omar's a big tabby, with a head like a melon and a personality that's hilarious, more dog than cat.

Starving, I head toward the kitchen and make a veggie burger. Omar stays very close and is unusually talkative. He begins to howl.

"What's up with you?" I ask, scratching his head. He's inconsolable, and I think it's the windy heat, although perhaps it's something else. Thoughts of an earthquake again flit across my mind.

I take the veggie burger upstairs, heading toward my office and CNN. The second war against Iraq is six days old and turning ugly. As I approach my office I can't see the rug, an antique kilim that was part of my great-grandmother's dowry. Omar must have bunched it in the corner during one of his hunts for a pen to gnaw on.

When I walk into the office I see that the rug is gone. The computer is gone. And, inexplicably, a $30 Ikea chair is gone. Shaking, I put down the food. *Shit . . . shit! No no no no no!* I try the back door. It's shut but unlocked.

I am stunned, and for a split second my awareness collapses around me like a deck of cards. I call a friend and burst into tears.

"It's gone. The book. It's gone. The zip drive is gone. . . . I've got a hard copy, but it's two months old. I'm screwed! I'm totally screwed!"

"Wait a minute," she said. "Weren't you e-mailing it to yourself?"

"Yes. But it dropped off AOL yesterday. They only hold it twenty-seven days. I was going to e-mail it again tomorrow after I finished this chapter. It's gone!"

I am hysterical. The laptop was old enough to be a paperweight, but it held my entire intellectual history, including scripts, essays, poems, love letters, e-mails, theses . . . everything. But most importantly, it held *City Dharma*. The book is due in a month and I am behind, and I know the ideas I wrote over the past two months are gone forever.

I have often said that if my apartment was on fire, I would grab Omar and my computer. The rest I didn't care about. I have some nice stuff, but it was just stuff, never a priority, always replaceable. The only things important to me were the ideas on that computer.

Now I am getting a horrible—and in my mind unnecessary—reminder of the impermanence of everything. City dharma indeed, but I didn't need to live it!

This lingering identification surfaces, and I am forced to confront it: "I'm a writer, see . . . there's my writing." Now I have just lost the only thing besides people that has any meaning to me: everything I'd written in the past ten years. And my book is gone. My book is gone!

So much of life can be an almost systematic denial or loss of everything we deeply desire. A thought flashes through my mind: one of the guiding principles in my book is learning to realize that freedom is indeed free, not dependent on any externals. That to lose or be denied everything I desired is to be offered the opportunity to learn the spiritual lesson that nothing is necessary for happiness.

Fine. But it's one thing to say that, another to live it. In confronting this loss, I am momentarily devastated.

It won't be until much later that I realize this loss is a final shedding and a positive experience.

The police come, a report is filed. There is no sign of forced entry, and the police officer theorizes it might have been personal. How many people know about the key hidden outside? Lots of friends. What is my relationship with my ex-girlfriend? Somewhat acrimonious, I say, but not felonious. The officer concludes it was probably a transient who saw me hide the key. Or the door was left unlocked by accident and somebody who was jiggling doorknobs took advantage of it—a crime of opportunity.

"But an Ikea chair? An old rug that looked worthless? A completely outdated computer while leaving an expensive Palm Pilot right next to it? It makes no sense."

"I got a call last week where the only thing they took was the closet door. None of it makes sense," the amiable cop says. "Nothing to do but get on with it,"

None of it makes sense; get on with it. He is right, both practically and spiritually. This is a terrible loss, but in comparison to what is happening around the world, it is a piddle. I take a deep breath and the moment springs back to life, no longer crushed into a horrible box in my mind. Eight years ago an event like this would have flattened me for months, creating story upon story. Now, after the initial shock, it is gone. The awareness has grown smooth enough that the mind, ever vigilant to assert its primacy, can't get any traction.

After a week of dealing with the insurance company, buying a new computer, loading software, and scanning an old version of the book into it, one task at a time, I am starting over. I am rewriting from the beginning what was essentially notes of the book to come, and have let go of the six completed chapters, now lost forever.

They are gone.

What is here is right now.

WHEN I WENT TO MY FIRST dharma talk in 1995, I was very caught up in the highs and lows of my dramatic life. If I thought I was doing well, given the external indicators of money, girlfriend, and a lucrative job, then I was happy. If these externals took a turn for the worse, then I was unhappy.

Like so many people, I rode the roller coaster of my life, caught up in the story of me—my successes and my failures. It was exhausting and, like Neo in the Matrix before he takes the red pill, I had a feeling that something was missing. I had been reading, practicing yoga, and attending different spiritual gatherings for a long time, searching for answers. Yet I was dissatisfied—there must be more to life. There had to be a spiritual way to be in the world that wasn't dependent upon blind faith, superstition, or dualistic religions, but I hadn't found it. Although some had aspects that resonated, they all seemed to ask me to check my reason and logic at the door—something I wasn't willing to do.

All that changed when I met my teacher Catherine Ingram. Catherine came from a lineage of Advaita Vedanta that started with Ramana Maharshi and continued through H. W. L Poonja, two famous Indian masters. She had been studying Buddhism for seventeen years before dropping it and waking up with Poonjaji.

It was in Catherine's dharma dialogues and retreats that I was first exposed to the teachings that would change my life. With endless patience and kindness, she answered every question. But unlike in the Matrix, she didn't offer a red pill; instead she offered the dharma. And after I accepted this gift, it became impossible for me to look at the world in the same way.

For many years I attended silent retreats and dharma dialogues held by Catherine. They were beautiful experiences that gently guided me toward wakefulness. Eventually she inspired me to begin teaching, and I started holding my own dharma conversations under her generous sponsorship. It was out of these dharma conversations that the idea for this book was born.

Most of the concepts I first heard from Catherine, and without her this book wouldn't exist. I sincerely hope it honors both her and the dharma.

WHEN I FIRST STARTED conceiving the idea of *City Dharma,* it was the summer prior to the terrorist attacks of September 11, 2001. My intention was to discuss being peaceful and awake within the challenges of modern city life, coping with all that is stressful, irritating, and occasionally dangerous. How do you maintain balance in an environment that promotes imbalance, comparison, and competition? Everything from driving a car to dealing with noisy neighbors is either a burden or an opportunity, depending upon one's point of view, and I wanted to illuminate city life from the point of view of the dharma.

I also wanted to write a "spiritual book" that is informal and gritty and that goes places other spiritual books shun—something out of my own experience that would be practical for those who don't necessarily consider themselves "spiritual." I also wanted to write it not as a teacher but as somebody who is a fellow traveler, perhaps further down the path than some and not as far as others, but, I hope, relevant to all.

After the tragic events of September 11 our world here in America changed. Certainly people have more important things to be stressed about during this time of war and terrorism than the daily annoyances of life. When more than three thousand people die sudden and horrible deaths while simply at work or flying in a plane, being cut off in traffic shouldn't seem like that big a deal.

One potent result of September 11 is that people are questioning everything, including their most basic assumptions about whether they will make it through the day and what that day should be about. With sudden death made real to friends and colleagues no different from themselves, people's illusion of invulnerability has been shattered. With death as an immediate possibility rather than a distant (and much denied) abstraction, life takes on a different meaning. The eternal lesson of impermanence has been driven home in financial ways with the contraction of the stock market and corporate debacles such as Enron and WorldCom making jobs and life savings disappear overnight. Tomorrow isn't a guarantee. It never was, but now we feel it on a deeper level.

As I watch what is happening here in America and around the world, I feel that *City Dharma* is even more relevant. Because we are all in the process of reevaluating what is important and what is real, we are looking for guidance. We now see the end result of belief systems run amok. We have witnessed the carnage of perverted spirituality, whether it's rampant sexual abuse in the Catholic Church, born-again antiabortion fundamentalists who shoot and kill doctors, or terrorists following their version of Islam. Increasingly the schism seems to be between the modernists and fundamentalists of all stripes, between those who can accept the world as it changes and those who cling with great fear to a past that never really existed.

As a result, many of us are looking for a different philosophy besides blind belief to frame our experience. Intuitively we know that all belief systems, whether benign or not, need to be examined. Indeed, the very dynamic of belief should be held under a microscope. Is humankind ready to evolve out of belief, superstition, and faith? What will replace it?

This, in part, is what *City Dharma* is about—these weighty issues examined from the daily and accessible vantage of city and suburban life. Although we live in a time when turning on the news fills us with dread, divisiveness is the national language, and the simple act of opening a letter can result in death, this hasn't eliminated the daily stresses and challenges of modern life—what I would call microstresses. These daily stresses have only gotten worse under the apocalyptic events facing us today. They haven't been eclipsed; they've been compounded by the threat of war, global terrorism, and new diseases such as SARS.

In addition to the looming horror of more war and possible future terrorist attacks, we live in a time when 70 percent of Americans feel "burned out" and "used up" by their jobs. As much as we are told the enemy is without, it is actually within. Stress is high as people juggle work and family obligations, and 80 percent of people report feeling like they have too little time. People are sleeping less and doing more, fueled by an IV drip of caffeine.

Road rage is at an all-time high; patience and perspective are scarce commodities. Recently a man was sentenced to three years in prison for throwing a woman's dog into oncoming cars during a dispute. A suburban father beat a man to death in front of eleven children in an altercation over a hockey match. These are not monsters; they are normal citizens who snapped under some internal strain.

As times get tough and Americans, even though hung over from a decade of unparalleled consumerism and facing an uncertain future, make no effort to break the habit of striving for more and more, the following statistics will surely get worse:

- Forty-three percent of adults suffer adverse health effects due to stress, which has been linked to the leading causes of death—heart disease, cancer, lung ailments, accidents, cirrhosis, and suicide.
- Up to 90 percent of all visits to primary-care physicians are for stress-related complaints or disorders.
- On the average workday, up to a million workers stay home because of stress-related problems. One large corpora-

tion estimates that more than 60 percent of all absences are attributable to stress.

All in all, job stress costs industry $300 billion each year in absenteeism, diminished productivity, employee turnover, and direct medical and legal expenses. Some estimates say that figure will rise another $100 billion due to the increased anxiety people are now feeling. The murder and spousal abuse rate has gone up. Antidepressant sales are up 30 percent, and people, pushed to their breaking point, are drinking more and engaging in more casual sex. This trend is unlikely to change as economic times get tougher and war or further terrorist attacks play out. Even during good times, modern life just seems to be accelerating out of control.

So the challenges of leading a wakeful life haven't diminished; they've actually gotten more intense. The impulse to "check out" of the present moment using any number of distractions, projections, or addictions grows with every viewing of the nightly news. In addition to all the usual suspects, radical belief systems and superstition are on the rise.

So what are we to do? Move? Run for the hills? Will this bring peace of mind? Will this offer us a sense of connection and spirituality? Is it even practical?

"It's easy to feel peace, to feel connected and to experience the presence of God or consciousness while sitting on a mountain, in a yoga class, or on a silent retreat," an earnest young woman commented one evening. "But how does one keep that awareness in the hustle of daily life? In living and working in a city? It seems impossible, especially now."

We were nearly at the end of a dharma conversation, the Socratic dialogue on the nature of consciousness that I lead every Monday night. A breeze gonged the wind chimes hanging outside our tiny meditation center, a gentle noise that competed with the sounds of cars and boisterous partiers heading off to the pub across the street.

I answered that the awareness I was speaking about wasn't dependent on a lack of sound or people or bustle. The silence is the diminishment of the little self, the ego-mind caught up in its drama, story, and conditioning of "I,"—who "I" think I am, what "I" think about my place in the world, what "I" desire.

Awareness is not a state of egolessness; we all need functional egos to get around in the world, and the absence of a functional self is psychosis, not sagacity. It's just that the identification with and attachment to the material world, as ephemeral as it is, creates an endless cycle of suffering. Our minds actually manufacture much of the stress we are feeling, and when we stop believing the mind's story we become free of that suffering.

It is possible to be fully relaxed in the present moment, no matter what the circumstances—on the top of a mountain or in Times Square. In this relaxed awareness, a sense of connectedness arises and replaces the feelings of competition and separation that are so common in crowded suburban and city living.

The young woman nodded, but her eyes were filled with doubt. As I walked home I reflected on her inquiry. It seemed to be a core question for all spirituality. What good is it in real life under real stress? I realized that there wasn't a simple answer, no red pill like in *The Matrix*, for her question.

The young woman's question led to many more, and thus this book was born.

Given the stress of life, is it possible to be peaceful and nonreactive? Is it possible to feel connected to everything, to experience oneself as God and everything else also as God? Is it possible to deal with a rude motorist and experience oneself in a state of wakefulness? To have, as my teacher Catherine Ingram has said, the sense of oneself in the world as "seeing God with God eyes"? To see any rudeness, any stress, any person as a manifestation of the consciousness that informs everything?

There is a famous Zen quote that says, "When you wake up, the whole world wakes up around you." It has been my direct experience living in three large cities in the country—New York, Boston, and Los Angeles—that this is true. After working as a management consultant, an advertising executive, and a screenwriter in the film industry, I have felt the pressures and competition of urban life. They are sometimes subtle and sometimes as subtle as a jackhammer.

Yet after being exposed to the dharma, I have found it is possible, even in the most stressful situations, to often be in a state of relaxed wakefulness. It is possible, even in an ostensibly competitive situation, to keep the recognition that the other person is just another "chip off the consciousness block," the same block from which everything falls. And if there is a contraction into fear, competition, or identification, it is short, lasting minutes instead of days.

Once you have shucked off the straitjacket of your mind, it just feels too uncomfortable to put it on again, because after being exposed to the dharma, you know when that straitjacket is on. You know when you're obsessing; being overly anxious; feeling envy, greed, or desire; and believing that every thought to cross your mind is you. And it feels tight! Before these teachings, like Neo, I had no idea I was even in bondage. I thought it was "normal." Now, each contraction or slip in awareness feels terrible; a new normal has been created.

The dharma, which means "the way" or "the path," teaches one to remain peaceful while the external world wobbles on the brink of chaos. The time is ripe to make these ancient teachings widely available to city dwellers and suburbanites, providing a life raft right in the middle of the maelstrom.

This book illuminates the dharma in the context of tough cities and even tougher times, taking a look at twelve types of stress in urban life that have been further magnified by global events. *City Dharma* analyzes these stresses and offers ways to perceive and defuse them without adding on more belief systems or practices. In fact, the opposite is true. By stripping away everything that obscures our true nature and the nature of reality, as a natural by-product, the dharma teaches us how to behave based on love and connection, not fear and separation.

Along with addressing the constant fears and stories generated by the mind, *City Dharma* posits the radical claim that true freedom is available in the here and now, no matter what the circumstances. And while it will take into account the recent terrorist attacks as well as war and its impact on our lives, the book mostly zeroes in on daily life when bombs aren't going off. It focuses on finding peace and happiness in all aspects of the accelerated modern world.

"HELL IS OTHER PEOPLE"

Was Jean-Paul Sartre Right?

To straighten the crooked you must first do a harder thing—straighten yourself.
—BUDDHA

In a cartoon in the *New Yorker* a woman walks down a Manhattan street and, in reference to the changed atmosphere of New York post–September 11, says to her friend: "It's hard, but slowly I'm getting back to hating everyone."

This is funny and startlingly honest. So many spiritual teachings and books sugarcoat the reality that people are difficult. But there's no denying that people are difficult; greed, selfishness, and narcissism run rampant in the human species. And as world history continues to demonstrate, many millions are schooled in repression, brutality, and deprivation. All of these disparate aspects of consciousness can be found in crowded urban and suburban areas.

My main impetus in writing this book is to help other people in the way that I have been helped by the teachings of the dharma. There is no getting around the fact that most of life's difficulties, excepting illness, are caused by people's relationship to *themselves* and those around them. This is true whether the conflict is between nations or the two people fighting in the apartment next door.

The dharma doesn't deny these difficulties; it simply lessens them in a couple of ways.

We assume that other people are the cause of our unhappiness, the source of our "hell." When we look around us there is much to support this assumption. From rudeness to murder, it seems as though all the hell is coming from outside ourselves. *Other people* are making us mad, crazy, unhappy, and unfulfilled. They cut us off in traffic, they sleep with our spouses, they don't give us the promotions we deserve, they lie, steal, and cheat—they create hell on earth in ways great and small. We tend to think, *I'm not an angry person; they* made *me angry.*

Then, after some reflection, we begin to recognize that most of our hell is actually inside us. Negative things happen, people act badly, and the world is an imperfect place. However, when we think about it, there is very little that happens to us on a daily basis that is really "bad," and when it does occur, it passes quickly. But we then create endless suffering through our interpretation, our conditioning, and our identification with the thoughts around the event.

In other words, bad things happen to good people, but most of the suffering comes afterward, in the netherworld of our own mind, as we rehash the incident, unable to let it go. For instance, after my computer was stolen, I went through a few moments of berating myself: *If only I had sent the book to myself by e-mail* or *This shouldn't be happening to me* or *I should have known better than to hide my key outside.*

We each react to the situation according to our own conditioned thought, which almost always creates more suffering. In my case it's usually something along the lines of *I should have known better.* Instead of reacting with compassion for myself, I was filled with self-recrimination. But the reality is, I don't even know how the thief got into my apartment. Anything could have happened, including someone picking the lock.

Another person might react to the situation by focusing on the people who stole the computer, going on a rant about criminals, and becoming more hardened and suspicious of the world. We will all have different reactions based on our different conditioning.

How strongly we react is dependent upon how *identified* we are with our thoughts. By identified, I mean how attached we are and how much we think those thoughts define us. For instance, the thought comes up: *I'm stupid.* If we are identified with that thought, then we believe it to be true and it becomes part of our identity.

So why do we believe these thoughts and give them such power? Because all the random conditioning hardwired into us by a combination of nature and nurture dictates our reactions.

For instance, in the nature end of the spectrum, they have just found a gene called 5-HTT that determines why some people react to stressful events such as death, abuse, or job loss by falling into deep depression or paralyzing anxiety, while others are much less affected by the same events. According to the journal *Science,* it turns out that those with two copies of the long allele of this gene are able to withstand such events much better than those with two copies of the shorter allele. This is a person's *nature,* made up of our individual inherited and biological reality.

The other aspect that determines our behavior is our nurture, our early experiences in our family, our culture and our society. For example, if your father told you, "You're stupid," or if your mother was hyperimpatient with everything you attempted when you were a child, that negativity becomes ingrained. It becomes a part of the voice in your head that plays every time a difficulty arises. These experiences are our *nurture,* which is either negative or positive or a combination of both, and continues all our lives.

So we create our own hell because of our own internal conditioned thought patterns, created by our nature and nurture. The way of lessening the hell of the outside world is not by getting other people to change but by lessening the hell inside ourselves.

How do we do this?

By not identifying with your internal story, judgment, and belief systems as they arise in the form of thought, you are in a sense *empty* of your conditioned response. This doesn't mean reactivity is going to magically disappear—it's incredibly difficult to be human. But although reactivity may happen, you don't hang on to it; you release it as soon as you recognize the conditioned response. In short, you are now *awake* to it. You simply don't believe the thoughts to be true and you don't project them onto the outside world. Because you're not contributing anything extra to the conflict or negative occurrence, you create peace. You experience much more internal freedom, and you lessen your hell and that of everybody around you. It's akin to the old saying "If everybody swept their own doorstep, the whole world would be clean."

The dharma goes one step further and suggests that the ultimate recognition is to realize there is no "I" at all, that "I" is a construct of the mind.

What is the answer when we ask ourselves the age-old question "Who am I?" Are we our education? Our beliefs? Our jobs? Our families? Our thoughts? Society would say yes. But is it true? This is one of the main inquiries of this book.

The dharma says we are not any of these things. We are not the small self, the little "me, me, me" of conditioned personality imprisoned by our attachment to and identification with people, experiences, and material possessions.

If we are not the small self with its constant striving, filled with desires and fears, thinking constantly about acquiring and then protecting what we have acquired, what is the truth of who we are?

We will get to that. But first we must take a long, deep look at *who we have been trained to be*.

THE HELL OF CONDITIONING

All things change, nothing perishes.

—NIELS BOHR

Most beliefs are a result of familial, cultural, or religious conditioning—the small self programmed from birth to think, feel, and act a certain way. We are all strongly attached to our beliefs, but this conditioning is simply an accident of birth—a version of the Crips and the Bloods, the Muslims and the Jews, the Protestants and the Catholics, who, if they were born on a different block, would be fighting to the death for the opposite set of beliefs and values.

You are born in one family and you are a Jew. Another and you are a Muslim. Another still and you are sacrificing goats to worship your god. Or you are born white, black, or brown . . . and the conditioning begins.

The conditioning is founded in a truth, but it is not the ultimate truth. It feels real, but it is not the ultimate reality. We will look at what lies underneath this apparent reality, but first let's look deeply at conditioning—how it is created and how it is passed on from one generation to the next.

Recently I was in Johannesburg, South Africa, a city undergoing a massive shift in thinking after the end of apartheid. While there has been incredible progress in the cities of South Africa toward integration and upward mobility for blacks, visiting the countryside is sometimes like stepping back in time. I traveled deep in the Drakensberg, a stunning area of South Africa characterized by mountains, mesas, and rolling farmland. Although miles from the carjackings that occur in Joburg, I had an experience that demonstrated the extent to which conditioning is inherited, created, and reinforced—a process that is repeated in cities and countries the world over, whether the conditioning is homophobia, misogyny, or racism.

It all started innocently enough. I was hiking with my friend Helena, her nephew Drumie, age nine, and two dogs. The sun shone hot and bright as we followed the trail along a muddy river and into a deep canyon. We were miles from civilization and picking up African porcupine quills, shouting out each find and inspecting the beautiful white and black quills with the avidness of connoisseurs.

After a while we heard the sound of a lamb bleating its head off. We grabbed the dogs to keep them from attacking it and tried to locate the lamb. I saw a flash of white and floppy ears disappear into tall grass across the river. I couldn't believe my eyes. How had this lamb gotten here, so deep into such pristine wilderness? After some discussion, we decided that Drumie and I would swim across and rescue the lamb, while Helena would take the dogs further upriver to look for a crossing point.

As we made our way across the river and scrambled into the tall grass, the bleating stopped. After locating our tossed shoes, we started searching the grass until I almost stepped on it. The lamb was tiny and had collapsed. It tried to stand but was too weak. I gently picked up the lamb, which didn't struggle, and gasped at the fresh beauty of it, with its spindly legs and white fleece (the softest I'd ever felt). It had long eyelashes and floppy ears, and smelled of lavender—magical and otherworldly. It weakly nursed on my finger as we carried it three miles over hills and barbed-wire border fences to the nearest dirt road. Both Drumie and I agreed it felt like we were holding God in our arms.

We were trudging toward a distant farm, under a now relentless sun, when a battered pickup truck approached us and stopped with a skid, spewing dirt from its tires. At first I thought it was an old man driving, seeing only the glasses, the sandy hair, and the stocky body going to fat.

"We found this lamb in the wilderness by the river."

"It's from my dad's farm," the driver said. "Come, let me take it."

The driver got out of the truck, and at that point I realized he wasn't an old man at all. He was a heavyset boy wearing thick glasses and carrying a stick, which he used as a pointer.

"Can we come with you?" I asked, reluctant to relinquish the lamb until I saw it to its rightful place by its mother.

"Sure," said the boy. "Get in—I have to get diesel where this lamb belongs, anyway."

Drumie and I got in the truck, the lamb on our laps. The boy's name was Thabo, an African name and an unusual one for a white boy. He was thirteen and the son of the farmer who owned the land bordering the wilderness area in which we were hiking. He had been driving the pickup since he was nine, something that fascinated Drumie, who immediately had visions of driving. Thabo brought us to the farm where six other tiny lambs were in a pen, being bottle-fed by a farmhand. He got out of the truck and pointed at the black farmhand with his stick.

"You. Fill these containers. Diesel."

Thabo tapped the containers imperiously. I looked at him more closely—the blond hair, blue eyes, and chubby sunburned arms. Thabo had the air of a forty-year-old man with a baby face. But his demeanor toward the blacks was more Hitler Youth than anything, both funny and frightening at the same time. The farmhand's face revealed nothing as he slowly started working.

"This lamb,"Thabo said in his thick Afrikaans accent, "is a day old. He was born in the storm last night and got separated from his mum."

"So we saved its life?" Drumie said as he began bottle-feeding the lamb.

"It wouldn't have lived another six hours,"Thabo said. "It's a good thing it was you who found it and not some of the blacks around here. The kaffirs steal everything they can."

I looked at Thabo, surprised and uncertain what to say. I knew that *kaffir* was derogatory, akin to *nigger* in the United States. I didn't respond, but he must have seen my face.

"It's on the radio every night,"Thabo said. We parted reluctantly from the lamb and got back in the pickup truck. "They steal everything, even the ones that work for us,"Thabo told us as he started driving down the dirt road. "What are the blacks like in America? Do they all steal and kill people?"

"They are just like the whites," I said after a moment, pondering the best way to answer his question. I began to see the hell of the racism that lingered after apartheid. "There are good and bad in every group."

"Last week some kaffirs got caught stealing cattle. I caught them stealing corn just yesterday. They are rotten. All of them. On the television they are like animals. They killed a man for a cell phone in Joburg yesterday."

"I heard there was a fertility cave somewhere around here," I said, changing the subject.

"Yes. It is here. On our land."Thabo frowned for a moment, then his face brightened. "I'll take you there."

This seemed like a continuation of our adventure, and after picking up Helena, who had finally figured out how to cross the river with dogs, we drove down another dirt road toward the fertility cave. At a gate Thabo honked his horn impatiently. After a while a couple of young blacks came down from their huts and unlocked the gate. They were sullen and unimpressed with Thabo.

"This is our land, and they keep a gate locked and charge people to drive toward the cave," said Thabo bitterly, driving a mile down a dirt road, where he parked next to a few other vehicles. We got out, and Drumie, Helena, and I followed Thabo toward the cave.

We hiked for about an hour up a gentle trail, catching glimpses of a towering mountain through the rustling leaves overhead. As several devotees came off the mountain wearing colorful robes and carrying pots and pans, my anticipation heightened. We were going to a sacred place, a destination for hundreds of years for people from all over Africa. The walk itself began to take on the heightened feeling of a pilgrimage.

Thabo walked with us, holding his stick under his armpit.

"See this?" He pointed at a piece of garbage. "They come up here and leave trash everywhere. They cut down trees for fires. They steal the plants."

He continued his litany as we walked up the mountain, at one point stopping and sniffing the air.

"They turn this place into an open toilet."

I exchanged glances with Helena. She just shrugged, as if to say, *This is the way it is in parts of South Africa.*

We crossed a river and hiked up a short, steep trail amid the smell of urine and human excrement. Streams of devotees were trudging down the mountain trail, some carrying blanket-wrapped bundles balanced on their heads. I looked down the steep cliff and saw camps set up along the river, clothes hanging on trees to dry. We climbed up further, and suddenly there was the cave. It was a huge gash in the mountain, shaped like a shark's mouth. We stepped out of the hot sun and into the cave. Cool air greeted us along with unfamiliar smells. I could hear singing in Sotho. As my eyes adjusted to the twilight of the cave, the first thing I saw was a bloody rock. Thabo saw me looking at it.

"They kill the animals they steal from our farm, and cut their hoofs off one by one, before they slice the throat," he said bitterly, making a slicing motion across his own neck.

People squatted over open fires, cooking. A group gathered around a *sangoma* (diviner and heales) who led them in a call-and-response song and a shuffling dance. The twenty or so worshipers watched us, some furtively, some openly staring. I felt very Western in my khakis, hat, and hiking shoes, compared with their colorful outfits. The walls of the cave were blackened by years of cooking fires and covered with written prayers and symbols. The feeling in the cave, to me, was heavy with the weight of superstition.

"They say they worship God, but they don't because they do this to the animals,"Thabo said. "Nowhere in the Bible does it say to sacrifice animals."

Repulsed and fascinated, I walked further into the cave by myself, wanting to escape Thabo's running commentary, the oppressiveness of his judgment—and my own, which was running in my head.

It was darker here, with water trickling down the rock walls. I saw a shape gleaming in the darkness. I hesitated and then stepped closer. It was a gutted and skinned animal, lying on a rock, its muscles glistening with blood, its hoofs missing. Nearby was a skin of some sort. I squinted, crouching down for a better look. It was a sheepskin, crumpled and discarded like a used handkerchief. The skinned animal I was looking at was the former owner of the skin. The hair prickled on the back of my neck; I stared at it for a long moment, wondering what it must have felt in its last moments.

I was suddenly ready to leave the cave, the smoke, the clouded feeling of lives being lived through the prism of primordial belief systems.

When we stepped out into the fresh air and sunlight I looked at the magnificent cave, a geologic wonder, its receptive opening beckoning to all who had made the climb. I couldn't help but feel that the cave in just its natural state would have had a soothing and awe-inspiring effect. I pictured it without the dead animals, the bloody rituals, and the belief systems that hung like a dark pallor over its cathedral-like beauty. African animism, a paganism that predates Christianity and is one of the earliest forms of worship, simply felt heavy in that cave. Humanity's ritual acts felt worse than a subtraction; they felt like a defamation, an obscenity upon nature's gift.

Even as I had the thought, I realized it was the product of my own conditioning, a culturally determined accident. I could have been born into a family that had a monthly practice of sacrificing a goat, and that would be the most normal thing in the world for me. Our thirteen-year-old host could have been born a poor black farmhand instead of the son of a wealthy farmer. It is for this reason that my approach to entrenched belief systems has gone from fierce argumentation to wry acceptance.

On the way out, hiking down the mountain, Thabo stepped up his diatribe against the blacks until he finally stopped an old woman who was picking herbs by the side of the trail.

"Put it down!" he barked at her. He continued his harangue in Afrikaans, the guttural syllables grinding in his mouth like broken glass. The old woman, heavyset and amiable, dropped the small handful of weeds. I looked at Helena, who had been born in South Africa, and she shook her head.

"You can't get involved here," she whispered. "There's a whole cultural history at play."

All the way down the trail Thabo, dictatorial with his stick, brusquely stopped the blacks, mostly elderly women, and searched their bags. The sight of him roughly opening the bags and emptying their contents was almost unbearable.

We walked ahead. I felt terrible, trapped in a cultural war that I didn't understand, feeling as though I should do something, but not having the tools or the understanding to bridge the gap. It was in that moment that I just had to accept that these people, living on the same land, were locked in a battle that I wasn't going to understand or begin to ameliorate as a foreigner visiting one afternoon.

Thabo caught up to us.

"I hope you understand," he huffed. "If we don't stop them, there will be nothing for them to pick in five years."

I doubted that very much, looking at their tiny bags and the dense foliage on either side of the trail. I just didn't know what to say. His conditioning was so set at the age of thirteen, it seemed futile to even try to change his perspective. I began to develop a dislike for the boy, his bullying, his stick, his self-satisfied air. I could see the boy's father resting in him as clearly as the wealth of his family, contrasting deeply with the poverty of his victims.

"It is hard to understand," I said, trying to speak carefully. "But it must be difficult to have the cave on your land."

"It is the stealing and dirtiness all the time," he said. "They've even killed the baboons in the hills. It happens all over the world. The blacks. Just look at the news."

There was a pause while I contemplated his ruddy face, trying to summon up my compassion. He was still a boy, and there was a parroted quality to his actions and statements that bespoke his background. I pictured him watching the nightly news with his parents, shaking their heads at the worst the blacks have to offer. Still, his cruelty was compounded by his youth, his blondness, and his blue eyes. Again, the poster child for Hitler Youth raced through my mind.

"Four years ago my grandma and grandpa were killed in their farmhouse for their money," Thabo said, with no extra emphasis. "The kaffirs killed them for four hundred rand." Four hundred rand is about fifty American dollars.

Suddenly his conditioning all made sense. I was overwhelmed with empathy for the boy.

"They did the same thing they are doing every day in Johannesburg," he continued. "The same thing."

"I'm sorry," I said. And I was.

Later I found out that the boy's grandfather used to flash huge wads of cash, buying cars outright with it in a land of crushing poverty. He had an ongoing war with the local blacks about the cave, at one point requesting government permission to close it with dynamite. The inciting incident that caused the murders was brutal; he had chased some cattle rustlers into Lesotho, and when he found his cattle with their ears cut off to hide the rightful ownership, he cut off the ears of the cattle rustlers. The local *sangoma* said that any man who did that to another man no longer deserved to live. The murders, although ultimately done by cattle rustlers from neighboring Lesotho, seemed like the inevitable culmination of the man's long-standing attitude of domination over the local black population. The attitude had been passed on through Thabo's father and down to Thabo himself.

Of course, none of this justifies the murders or would matter to a nine-year-old boy who had lost his grandparents. It just demonstrates the generational nature of conditioning.

When we got back in the truck and drove to the gate, it was padlocked again. Thabo honked the horn impatiently. Ten minutes passed, and then the same two guys who had unlocked the gate for us earlier sauntered down, obviously having made us wait. They made no motion to unlock the padlock.

Swearing under his breath, Thabo got out and strode to the gate. The conversation was in Afrikaans and I was too far away to hear it, but the body language was unmistakable. Impasse. Three hundred years of history boiled down to these two parties, one black, one white, on opposite sides of a country gate. Both sides of the story in full living color, neither right, neither wrong; neither good, neither evil; both firmly entrenched in their conditioned reality of hatred.

Thabo stormed back to the truck.

"The bloody kaffirs want ten rand to unlock the gate," he huffed. "I'm going to get my father and teach them a lesson. We're not going to pay. We'll sit here till midnight if we have to."

It was now about five in the afternoon, and we had a long hike in front of us. Ten rand is a little over a dollar, but I didn't have it on me. And I didn't feel I should get involved in trying to change the situation. After a few minutes of baleful staring on both sides, the men unlocked the gate, suddenly laughing. They were giving Thabo, the little dictator, a hard time. Sitting in the back of the pickup as we drove away, I flashed them a peace sign, which they both returned with knowing grins.

When we got to the farmhouse Thabo disappeared into the house and returned with a fluorescent green liquid that was some kind of Kool-Aid. We thanked him profusely for being our guide and wished him well.

I pondered Thabo's future as we hiked through the deepening African twilight. In a way he couldn't live anywhere else in the world except the Free State region of South Africa. He was a complete product of his environment, as were the blacks with whom his family was locked in battle. The blacks hate the whites and treat them badly, and the whites hate the blacks and treat them badly. Their conditioning is set and reinforcies their reality every day. And as they point the finger at each other, their reality reinforces their conditioning. They are, in a sense, mirroring each other, locking each other in a hellish prison.

A version of this scenario is playing out in every city and suburb in the world, between neighbors and strangers born on different sides of the fence. Each of us is inculcated beyond our control into a conditioned reaction; each of us has a set of beliefs to which we cling as if to life itself. Some of it is a result of our direct experience, but most of it is handed down. Either way, it doesn't matter.

Of course, the blacks that killed Thabo's grandparents were not the blacks that were on the trail, but Thabo's prejudices, his *prejudg-*

ment, made it impossible for him to make the differentiation. They were all just kaffirs. This is not to judge Thabo; don't we all carry our own baggage, which makes it impossible to meet each moment fresh?

On a macro level, a version plays itself out between nations and tribes the world over. We are now a global village, staring at each other over the digital fence, fingers on the trigger. Our conditioning is killing us, making a hell of heaven.

We are all connected on this planet—we are all manifestations of consciousness, whether on the level of individuals or countries. This was always the case, even when it took years or months instead of hours to traverse the globe. The world had just gotten small enough in the past hundred years for the point to really be driven home on the level of nations.

Now we enter an age when a disease that starts in China shows up in Canada a week later; when nuclear weapons can fly around the planet in minutes; when a small group of committed individuals with major grievances can greatly affect the richest and most powerful people on the planet. What happens in a poverty-stricken country such as Afghanistan, ignored and discarded by us after their war against the old Soviet Union, is important. It was *always* important. We just weren't aware of it—our consciousness hadn't expanded enough to include it.

Deepak Chopra called the terrorist attacks a planetary autoimmune disorder. Ram Dass, another spiritual teacher, called them a planetary stroke. Both descriptions, using medical metaphors, point to the fact that we are one world. No corner can be neglected or exploited without it coming back to hurt the entire system. As Robert Wright, author of *The Moral Animal*, wrote recently in the *New York Times*: "All along, technological evolution has been moving our species toward this nonzero-sum moment, when our welfare is crucially correlated with the welfare of the other, and our freedom depends on the sympathetic comprehension of the other . . . a religious motivation isn't necessary. Simple self-interest will do. That's the beauty of the thing."

Although we are all different manifestations of consciousness, we are all connected, whether we want to be or not. This is true on the level of families, neighborhoods, and nations.

Who is right? Nobody.

Who is wrong? Nobody.

TRANSCEND THE CONDITIONING

When you look into a mirror you see your face as it is; you may wish that some parts of it were different, but the actual fact is shown in the mirror. Now, can you look at your conditioning in a similar way?

—KRISHNAMURTI

Most thought is generated in an automatic, reflexive way, creating our inner hell. In fact, most of this habitual thought is neurotic; 90 percent of it we thought yesterday, and 90 percent we will think again tomorrow. Our internal hell can be created with endless thoughts of *I wish I were rich, all my problems would disappear* or *This friggin' traffic* or *My life sucks* or *My boss is a jerk.*

So how do we escape the constant pummeling of conditioned thought, whether it's Thabo talking about the kaffirs or somebody berating himself that he should be more successful? How do we wake up from it?

One hint is that by simply bringing our attention fully into the present moment something important happens: the internal cacophony of our story dissipates. It's almost as if the present moment and the story can't occupy the same instant of time.

Picture yourself in a pitch-dark room with a flashlight. You are running the flashlight across the ceiling. In that moment a portion of the ceiling is illuminated, but in the moment before and the moment after that part is dark. You can see only what is in the beam of light in each instant. In the way that a beam of light illuminates a dark room, the present moment pierces the mind's confabulations.

Let *right now* be that beam of light, drenching your awareness, making the shadows of neurotic thought disappear.

When your attention is right now, the past and future disappear. They have to disappear because . . .

The past and future can only exist in the mind.

Think about it. The past is a memory.

The future is imagination.

Only right now exists

When you are in the present moment it doesn't mean that the thoughts stop. It means you simply witness them come and go. You may never eliminate them—that's unncessary and perhaps impossible—but you just don't identify with them. You don't think they are *you*, so you're just not paying attention to them anymore.

Or perhaps the thoughts may eventually disappear—great! But neither condition is necessary for wakefulness, which is a state of being in which you're present, awakened from the story your thoughts are telling you.

I'm reminded of a friend who was driving her car one day and kept hearing a car alarm. The alarm was really annoying her. Then she realized it was her car alarm that was blaring. Oftentimes this is the case. We think it is other people, but it's really the blaring alarms of our small self, caught up in its drama of *me, me, me*.

This drama is put on by a stream of neurotic thoughts that we believe to be the truth.

The neurotic thought jumps on center stage like an unbidden actor. An entire imagined drama plays itself out, filled with highs and lows. While watching the drama we may go along with the ride completely—palms sweating, laughing and crying, hoping and fearing. Then, as quickly as the play starts, it ends. The thought that rushed in and filled the stage of our awareness lurches off, leaving this awareness empty and untouched by its arrival and departure.

In bringing your attention to right now, you simply don't believe the actor is permanent or real. What is left is the stage of awareness.

For instance, I know a woman who believes that she's not as attractive as other people. It's a litany of "I wish I were thinner" or "I wish I were taller." She obsesses about occasional outbreaks of acne and was considering a three-month course of a dangerous drug with many side effects, including suicidal depression, to clear it up. This is a beautiful woman—everywhere she goes men are falling all over her—but no amount of discussion with her changed the critical thoughts (a legacy from her mother) or ameliorated her suffering. She was identified with her thoughts, believed them to be true, and believed they defined her.

Nothing worked or changed until she began to simply watch her thoughts. She watched them come and she watched them go, without believing they were real. In doing so she disarmed the thoughts of their power.

When you have a witnessing relationship to your thoughts, it changes everything; you can sort out the neurotic from the useful. In this way you develop a different relationship to your mind, which is a major step in reducing your internal hell. Our gateway into this witnessing relationship is as close as the present moment.

When we are fully and directly experiencing right now, the baggage of belief and neurotic thought can't stay long. There's simply no room on the stage, because when we are blasted awake in this very moment, the mind is superseded by the sheer intensity of life. When we are fully absorbed in the now, what emerges is a kind of attentiveness, a simple and harmonious beingness that is relaxed and always present, without projection, story, or belief. You never lose sight of the stage of your awareness, no matter how intense the play of the mind.

The thoughts may always flit across the stage—again, there's no need for them to disappear in order to experience wakefulness—but the key is that they don't stay long. And after a while, because we're not identifying with these thoughts, they can become a source of amusement rather than a source of suffering. As in "Oh, boy, here comes that thought again, for the ten thousandth time."

In this way you develop an internal compassion for yourself and your reactivity. This then allows you to have compassion for the internal hell of others.

In short, the now gives us the only livable moment in which we can awaken from the nightmare of reflexive thought and conditioning. Right now gives us the ability to witness, understand, and then drop our own habituation.

And when this happens, there is no external hell, there is no internal hell, because there is no little self there to experience it. There is just *experiencing*. Period.

For instance, if Thabo had been able to walk up that mountain path fully in the moment, without his conditioning, he might have noticed how small the pouches of herbs were that the old women had gathered. He might not have treated the gatekeepers so roughly because he might have seen how poor they were. He wouldn't have had room for the story of the "bloody kaffirs" as a group, but rather simply seen each person coming off the mountain as an individual. Instead of focusing on all the negatives, he might have been experiencing the sights, sounds, and smells of the beautiful hike. In each of the moments on the hike, everything was fine. The hell he was creating was his own.

Likewise, the gatekeepers might not have felt so angry and controlled by this little kid that they had to engage in a petty struggle over when they unlocked the gate. If they had been in the truth of their moment, they might have seen an insecure boy giving a tour to strangers, perhaps trying to impress us. They might have met him with kindness and broken through some of the pattern of power struggle and anger.

Again, the sights and sounds of the day were the same for everyone there. It was the perspective of conditioning that colored everything for the idividuals.

And the same is true of all of us. Can we take each step in our day as if we were newly born to the world? Can we walk without dragging around all the baggage of the past? It is both simple and hard to meet each moment fresh, especially if the conditioning is severe, as it is for Thabo.

But what is much more painful is meeting each moment *stale,* with all sorts of beliefs and conditioning obscuring our view of reality. Unfortunately, that is the human condition and our second nature.

I'm sure that to some of you, as you read this, it may seem impossible to get out of this human condition. The good news is that it is not. What the mystics ask of us is simply to show up moment by moment.

Even though freedom is instantly available, washing over you like a wave, it often takes time, more akin to water slowly eroding rock, in this case the bedrock of one's conditioning. In showing up moment by moment as much as you can, you are spending time in the water. With each moment of full wakefulness, more conditioning and reactivity will wash away.

When we are in this sense of experiencing, in this lack of attachment to our isolated identity, everything feels connected. In this recognition we have a feeling we are part of one blast of consciousness. This is the nondual taste. It is not so much a belief as a direct experience.

I am not asking you to take anything in this book on faith. Rather, conduct your own thought experiments. Check it out for yourself and see if you experience peacefulness when you stop believing your thoughts to be real. Use your mind as the tool it is, designed to solve problems and be creative, rather than a swamp generating the mosquitoes of neurotic thought.

As you relax into wakefulness, moment by moment, you become unchained from belief, thought, superstition, and conditioning. Instead of praying for peace, you *become* peace. Instead of looking for compassion and understanding outside yourself, you *become* compassion and understanding. And, particularly in cities, instead of "needing space," you become spacious in your dealings with people.

Because you are not protecting the fortified small self, the hell in yourself is reduced or eliminated. Understanding replaces judgment, which allows compassion and tolerance to arise.

This creates a self-fulfilling loop of love creating love. Reactivity gets reduced, replaced with the direct experience of:

I am you.

You are me.

We are they.

All is consciousness.

When we stay in our identification, when fear and judgment keep getting passed around, then more of that will be created. Humans have more than proven how adept we are at creating hell on earth.

WHEN THE HELL IS YOU AND YOUR MAD DESIRES

Ultimately, when you stop identifying so much with your physical body and with your psychological entity, that anxiety starts to disintegrate. And you start to define yourself as in flow with the universe; and whatever comes along—death, life joy, sadness—is grist for the mill of awakening. Not this versus that but whatever.

—RAM DASS

Anybody can create a private hell at any time, even during something as innocuous as ordering dinner at a restaurant.

I have a friend I'll call Charlie. He's a vegan (he eats no meat, fish, or dairy) and is a very mellow guy who is into yoga and has done a lot of work on himself in therapy. One day we were having brunch at a predominantly vegetarian restaurant. We had just practiced yoga and were starved. He knew exactly what he wanted, the tofu scramble. But when the waiter arrived, he informed us that they were out of tofu.

"Out of tofu?" Charlie asked, incredulous and exasperated. "How can that be? It's a vegetarian restaurant."

The waiter shrugged, indifferent. "No tofu scramble. We're out of tofu."

"Maybe you want to get something else," I suggested. "How about a veggie burger?"

"I don't want anything else!" Charlie snapped.

"I'll be back in a minute," the waiter said, heading toward the safety of another table.

When the waiter came back a few minutes later to take our order, Charlie was still fixated on the tofu.

"What if I give you some money and you run next door and buy some tofu? Can you cook that up?" Charlie asked, succumbing to low-blood-sugar madness.

The waiter just looked at him dumbly. "Next door?" he said.

"No, wait. You're busy, right?" Charlie said. "What if I go and buy some tofu and bring it back? Then can you make a tofu scramble?"

"I don't think so."

"Could you check?" Charlie asked.

The waiter walked away, shaking his head.

"Sure you can't find anything else on the menu?" I asked Charlie.

"This is crazy. I can't believe they don't have tofu," Charlie said, getting up. "I'm going to talk to the cooks and see if they'll cook it for me if I buy some." Charlie walked over and began talking to the cook. That's when he saw a tofu scramble being taken out to a table by another waiter.

"What's that?" Charlie screeched at our waiter. "That's tofu! I thought you were out of tofu!"

Charlie stabbed his finger into the chest of our waiter, who pushed Charlie back. Another waiter stepped between them. Charlie walked over to me and said huffily, "I'm out of here."

I went over to apologize to the bewildered staff.

"What's that guy's problem?" asked the waiter.

"He's . . . he takes his tofu seriously," was all I could think of saying. Then we both burst out laughing.

To this day, I can't say the word *tofu* without a smile coming to my face. Charlie and I now laugh about it, calling it the "tofu meltdown incident." But this was very painful in the moment for everybody concerned. And it was even more painful for Charlie later on, when he came to his senses—he felt terrible and ended up going back to the restaurant to apologize to everybody.

This was simply a case of a good person being focused on his desire, to the point of missing the larger picture. When the small self is consumed with its wants and desires, the present moment is lost and other people are reduced to obstacles to be run over.

You might be thinking, *He's not me. I'd never do that!* But haven't you ever gotten in a huff when you haven't gotten a job? When you've been turned down for a date? Or when you're behind a really slow driver with his blinker on and you lay on the horn in exasperation? How are these moments different from Charlie's? And what did it do to you? The truth is, every once in a while we all lose sight of what is versus what we think should be. It's human.

But if you are in desire, you are not awake to the exact present moment in which the desire is arising. When desire arises, whether it's for tofu or for a house, it's usually about getting something in the future. And even if it's a minute in the future, the immediate moment is lost. This "futurizing" is epitomized (and drummed into us by a constant stream of advertising) by the "if, then" belief system. *If I had this car, that house, that girl, or* (in this laughable case) *that breakfast, then I could be happy.* This is the big material lie as experienced by so many people who finally get everything they thought they wanted, only to find that happiness still eludes them.

Desire precludes being happy right now, which is the only place we can be happy. You can't be happy in the future. Past happiness is a memory. You can only be happy in the now.

Most of us, moment to moment, have everything we need. We can, as Catherine Ingram likes to say, put down our begging bowls.

We don't have to live as hungry ghosts, wandering the earth for a fulfillment that is already here in each vibrant moment.

This is not to say that desire doesn't arise in the moment or that it's necessarily bad. But when the desire obliterates the stage of awareness, it can become a kind of internal madness. And when this madness spills over into the lives of other people, there is inevitable suffering.

When fully awake in the present moment, when fully living life second by second, it is much easier to accept what is in the here and now. Desire is reduced to just another phenomenon, ephemeral and fleeting. When it happens, we realize it is surrounded by an awareness that holds it.

REALIZATION

> You don't want to create an image of yourself, a stone Buddha . . . always sitting in the lotus posture and discerning marvelous wisdom . . . take the practice into everyday life to practice moment to moment. You can learn everything I've said just as well by cleaning the toilet.
>
> —LARRY ROSENBERG

Inevitably, these "tofu moments" will happen to all of us. Occasionally we all lose balance and perspective. When this happens, the feelings of contraction can be intense. The mind can be particularly relentless, beating you up with all sorts of guilt or shame, with thoughts about the thoughts, as in *I shouldn't be thinking this,* spiraling down into a never-ending loop.

The first thing is to congratulate yourself on noticing when you are fully identified and on the rack, suffering mightily for your attachments. This witnessing is a huge step toward wakefulness.

At this point it is necessary to access internal forgiveness. Compassion begins at home. We see our conditioning and have empathy for ourselves and the lack of consciousness that gave us the conditioning. We treat ourselves tenderly, for we are suffering.

It is a challenge to have compassion for ourselves and our conditioning. It's hard. And if we encounter people being nasty in pursuing their own desire, our knee-jerk reaction is judgment. But if we can get to a place of compassion for ourselves, we internally soften our stance. Then when we encounter people who are trying to run us over in acting out *their* desire, we will see it as suffering and will have compassion for them. We do not take it personally, because we understand. We've been there.

In this way we gently lose our identification with the small self. What replaces it is a merging with the big Self (all that is), and out of that comes a direct experience of nonduality.

This is the heart of the mystical experience. But what exactly does it mean?

I will get into specific and less conceptual responses later in the book, but the short answer is that everything is consciousness or God or *atman* or *brahman* or whatever culturally relevant name you have inherited. You are the instrument through which universal consciousness is perceiving, expressing, and creating.

If it's either all you or all consciousness, then how do you have an experience of this nonduality, a mystical sense of connection? By simply dropping your identification with your small self and merging your awareness with all.

Picture your small self painted on a large piece of glass that we will call awareness. This awareness is pure, clear, and unstained, and it infuses everything. It is always present, even when what people see is the "you" carefully painted on the glass, even when all that you yourself see is the painted "you" on the glass, with no idea of the awareness underneath it all.

Now suppose you want to end your suffering, come out of your "hell." You want to improve the "you" painted on the glass. You tell yourself that you're not good enough, that you need a touch-up—

you need to lose some weight, work out more, get a better job or a better car. So you fiddle around with this painted "you."You make all sorts of changes to the personality, trying to become happy. Using your mind, you try to think better thoughts or try to eliminate the thoughts altogether, which is like trying to cleanse the lens of awareness with a dirty rag.

In various ways, and there is a self-help book for every way, you change the painting. You try to improve "you," but you're never satisfied—it's a never-ending process.

Then you might try to stifle your self or pretend it doesn't exist, but that tack results in a form of denial or mental illness.

Then you try to fill yourself up from the outside—you do more, experience more, seek more pleasure. You keep painting on layer after layer, but after the pleasure or experience is gone, there is a sense of loss or emptiness. Even while the pleasure is happening, there is a feeling that the end is coming, at which point you won't be as happy.

This is because you are identified with this small self having these experiences. You still think the painting is what you really are. But it's not.

Your true nature is the clear glass of awareness upon which "you" are painted. This awareness is steady and unchanging, no matter what story is being painted on the surface. All you have to do is recognize this.

The trick isn't to be happy when everything seems to be going your way. That's an easier path, if still a fruitless one; for however long the material cushiness lasts, you seem to feel better. And then it is gone, along with your happiness. The real trick is to be happy when *nothing* in the material world is going your way. For this to be possible, we must realize that none of it has anything to do with peace and love and joy and freedom.

Now suppose you finally realize this or you finally become exhausted. Still unhappy, you finally want to drop the identification with the small self. The highs and lows, the judgments about losses and gains, and so on are causing you misery and suffering. You never get ahead. You never feel happy. Always anxious, you keep striving. You're in hell and you think the whole world is hell. You finally see that this identification with the small self is killing you and separating you from your fellow human.

So you try to get rid of it. You've got to do something! You buy this book. It's the least you can do, right? And you're reading this book, right now, hoping for something, anything that will help.

What can you do?

Nothing.

As written in the Mundaka Upanishad: "Those who dwell on and long for sense-pleasure are born in a world of separateness. But let them realize they are the Self and all separateness will fall away." The key word here is *realize*. Simply realize that you are the big Self. There's nothing to *do* because you already *are*; simply recognize that the mind, with its story and its identification with the small self, is apparently separating you from consciousness. This is what the mind does.

But it's an illusion. It's impossible to separate you from what you are, which is consciousness itself.

It appears that painted on the clear glass is reality: you against a background of city, sky, and ground. The glass is unseen, painted over. But awareness is the clear glass that informs, supports, and ultimately is untouched by it all. You are fused with this awareness, and the painting can't exist without it.

Begin to check it out for yourself. The less identified you are with the small self, the more you will realize that you are a manifestation of consciousness. The less "you," the more connection and peace you will feel with all.

God is not outside you. You are inside God. When you are so connected, you leave hell forever. It simply doesn't apply anymore.

As you read the book, simply ask if it resonates. Do you recognize your own true nature in the stories and teachings?

Perhaps this is too much, this overview of nonduality. Don't get bogged down with it here. There will be many stories and metaphors to explain it later in the book. And if it doesn't resonate, then please do not try to force yourself to believe it—that would be counter to everything the dharma is about.

Simply continue to gently direct your attention into the present moment, which is the golden gateway to this awareness. As you become more fully present, there is no room for anything else, including the small self, with all its constant anxiety and desire. Become so drenched in the present moment that you allow it to obliterate neurotic thought.

The small self will drop away naturally and easily, and a sense of connection with all will replace it.

THE TOUGH CASES

Enlightenment is intimacy with all things.
—JACK KORNFIELD

Perhaps you can't get beyond the idea that everything is a product of the divine consciousness that informs everything. The mind rails against the very idea: *What about my boss, who chases me around the desk every day? What about my husband, who beats me? What about my partner, who stole my idea and absconded with my money? The real bastards who create hell for me every day of my life—how are they God?*

Let's not stop there; let's take it to the furthest extreme.

What about the September 11 terrorists? Surely they can't be manifestations of God. They have done this evil and cowardly act. They are evildoers.

Although it is understandable to see them as such, with enough compassion and understanding it is also possible to see that the terrorists' conditioning, perverted beliefs, lack of love, and plain mental illness caused them to kill themselves and thousands of other people. With compassion we can see them as the extreme product of an indoctrination that perverted their basic human impulse toward spirituality. Their personalities succumbed to a cult of death no different from that inculcated in Nazi Germany.

Those terrorists weren't present in the moment; they were living in a future heaven and creating a present hell. If they could have woken up for even a second, the horror of what they were doing would have become apparent. Without the straitjacket of fanaticism locking their minds into this action, their hearts would have seen with revulsion the violence they were perpetrating. If they were awake, the terror they were causing innocent people would have stopped them in their tracks.

Think of the most reprehensible act one person can do to another. Even as you read these words, chances are it is being done in some torture chamber, bedroom, or boardroom somewhere in the world. Yet even though the perpetrator's actions are the result of tortured beliefs, sadistic conditioning, and twisted psychological compulsion, his or her true nature remains untouched.

If we can see this true and divine nature clearly, if we can find compassion in our hearts for what this person did, think how easy it will be to forgive those guilty of lesser crimes.

When awake, without the filters of conditioning, the love that we naturally are blossoms. It is as tenderhearted as that newborn baby lamb.

As the Buddha said: "See yourself in others. Then whom can you hurt? What harm can you do?" This kind of awareness and compassion is at the highest level, the level of Buddha or Christ. But it is useful to hold it in our heads as an example of the highest form of love, seeing the divine in everything.

Either it's all God or none of it is. And our direct experience of that loving reality is entirely dependent upon how free we are from story, conditioning, and beliefs.

Don't take anybody's word for it. Alan Watts said, "When you confer spiritual authority on another person, you must realize that you are allowing them to pick your pocket and sell you your own watch."

In other words, the truly is already yours—you know what time it is—so don't look for a "higher teacher" to give it to you. Teachers are fallible humans.

As you read the book and begin to check out the world through this paradigm, simply see what happens as you relax the beliefs, conditioning, and thoughts that appear to separate you from right now. See if your hell diminishes in a very practical way.

Every moment of every day you will have an opportunity to meet the moment either fresh or with all your conditioned ideas of the world. Just be open to what is. Trust your direct experience. Don't be "spiritual."

MEET THE MOMENT

The guru is the Formless Self within each one of us. He may appear as a body to guide us, but that is only his disguise.

—RAMANA MAHARSHI

You certainly don't need to travel to Africa, the Middle East, Afghanistan, or another part of the United States to encounter the madness of mind. Nor do you need to engage in global events to experience the hell of other people. As we will explore in this book, sometimes you only have to look as far as your own family or step out the door of your house in any decent-sized city. There you will have endless opportunities to see if kindness and compassion can reach across seemingly unbridgeable distances.

This can happen only when you meet the moment without an agenda.

One day I was standing in a long line at the bank, waiting to close out an account. There were only two tellers, and in front of one was an extremely agitated man. His blue eyes were rheumy and his fingernails were long, protruding from hands the color of aged newspaper. His coat was tattered and he was shouting at the teller what he was saying was unintelligible except for the phrase "two hundred dollars." The teller, a young man, just stared at the man with wide eyes.

The portly man next to me in line was sighing and clearing his throat impatiently. Other people in the line were tapping their feet and looking at watches. The old man began demanding in a raised voice that the teller give him his name.

"Albert," said the teller.

"Albert. Last name! Last *name!*" shouted the old man.

"Come on," muttered the portly man, becoming visibly agitated. The old man continued shouting as the teller tried to get him to move to an empty window so a supervisor could come and deal with him.

It was at this point that I thought I could be of assistance by demonstrating the power of the dharma. Putting on my most winning smile, I stepped up to the old man, just as the portly man said loudly, "Come on, move over! Get the hell out of the line."

The old man whirled around to face me, his eyes rolling maniacally. He began swatting at me with his arm.

"Who? Who? What did you say?" The man spat the words at me, thinking I was the one who had just shouted at him.

I smiled and reached out to him, gently touching his elbow. I thought touching him would be reassuring and ground him in the reality of the moment. I truly wanted to help.

"Let me help you," I said.

That's when he reached over, grabbed his cup of coffee from the counter, and threw it at me. I barely dodged it, and the cup landed on the floor, splattering everybody.

"Help me? Help *this!*" The old man grabbed me by the arm and began swatting me with a rolled-up newspaper. I struggled to escape his grip, which felt like talons on my arm.

"Who do you . . . what do you think you . . ." The old man, feeling extremely threatened, was getting hysterical.

I just stood there for a moment in shock. Finally I broke free of his grip and quickly retreated to my place in line. The old man returned his attention to the teller. "What's your name, huh? Huh?" he shouted at the teller.

At this point the bank manager came out. She was a matronly woman with gray hair and a twinkle in her eye. She bustled over to the man.

"Come on," she coaxed the man. "It's okay. Come with me." She was so friendly and warm, making little gestures with her hands, that she got the old man's attention.

"He . . . he . . ."The old man pointed at me.

"I know. Come over here and tell me about it." It was as though she were talking to a scared little boy or even a dog. She kept her distance, never getting within four feet of the man, and kept smiling at him with incredible warmth. It totally penetrated the old man's alienation, and with one final glare at me he followed her, docile as a lamb.

"He's obviously demented," I said to the man next to me.

"No shit, but he's holding up the fucking line."The portly man shook his head in disgust, moving up to the teller. It's a comment I'll never forget.

I looked over at the bank manager, who had managed to get the man seated by her desk. She came over to me and apologized. She had handled everybody with such compassion; I wanted to sit at her feet.

The lessons I learned that day were innumerable. I had approached the man as a way to "practice the dharma." I was going to "lessen his hell," make him feel better, and be of service to everybody in line. It was coming from an ego-driven place and a belief that I was special. Even if the portly man hadn't shouted the man into further agitation, I doubt I would have been successful. I hadn't seen the situation correctly; touching the man on the elbow was a mistake, invading his boundaries and freaking him out.

Chögyam Trungpa wrote on the basic openness of compassion: "If you can afford to be what you are, then you do not need the 'insurance policy' of trying to be a good person, a pious person, a compassionate person."

The bank manager, even though it was her job and she had an interest in moving the man along, had approached the man in a way that could be heard and understood through his dementia. She had practiced true compassion and had met the man in the moment, without belief or spiritual agenda, without a personal sense of "me, making the situation better."

When you meet the moment fully, then you have the opportunity to see what is true, without the projections and desires of the small self. You meet people where they are and let them *be* where they are, even if it looks like hell. It is a surrender to what is, rather than to what you think should be. This allows a complete acceptance and openness to all situations, emotions, and people, which is freedom itself. As the Roman playwright Terence said: I am a human being; nothing human is alien to me.

A month after September 11 a major movie star addressed a crowd in Madison Square Garden during the Concert for New York. The crowd consisted mostly of grieving firefighters and police officers. It was as red-blooded-American a crowd as you could get. When the movie star came out, he said that what we really needed to do was practice compassion and forgiveness, giving peace a chance.

It came off as patronizing, and he was almost booed off the stage. The crowd was infuriated at being told how to feel in their time of grief. At which point the movie star acknowledged that perhaps this was an unpopular statement to make at this time.

Somebody brought up the incident in a dharma conversation later that week, and did so with a sense of judgment for the "unspiritual" response of the crowd. This person applauded the movie star's attempt to raise the "dense" consciousness of the audience and wondered, "What hope do we have for the world if people are booing sentiments of peace and love?"

But the movie star wasn't being "spiritual," whatever that means. He wasn't even being loving. He didn't meet the audience in the moment where they were, which was in a state of shock, grief, and anger at the murderous attack. In much the same way as I did in the bank, he approached the crowd with an agenda, which came across as being condescending and had the opposite effect from what he intended.

DON'T KNOW

If there is any peace it will come through being, not knowing.

—HENRY MILLER

Something that spiritual seekers need to be particularly vigilant about is a vague superiority, a belief that they "got it" and the rest of the world doesn't. The ability to parrot spiritual jargon can be easily learned. It can become just another narcissistic presentation, another path to separation, pride, and ego. In short, spirituality can create hell for you as easily as anything else.

When you don't know, you are open to what is. You are fresh in your approach to the world. You are not waiting for an opportunity to plug in the tape where you pontificate, telling everybody the secrets of the universe. You are not experiencing the world through the prism of mind, with its attachment to the past and its projections upon the future.

With this recognition, why does our beautiful planet need a heaven? We need only to open our eyes to have a direct experience of it here and now.

And don't we already have a hell that we create right here on earth, often due to our thoughts and belief systems? A hell that we impose on ourselves and other people, either locally or globally?

And why do we need New Age "miracles"? Isn't the dance between a flower and a butterfly miracle enough?

In the full blast of Now, as Catherine Ingram likes to say, the ordinary becomes extraordinary.

The Germans have a word, *Weltschmerz*, which means eternal disappointment in life as it is. It can lead to a sense that there's always something better around the corner. This can hold true in the spiritual path as well, as people move from tradition to tradition, teacher to teacher.

For this reason it is best to give up the term "spiritual seeker" altogether. It's an oxymoron. As a manifestation of consciousness in this very moment, who is doing the seeking and what is it that is being sought? "Spiritual seeker" is often just another form of identification, a way of being somebody; it can result in a vague smell of superiority, which doesn't feel emotionally connected or true.

We can also drop the idea of seeking self-improvement. *Someday* we will wake up. *Someday* we will be free. *Someday*, after seeking a bit longer, we will be spiritual.

What about today? What about right now?

Everything you need to become awake is right here, right now. It's also the only moment when freedom is available. When you don't claim to know with certainty what is happening, you meet each moment, whether emotional or not, without an agenda. No manipulation is happening. Whether it is a conflict with your spouse, standing in line at a bank, or a moment with twenty thousand people in Madison Square Garden, there is no *Weltschmerz,* just welcome.

PLAY

> Always remember: Joy is not merely incidental
> to your spiritual quest. It is vital.
> —REBBE NACHMAN

So what is a characteristic that embodies true spirituality? Is it a lack of habitual thought? Is it pure devotion? Is it earnestness?

Maybe. But is this the way we want to deal with other people? By becoming all sweet and perfect and spiritually correct? By only speaking in hushed, measured tones and artificially containing our personality?

Ugh! What fun would that be?

I find that true spirituality embodies meeting the moment in a fluid sense of play. Play is the opposite of hell, either internally or externally.

When you play, you deeply don't know.

Play doesn't exist only when you're having fun; being playful means you are present to what is, whether it is suffering or joy. And play can only happen in the moment, along with true emotion. Also, when you play, your conditioning, your presentational self, and your reflexive thought recede to the back of the stage. Playing in the moment with people can turn the hell of human interaction into pure joy no matter what is happening.

As you wake up, it's not that you're not serious. You are—you're just not solemn. You're too serious to be solemn. True spiritual adepts reveal themselves in a lightness of being; they have done the work and are free, meeting each moment with a playful emptiness.

I am speaking about play from its most ordinary form to its most exalted. One of the reasons we are attracted to professional athletes, musicians, and actors is that they are completely absorbed, playing in the moment. They are accessing their joy—passionate, intense, and emotional, letting the full range of experience be felt right *now*.

Athletes can't be in the past or the future, because they will drop the ball. Literally. Musicians can't be thinking about the next note, because they won't be able to fully inhabit the note they are playing. And in theater, acting is *reacting*, moment to moment.

This is the joy that performers talk about, complete absorption in the moment. An actor might put it in terms of "being more comfortable as somebody else," an athlete might talk about "being in the zone," and a musician might speak about "hitting the groove." But what they all have in common is that they have lost themselves (their small selves) in moments of play. It is so powerful that we like to watch them; they enable us to lose our small selves too.

Play can also be experienced in more ordinary exchanges, whether it's buying groceries, ordering in a restaurant, or paying for a cab ride. In fact, every exchange with another human being is an opportunity to play and to connect with somebody in the moment, whether through a smile, a gesture, or a word. But this can only be done when not obsessing about the past or worrying about the future or thinking we *know* the present.

Improv your way through the moment. Riff and play and nudge yourself and other people, with a twinkle in your eye, into being more present. Notice how lively everything feels. You are awake!

Notice how in this playfulness the world turns into heaven instead of hell.

WHEN HELL IS A FEELING, TRIGGERED BY THOUGHT

When mind is quiet, all is Self.

When mind moves the world arises.

So be Still, throw away everything and be Free."

—H. W. L. POONJA

I am often asked in dharma conversations, "What about feelings? How do you stay open to your feelings in the moment while living in a big city? Don't you need to put up a tough exterior?"

To which I usually answer, "Who and what need protecting? And what is the cost of protecting oneself?"

The cost of carrying the tough exterior actually far outweighs the benefits. Yes, it can be a buffer between yourself and a difficult reality, but it is also armor, heavy and exhausting to carry around. Better to be almost childlike in one's approach to direct experience. Not childish, which connotes immaturity and naiveté, but *like* a child, fully engaged and laughing one second, vulnerable and sad the next, with no need to protect.

Daniel Gilbert, professor of psychology at Harvard, did a study revealing errors we make in overestimating both the intensity and duration of our emotions, something he calls "impact bias." Our natural tendency is to think that good and bad events alike will cause stronger emotions than they actually do. For this reason, it is important to differentiate between what is a direct feeling and what is a product of mind. This is both easy and not so easy.

When I was first exposed to these teachings seven years ago, I was in the middle of a difficult breakup. It had been a short but deep relationship with Tracy (not her real name), and we had said a lot of things to each other and made a lot of promises that I took seriously. When it ended, I was heartbroken. I felt betrayed, angry, and sad. Six months later I was still inconsolable. I couldn't stop thinking about her. *If only she would be less afraid and change her mind! What if I had just done this or said that?* It's hilarious to me now, but I was actually thinking: *Should I write her letter number seventeen?* I was constantly running strategies in my head to win her back or producing fantasies of what the relationship could have been.

When I went to my first dharma talk, I was in a kind of crazy agony, on the rack of my emotions. I was in pain! I listened intently as my dharma teacher, Catherine Ingram, spoke about the freedom to be fully in each moment. I raised my hand.

"What about emotions?" I asked. I fully expected some system that denied emotions.

"Emotions are important, and they must be honored when they arise," Catherine said. "But make sure they're part of a direct experience and not about some recurring story."

That struck home for me. I had thought I had a problem with Tracy—what she had said and done, how she had made me feel so sad. But I really had a problem with *myself*—I was creating my own hell. The direct grief of my relationship ending was long over. What remained was the story of Tracy: the beautiful, intelligent, and funny woman who got away.

Many times our moods are affected by our thoughts and not vice versa, and the mind can use anything—an incident at work, the neighbor's barking dog, or our lack of money—to steal the moment.

In this case I was thinking the thoughts of the tragic romantic: *I'll never again find another woman to whom I'm so attracted. She just doesn't exist*. Then I would experience pain or depression. Although I had truly loved Tracy and had given my full and tender heart to the relationship, it was time to get on with life. But I had no idea how to go about it.

I decided to conduct an experiment. I would see how often I had a "Tracy thought." I bought a small clicker, and every time I had a thought or image relating to Tracy, I clicked it. After an hour I had 127 clicks—a thought every thirty seconds. And the pace didn't decrease throughout the day, ending up in the thousands.

For a couple more days I would just watch the thoughts as they tumbled, unbidden as drama queens, onto the stage of my awareness. I didn't believe them, identify with them, or go along for the trip. I did nothing except watch and click the clicker. By simply staying in a witnessing position, it allowed me a bit of objectivity in terms of my predicament. (Feel free to try this with any story you might be experiencing. It is a fine way to work your way into a witnessing position with your mind.)

The thoughts were strong and persistent and most unpleasant, pulling me down into a kind of sleep. But as I clicked the clicker I woke up into the present moment. It worked because, as Catherine said in that same dharma talk so long ago, "If you have to choose freedom ten thousand times a day, that is ten thousand tastes of freedom."

In my Tracy trance I was well on my way toward that number, so I clearly had my task cut out for me. My hell was in my head, and it was creating feelings of depression, lack, and loss. It was robbing me of my freedom, my joy, and my sense of play. In short, I (my small self) was stealing my life thousands of times a day.

The next day, instead of simply witnessing the thoughts or images, I decided to fully indulge them, lingering over this dinner we'd had, that conversation. I would follow every thought, and my energy sank as I drifted into the reverie of what was and what might have been. Then I watched as my emotions tanked into the malingering funk I'd been in for the past six months. The dynamic was clear: my thought (the Tracy story) was causing my emotions, not the other way around.

After I confirmed the connection between my mind and my emotions, I decided to continue to witness the thoughts as they came up. But in addition to witnessing, I would bring my attention back into the now. By gently steering my attention into what I was doing—driving, making dinner, doing my laundry—I could get glimpses of freedom, if only for a second, from my nightmare. I kept at it.

Gradually, as I brought my attention from the story of Tracy to the present, the gap between the thoughts grew longer. I began to come out of my fog of my depression. The story (in the form of imagination and mind) was like constantly burning embers, and my attention was like gasoline. If I turned my attention to it, then it would flare up, filling my screen of awareness. If I let the embers burn in the background, without feeding them, and paid attention to chopping vegetables or taking a walk, then I could appreciate the now. Anytime I slipped, the moment was instantly consumed and I was checked out, back in the trance.

Right now is like a life raft to a drowning person.

Gradually I played with this awareness, spending more and more time in the present. Eventually, as though I were coming out of a deep hole, I was freed from the misery of my story. It was my first and most profound realization of the vigor and intensity of now.

It became clear to me that the "story of Tracy" was equal to death—it was literally robbing me of my precious life. The emotions weren't real, they were dead bones of thought that I was gnawing on. Only the present moment was life. It became as clear-cut and absolute as these equations:

STORY = DEATH
NOW = LIFE

All of our stories, no matter what they are, whether about a relationship, work, money, or death, will obscure our freedom. This is true no matter where you are on the so-called spiritual path. Whether you are a master or hearing these ideas for the first time, the mind will seize on anything, even your spirituality, to steal your life, moment by precious moment.

Thoughts are like wild horses. You can jump on and ride them to hell and back, suffering all the way. They can range from *That crazy guy shouldn't be in the bank* to being racked by guilt by the thought *I'm a horrible, unspiritual person because I upset the crazy guy in the bank.* No matter what they are, if you identify with these thoughts, you will have no peace at all.

Another favorite alternative for dealing with thoughts is to try to corral them, which is what most spiritual practice does. This is akin to trying to catch the wild horses and put bits in their mouths, attempting to control or break them. The idea is that you can train your unruly mind and thus not think these thoughts. But usually all this does is suspend the mind. As soon as the steel bit of technique is released, the stream of unwanted thought comes galloping in. And in addition to this stream comes another one: *I've failed at my spiritual practice because I'm still having these horrible thoughts!* The mind will pick up anything, including spiritual yearning, to bludgeon you with more thoughts.

Just as the most effortless way to experience a herd of wild horses is to sit on a fence and enjoy the spectacle, the most effective way to deal with mind is to simply witness the thoughts running free, whether this is during meditation or walking down the street, No need to believe the thoughts or try to stop them or say that they are your true nature. They're not, any more than the wild horses are your true nature. Witness the wildness or the craziness, but don't jump on and go for the ride.

This is true for happy or sad thoughts. Whether it's a daydreaming reverie or a panic attack brought on by neurotic thought, either one will take you out of the only livable moment, which is right now as you read this book.

Again, use the mind as a tool that you pull out of the tool box for specific tasks. Then, when you're finished, put it back and enjoy the now.

As for the rest of the running commentary, the unbidden thoughts? Think the thoughts, and think nothing of them.

FEEL IT ALL WITHOUT INTERPRETATION

Do not try to become anything. Do not make yourself into anything. Do not be ameditator. Do not become enlightened. When you sit, let it be. When you walk, let it be. Grasp at nothing. Resist nothing.

—AJAHN CHAH

This doesn't mean that there isn't real emotional turbulence in life, because obviously it arises and must be experienced. It can be hellish or not, depending upon our interpretation.

Once in our dharma conversations a woman named Darcy spoke about losing everything on her computer because the hard disk had crashed. Her entire livelihood, her intellectual history, a large mailing list—all of it was gone (something I have even more sympathy for now, having experienced a similar loss). When she went to check the backup file, it was corrupted. She had just encountered one of the most frustrating aspects of modern cyberlife. It had happened two hours earlier, and she was handling it well but was understandably upset.

After she was done speaking, a young man raised his hand and said, "That's all just attachment." Darcy's face crumpled as she slowly nodded. She was attached to all this work, which was also her livelihood. Now she felt that she had failed at an important spiritual lesson.

I almost jumped out of my chair.

This is a perfect example of a case when a spiritual belief system prevented somebody from showing up in a compassionate way for a person who was suffering right in front of him. By saying her feelings were just "attachment," he was invalidating the very real emotional turbulence that was coming up. He was like the movie star in Madison Square Garden after September 11 in that he didn't meet the moment and wasn't empathetic. Even though it was based on a "spiritual" principle, what he said actually lacked love. It isn't that thoughts and emotions ranging from anxiety to sadness don't come up: they obviously do. But to label them as attachment, with detachment being the higher virtue, is to impose an unsympathetic belief on what is.

It is also a form of spiritual up-leveling. The spiritual path is a terrific place to hide out from feelings, used as a perfect form of denial. But people in spiritual circles are often just as filled with unresolved psychological issues as the nonspiritual person, except they're often festering under the "higher virtue" of detachment. And why not? They get to hide out and be spiritual at the same time—a double win. But the desire to transcend difficult feelings leads to a strange kind of out-of-touchness. Emotions can be transcended for only so long. Scrape the surface and the patina falls away, revealing the long-repressed feelings that are raging below the surface.

The point of these teachings isn't detachment. It is more about *compassionate engagement*. It isn't retreating into a cerebral ivory tower—emotional experience is welcome, even necessary. In fact, emotions exist to tell you the truth of what is happening when the mind is in confusion. Emotions are an early warning system, a fuse that gets blown whenever a situation isn't right or true. As a product of the body, they don't lie. When you are in confusion between what you feel and what you think, the emotion will reveal the deeper truth and the thought, a product of mind, will be the untruth.

So emotions are invaluable and must be honored. If they are not part of some long story and are fresh in the moment, you let them blow through. Without trying to detach, you feel them fully and then allow them to fall away.

Everything is felt, nothing is kept.

So if frustration arises because of lost data, you feel the frustration but don't compound it with any additional interpretation. If the feeling is about a relative who died and you feel sad, you feel the feelings but don't add on the story that you "should have done more."

So much mental suffering depends upon the interpretation one gives to an arising phenomenon. It doesn't matter if the stories are about the loss of a love *(I'll never find anybody as beautiful or intelligent again)* or the loss of data *(I'm such an idiot for not making two backups)* or any judgment for having the stories themselves *(I'm not spiritual).* When indulging the story, there is suffering. But when the actual pain arises in awareness and when it is fully allowed, without excess interpretation, then it can be felt, witnessed, and released.

This is true of physical pain as well. If you are hurt and in this moment feeling pain, there is nothing to do. Pain is a phenomenon like any other, one that arises and, except in the case of chronic pain sufferers, usually falls away. There is the pain, and there is the awareness in which the pain arises. The idea is not to avoid the pain—which is, well, unavoidable—but rather to expand your awareness *around* the pain.

Part of this involves acceptance, and the other part involves not telling any stories about the pain. Don't get into "I'm going to die from this disease" or "I'm never going to feel good again" or "This happened to me because I created it" or the Puritanical nonsense "I created it because I'm a bad person." Pain happens in life Period. Simply have a direct experience of the it because it's all that is real in the moment. You don't know anything about what's going to happen next. In this way you feel the pain without adding additional suffering.

For example, I know from personal experience that prognoses for people with a terminal disease are often wrong. A person very close to me has been HIV-positive for almost twenty years. When he was first diagnosed, we were literally planning the funeral. He didn't even have any symptoms, but every holiday was our last, for in the mid-eighties people with HIV usually lived only a year or two. Yet twenty years later he is still healthy and very much alive. All the drama and suffering around the diagnosis were, in his case, premature.

So when dealing with loss, pain, or disease, avoid interpretation. Don't add a hell when it isn't there.

I overheard a funny exchange between a man and a woman standing in line at a grocery store in New York City. They were discussing beauty tips, including how to keep one's face clean amid the dirt and grime of city life.

"I've never had a facial," he said.

"It wouldn't help," she quipped.

"Oh, thanks a lot!" the man replied, laughing.

"Because your face can't be improved upon," she said, eyes dancing.

"Oh, thank you so much!" he said happily.

Interpretation can make the difference between happiness and suffering. Have the experience, the emotion, the thought—have it all, but don't layer an interpretation on it.

ESCAPE FROM HELL

I was riding in a convertible the other day when I noticed a fly buzzing against the windshield, trying to get out of the car. The top was down and the air was swirling around us. All the fly had to do was relax and it would have been swept out to freedom. And yet this fly, in its lack of awareness, just kept on bumping up against the glass.

This is us when we are caught up in our own mind and conditioning, unable to see the freedom that we already are. In a way it demonstrates what Alan Watts called the Theory of Reverse Effort. When you struggle in water, you sink. When you relax, you float. When you hold your breath, you lose it.

It is the same way with thought. Focus on controlling it and it often only gets stronger. The mind will take the spiritual urge to control thought and use that very urge like a cudgel to beat you up when you fail. In the nondual teachings, we understand that everything is a manifestation of consciousness. Everything is allowed, including thought. Feel the freedom and the lack of straining that comes from this.

There is nothing to do. Nothing to be added or eliminated. Nothing to be changed.

This is true whether the events are large or small, between countries or between lovers, whether it is the hell of other people or the madness of your own mind. It is always useful to inquire of yourself. *What is the reality (the phenomenon), and what is my belief, imagination or interpretation?*

When avoiding the hell of your small self, it becomes much easier to approach other people's hell from a place of peace, compassion, and love.

ROAD RAGE

Dealing with Mad Max Within and Without

Will you put out mine eyes?
These eyes that never did nor never shall
So much as frown on you.
—WILLIAM SHAKESPEARE, *King John*

You're moving in traffic with your blinker on, trying to get to the right lane so you can catch your exit. The Mercedes next to you speeds up, closing the car-length opening. The man driving doesn't acknowledge your existence—you're not there unless he makes the horrible mistake of actually looking at you—so he cuts you off, only to sit in traffic directly in front of your bumper.

Or you're sitting at a light and it turns green. Immediately the person behind you leans on the horn. A moment later that car is screeching by you, leaving only the driver's raised middle finger in its wake.

Welcome to another day on the congested highways of the world, where people are simmering just under the boiling point, ready to explode over the smallest perceived infraction. Caught up in a nightmare of ego, stress, and competition, driving can become dangerous and frustrating, a proxy ground for feelings of unresolved anger. In the anonymity of one's car, separated by speed, glass, and metal, it's easy to forget there is another living, breathing human just a couple of feet away. Cars contribute much in terms of convenience and mobility but also increase isolation, create stress, and decrease one's tolerance for diversity.

You can particularly see this in cities such as Los Angeles, where the car is the only practical form of transportation. In New York or Boston, where everybody rides the subway, there is a higher tolerance for the hurly-burly of life and all its different manifestations. You are exposed to people you wouldn't normally meet and thus, without a choice, your understanding is expanded. In Los Angeles this is not the case. We glide by each other like so many exotic fish, each in our own tank of glass and steel, swimming in our singularity. This leads to the sense of disconnection and isolation that depersonalizes the individual driving next to you.

Even normally nice people can become maniacs because in their anonymity they see other drivers, rather than human, as mere objects in their way. Recently a man was sentenced to three years in prison for snatching a woman's dog out of her car and throwing it into oncoming cars during a traffic dispute. The philosopher Horace said, "Anger is a short madness." This man's short madness ended up with the loss of a beloved pet, a traumatized woman, and for the man a life forever changed. In the blink of an eye, his screen of awareness was obliterated by anger, pain, and the impulse to hurt. The end result was three years in jail and a lifetime of regret.

Yet which of us hasn't felt a surge of frustration, anger or fear while driving? Which of us hasn't taken every last thing personally?

IMPERSONAL VERSUS PERSONAL

When things go wrong, don't go wrong with them.
—ANONYMOUS

I have a close friend, Sam, who becomes a lunatic behind the wheel. It's not that he is aggressive himself. He is simply hyperaware of every infraction that other drivers make. Somebody is driving too fast or too slow; another person didn't come to a full stop at the sign or is tailgating him. And if a driver is rude, appears not to be paying attention, or is trying to get ahead by "gutterballing" along the shoulder of the road, Sam goes ballistic.

Once, at a four-way stop, a driver followed the car in front of him through the intersection, not waiting his turn. Sam gunned our car into the intersection to block the offending vehicle, almost causing an accident as a result. Curses were exchanged as both drivers blared their horns at each other, each refusing to budge. When I asked Sam about it later, he said he hated when people broke the social contract and that they needed to be "taught a lesson." When I asked him about the wisdom of teaching a total stranger anything during a furious exchange, Sam laughed and said, "It's a tough job, but somebody has to do it."

People can seem like total jerks on the road. They can cut you off, drive dangerously, and be inconsiderate. This is challenging to deal with if their selfishness is directed intentionally at you. But even if it is, what does it ultimately have to do with you? Even if they are being completely confrontational, even if they have just sped up and cut you off and are screaming at you with veins bulging from neck and forehead, they have chosen you randomly.

This means it has nothing to do with you. So why be reactive?

Sam was actually making an error we all make at one time or another—the error of taking *anything* personally. The sad truth is that most people going through the day, actively pursuing their business, don't have any idea you're alive. Nothing is personal. They aren't trying to wound you; they're too busy protecting their own wounds. Often their behavior is unconscious. They are talking on the phone while driving, involved in an argument with their spouse, or overtired from working the late shift. Again, it usually has nothing to do with you. You are incidental, inadvertently experiencing their "jerky behavior" as a by-product of their inattention. It is only in referring every event back to "me"—*what that person did to me, how they cut me off*—that one's personal suffering is created.

How much better would it be to see the actions of other drivers in the same way that you see the weather? Unpredictable. Impersonal. Beyond your control. Nobody but crazy people would think of shaking their fist at an icy patch on the road or giving a thundershower the finger for getting them wet. Yet what control do unconscious people have over their actions in the moment? They are asleep, absorbed in themselves, not present. Why trade in your wakefulness and enter their dream state?

Now, my friend Sam says we should wake them up, that this is his job, to stop the rain from petting down and the snow from falling; he sees this as his own personal destiny, as a *calling*. I'm exaggerating, but you can see how funny this becomes. To see everybody as Buddha, *atman, brahman,* God, consciousness, awareness—whatever culturally derived name you have inherited—is to see reality clearly.

But if, as the Buddhists say, some of them are sleeping Buddhas, then, as with all sleeping people, you wake them at your own risk. They might be shocked or grumpy, you might be perceived as condescending or controlling, and the end result might be an explosion.

SUBJECTIVE REALITY VERSUS OBJECTIVE REALITY

You cannot control without being controlled.

—DR. ROBERT ANTHONY

There is a Sanskrit word, *avidya,* which means "incorrect comprehension" or "ignorance." It is the opposite of *vidya,* which means correct comprehension. I like these two terms because we are all operating under some misapprehension—this is the nature of our conditioning, which forms our subjective reality. We all experience life from a unique and subjective place, and if we didn't, then we would be completely free from *avidya.* We would have correct comprehension and, in fact, would be awake.

At one point during one of my dharma conversations, a young man said there is no such thing as objective reality, that reality itself is an illusion.

"What is illusory about reality?" I asked.

"Life is completely subjective," he responded, gesturing around the room. "All this is an illusion."

I rapped the table with my knuckles.

"My direct experience is that it all feels pretty real to me," I said. "It feels more real to me than the concept that it's an illusion."

"But just because you have a subjective experience that all this is real, it doesn't make it so," the young man countered.

"I would agree with you that we are all experiencing reality differently. Given our own psychological and physical conditioning, our different vantage points, and the unique filters we all wear due to our genetics and upbringing—our nature and our nurture—that is inevitable. But this doesn't mean there isn't an objective reality."

The young man paused, looking puzzled. "But how would you define objective reality?"

I picked up a plastic bottle of Evian, holding it above my head.

"Does everybody see this water bottle?" I asked, looking around the room. Everybody nodded. I dropped the water bottle on the floor. It bounced once and landed, miraculously, standing upright.

"See my magic powers?" I joked. Everybody laughed. "The objective reality is that the water bottle fell. Now, given the different vantage points we have, we may all have seen something slightly different about the way the bottle fell. But it did fall. That is the objective reality of gravity acting upon this water bottle."

I picked up the water bottle, looking around the room. I held the bottle above my head.

"Now, somebody in this room might have seen this water bottle hovering five feet above the floor. Maybe somebody is still seeing this," I said, laughing. "That would certainly be their subjective reality. But that doesn't mean that it's objective reality. Subjective reality is further distorted by time and memory. Any detective will tell you that given a crime and ten witnesses, ten different stories will arise between them. But, again, that doesn't mean that an objective reality doesn't exist."

I opened the bottle and took a sip, letting this sink in.

"In fact," I continued, "a definition of wakefulness could be the alignment of one's subjective reality with objective reality."

"Could you say that another way?" asked the young man.

"The more your subjective reality is in alignment with objective reality, then the more awake you are. It simply means that your individual filters of conditioning have been removed. The tape in your brain that you're running—what you want reality to be, what your desires and prejudices show you—no longer has a distorting effect."

I bring this up in the context of driving to explore the relationship between what you are experiencing and what you are telling yourself you are experiencing. The driver who cuts you off may not even have seen you. Your incomplete understanding (subjective reality) of the situation is going to create suffering because of the story you are telling yourself about what is happening.

I can hear my friend Sam protesting: "But what about the person who does see you? Or pretends not to see you? What if you are seeing objective reality clearly and it's taking the form of a jerk who cuts you off?"

Again, that is that driver's prerogative. How you react to it is yours. You can be outraged and disgusted by the asinine behavior of the human race, or you can be mildly amused. Either way, understand this: that driver doesn't know you! I can assure you that he or she didn't offer it personally. But if you want to take it personally, then the choice for suffering is yours.

SUFFERING VERSUS SURFING

Peace does not mean the absence of war.
Peace means the presence of harmony,
Love, satisfaction and oneness.

—SRI CHINMOY

You can suffer or you can surf. You can fight everything tooth and nail, or you can merge with the flow of traffic in the same way a surfer catches a wave. Surfing and driving are analogous. One miscalculation and the surfer gets dumped; one error in judgment and the driver crashes. This is literally true, and it is also energetically true. When you are met with a wave of another person's conditioning, do you fight it? Do you try to prevent it from running its course? Or do you relax and merge with it, accepting it as it is? Do you do battle or do you get out of the way? In surfing you either ride the wave or get out of the water. The same is true for human relationships.

One school of psychological thought says that anytime you try to impose change on another person, no matter how good your intentions are, it is a manipulation. It does damage, however subtle. On a spiritual level, if other people are indeed manifestations of consciousness, (even people who are annoying or dangerous on the road), then who are you to say they shouldn't be exactly the way they are? The truth is, they are exactly the way they need to be in that moment, pursuing their needs even if they are suffering. Maybe in that moment they need to speed. Maybe in that moment they legitimately need to get there before you. Are you competing with them because you have like needs or because you just want to win?

When you try to change another person's behavior you create suffering for both of you. This is true of deeper relationships as well as superficial encounters during the day. Even if you manage to control and change somebody's behavior (especially somebody you know well), the change is typically short-lived, with resentment building over time. Think about the times you have tried. Has it lasted? Does it stick or does it unravel? Although it is a truism that everybody is enlightened or awake, that nothing needs to be done except for them to realize it, you can't be the one to do it for them. You can't wake somebody up who's asleep. The most you can do is invite them to wake themselves up, and they have to *want to do it*.

For you to try anything else is a waste of your chi—your life force, your energy. This couldn't be truer than during a momentary encounter with a passing motorist.

WHAT IS ACTUALLY HAPPENING?

Everybody complains about traffic—how horrible it is, how frustrating it feels. But what is actually happening when we are driving? What is the actual experience? Most of us are usually seated in air-conditioned comfort, listening to music or chatting with friends on the phone. We might as well be in our living room, relaxing on the couch. Some cars even have televisions, so you can truly relax (at your own peril). So what prevents us from experiencing this direct reality? Mostly it's our mind, which is somewhere else. We're in a rush, impatient, aggravated because we think other people are preventing us from getting to our goal. Or because we haven't left ourselves enough time, so it's impossible to relax. Or else we're checked out completely. How often have you been driving and arrived at your destination wondering how you got there? It's as if your reptilian brain, the same part that regulates your breath and heartbeat, was automatically piloting the car without any help at all from your cerebrum.

No better metaphor exists to describe these nondual teachings. Asleep at the wheel and missing the journey, we arrive at our destination confused and disconnected from ourselves, our experience, our environment, and our fellow man.

So what is actually happening when we are driving? Are we going somewhere? Yes, of course, that's why we're in the car. But is that all that is happening? No. We already *are* somewhere. The next time you drive your car, understand that as you walk out the door of your house you have arrived. As you put your hand on the cool metal of the door handle you have arrived. As you sink into the seat you have arrived.

Each moment blooms and dies continuously, so fleeting that it is gone faster than a thought can grab it. Each scintillating moment is born from the future and dies into the past, yet the present always has a beautiful constancy, rolling along endlessly, infinite and sublime.

You can't not be in this moment; it is the only one that exists, whether you are at your "destination" or on the road.

GOING VERSUS BEING

I teach yoga, and one of the things I've noticed in myself and my students is that we often "fall asleep" during the transitions between poses. We rush or lack consciousness in our transitional movements. Often we are already moving ahead to the next asana (pose) before fully completing the pose we are in.

I remember a master teacher asking me, when I first started doing yoga ten years ago, if I was the type of person always thinking about the next activity, the next party, the next event. I said I probably was. I was always the person bugging my friends to go to the next place. Being the eternal optimist, I always thought it was going to be better than the place I was in. My teacher pointed out that this dynamic was apparent to her from my yoga practice. I was not filling my lungs up all the way and I was not exhaling all the way out, crucial to having a meditative experience during yoga. My breath was shallow, and so was my experience of my own poses.

How can you find the still point in every moment? In yoga it is by fully inhabiting each moment, breath by breath. Outside the yoga class, it is the same.

The difference between going somewhere and being somewhere is quite simply a change in perspective. It is the recognition that in the attempt to arrive, we never arrive. Paradoxically, it is only through releasing the concept of arriving that we can ever actually fully arrive, moment by moment, throughout the day.

TRANSITIONS DON'T EXIST

You wander from room to room
Hunting for the diamond necklace
That is already around your neck!
—RUMI

The truth is that there is no such thing as a transition. Moment by moment life marches by, and we are in it, engaged or not. So the idea that *this* moment isn't really important, that *this* moment is just a transition to a really important moment, like that party you're driving to tonight or the job interview you have tomorrow, is not seeing reality clearly. Even the idea that you can start being spiritual after you finish this page or book or seminar or meditation or retreat is a fallacy. No moment is more important than the next, because *each and every moment is the only place where life can happen.*

Again, no moment is more important than the next, because the present, this moment, is the only one that is livable. The past is dead, and the future never arrives. This is not a concept; it's simply a fact. The past and future are uninhabitable except in the imagination of the mind.

Thich Nhat Hanh, the Buddhist teacher, will not speed his step to catch an airplane, even when he is thirty feet from the gate. He would rather miss the plane than rush. If he misses the plane, what is the problem? He is just as happy sitting and waiting for the next one because there is no such thing as a transition in life. No present moment is better than the next. How could it be?

But let's say you're not an enlightened Buddhist monk. It doesn't matter. Even when you are going, let's say really going, like running for a plane, you are awake to each step, the feel of the strap of your carry-on bag, the slap of your shoes hitting the floor. You're not thinking about the consequences of missing the plane, losing the account, or missing the wedding; even in going fast, you are being.

It is possible, to quote Buckaroo Banzai, that "wherever you go, there you are"—to have a feeling of always already being there rather than always going. Feel the relief and relaxation of that recognition. The internal pressure and anxiety are instantly released, replaced by an endless stream of now.

Yet driving has become a metaphor for our society, which is obsessed with the idea of future happiness. We often make the deal that "once this happens, then I'll be happy."The same is true of driving: once we arrive, then we can relax. This is an illusion of the mind, and once you see through it you become unwilling to exchange the vibrant present moment for any future, which is ultimately, from the vantage of right now, simply an imagination or nightmare of the mind.

As we go through our day in a big city, people are going to be continuously challenging us, approaching us with needs and desires. Much of our own response to the dense proximity of people in city living is our constant strategizing about how to get what we want. This helps create a sense of anxiety about the future, which again steals the present moment. By definition, this has to be the result of imagination: it's not happening now, so it can only be happening in one's mind.

Time itself only exists as a concept of mind. Without mind there is only right now Everything else is imagination.

STEP OUT OF THE CAR, PART ONE—NOW VERSUS IMAGINATION

To set up what you like against what you dislike—this is the disease of the mind.

—SENG-TSAN

I can remember one time, early in my film career, when I was a production assistant for a music video being shot out in Huntington

Gardens in Pasadena, California. I was fresh out of film school, was completely broke, and had not yet been exposed to these teachings. Part of my job for the one-day shoot was to get to the location and unlock the gate for the crew so they could start unloading grip trucks, setting up catering, and so on.

Nothing could happen until I got there with the keys at five in the morning.

Well, my battery-operated alarm clock ran out of juice, and I overslept. I woke with a jolt and left my house at 4:45. The drive was forty-five minutes, and so I sped through predawn Los Angeles as fast as my old Ford Escort would go, which was about ninety miles per hour.

At least that's what the police officer said when he pulled me over.

As much as I pleaded with him, saying that fifty people were waiting for me and couldn't he cut me a break, he wrote the ticket. Slowly. It was a ticket for $148, two dollars under what I was being paid for the day. When he finally finished, I raced off to Huntington Gardens, where everybody was waiting for me to unlock the gate.

Now let me paint the picture of the day. It was seventy degrees and clear. We were filming in a beautiful rose garden. My duties were light and interesting, and the director was organized and civil. It was about as perfect a production job that could ever be. Even the song, by an artist named Abra Moore, was beautiful.

But I was in a living hell.

All I could think about was the speeding ticket. How I should have put a new battery in my alarm. How I shouldn't have been speeding. How I was essentially working the entire day for $2. How I needed the money for essentials. How I was going to get another point on my record and lose my safe-driver status and have to pay more money for insurance. On and on my mind went. There I was in paradise, learning my craft, surrounded by creative people, and I was just filled with misery. The day, which was even short by music video production standards, was ruined by my anticipation of my future loss.

Thirty days later I went to court for the ticket. It was dismissed because the police officer didn't show up.

This was such a powerful lesson for me. I often think how all of the worry and anticipation of the future was a complete waste of that beautiful day. What had actually happened when the officer gave me a ticket? In that moment, all he had done was *hand me a yellow piece of paper*. That was the reality of my direct experience. No money was taken out of my account. No final judgment had been made. Nothing had really changed.

Some people would look at this event another way. They would create a "magical thinking" story around it: for all I know, the police officer may have stopped me right before a terrible accident. He may have saved me from a horrible future that I wasn't worrying about as I was speeding. The what-if game works both ways, for the positive as well as the negative. Either way it's all in the mind.

Seeing clearly is forgetting the name of what one sees. If we don't immediately label our world as we process it, we will have a more direct experience of the world, see it more clearly, and have much less suffering. See what is real. See what is imagination. Forget about labeling what you "like" and "dislike," what is "bad" and "good." See reality stripped of projection about past and future. See it so clearly, with such wakefulness that you are experiencing movement, color, shape, sound, and taste without even giving them a name.

Just *now*.

Just this experience of the yellow shape the police officer handed me.

Everything else is extra.

All of my stress was about a future that never materialized—it was a complete waste of life. In the present moment, all was fine. In my imagination about the future, it was a nightmare.

Consider the difference in the next story.

STEP OUT OF THE CAR, PART TWO

Recently I was making a left turn onto a gridlocked freeway ramp. The light was yellow, and when it turned red I was stuck in the intersection. It was then I saw the bicycle cop staring at me. I had a moment where I actually thought: *Hey, he's on a bicycle. I should just swerve around the traffic and take a side street out of the mess. What's he going to do? Chase me on a bike?*

But by then he was already rapping on my window, which I rolled down.

"License and registration," he said brusquely. After fumbling around a bit in the glove compartment, I handed them over.

"Do you know why I'm stopping you?" The classic rhetorical question.

"Yes," I said, guilty as charged. "Must have had something to do with running that red light."

"Yes. And driving without your seatbelt."

I looked down. *Darn.*

"I—I'm sorry," I stammered. "I just got in my car."

"And driving without a front license plate."The cop continued his litany of charges. I began to see myself regularly taking the bus. "Where is it?"

I stared at his gun. "What?"

"The license plate."

"It's in the trunk," I said.

"That's not the right place for it, is it?"

"It all depends. I took it off because I kept getting photo tickets in the mail from the camera. It felt a little Orwellian, the photos . . . they were ugly photos."

The cop lowered his book and stared at me. But I couldn't stop myself—it was as if I'd been given some bizarre truth serum.

"Let me ask you something," I said, continuing on my journey toward permanent bus rider status. "You're on a bike. I'm in a car. I had this crazy idea when I saw you that maybe I should just take off. What are you going to do, chase me on a bike?"

This seemed hilarious to me, so I started laughing. The cop looked at me with amusement. Then to my shock he laughed with me, the remnants of his brusque demeanor evaporating.

"You'd be surprised," he said. "We can usually catch people at the next light or call it in to a cruiser in the area."

"Oh . . . good thing I resisted that impulse, huh?"

"Good thing. It's too hot to chase you." The cop pulled out his ticket book, seemingly ending our amicable discussion. "I'll tell you what I'm going to do. I'm just going to write you a ticket for no seat-belt. It's twenty-two dollars."

"Really?" I said. "How come?"

"Because you didn't give me any attitude." After a few more minutes of conversation, he gave me my ticket, a fraction of what he could have charged me with, and sent me on my way.

I began to think about his line: *You didn't give me any attitude.* What is the dharmic interpretation of that line? When you don't give someone attitude, you're not projecting any concepts or ideas or manipulations about who you think the other person is or what the interaction is going to be.

For whatever reason that day, what was disarming to the police officer was that I momentarily had no agenda with him. I wasn't defensive, and I wasn't trying to talk him out of anything. When two people push against each other, struggling to control the other person's behavior, great amounts of energy are expended, one's life force is drained, and the results are usually counterproductive, leading to a hardening of one's stance and even more intractable confrontation. But if one person stops pushing, the other is thrown off balance and may have to react in a different way to regain balance. That different way may be unexpected laughter. Whether with a police officer writing a ticket or with your spouse, it happens out of a sense of surrender to the moment and what is happening, rather than pushing for control or a particular outcome.

The result is play, which is derived from innocence.

INNOCENCE VERSUS AGENDA

My teacher and friend Catherine Ingram has said when you approach life with innocence, you meet each moment fresh, without expectation and without agenda. And it's not the innocence that's a result of lack of knowledge or experience. It's like the innocent part of a child that is awake and joyful to what each situation will bring. It is a matter of finding each moment and merging with it rather than trying to control it. Like a stream flowing into a river, this merging is fluid, flexible, and about connection.

The opposite is to approach life with an agenda, whether it's beating a ticket, manipulating a lover, or working a room. An agenda is never innocent, fluid, or free in the moment because the mind, with all of its concepts and strategies, is running the show. It is constantly selling out the joy of now for some imagined joy in the future.

But it's a Faustian bargain that never pays off because the future never arrives. As I've mentioned, life is, in reality, a never-ending string of now. So if one is in the habit of selling out now for future happiness by working an agenda, where does it end? It doesn't, because it's a reinforcing dynamic. The small self, with its habit of control, manipulation, and desire, gets reinforced, whether it succeeds or fails in its agenda.

For instance, if I had tried to cajole, plead or bribe my way out of the ticket, it would have succeeded or failed. The cop would have written me a ticket or not. Either way I would have agreed to be playing a certain game with certain rules. Let's call it the "me game." And what would that have entailed? Well, I would have tried to talk the cop into letting me go, thus allowing me to avoid paying a large fine and accruing points against my license. If I succeeded, then the dynamic would have been rewarded, and I would draw the conclusion that this is the way to be in the world, striving to bend people to my will. If it failed (as it so often does), I might have drawn the conclusion that the cop was a heartless jerk, creating judgment and separation in myself. It's only after many failures at this that I might stumble upon and question the actual dynamic.

So what's going on with the other living, breathing human being who is receiving my pleading and cajoling manipulation (in this case the police officer)? I would have been asking him to not do his job and thus put him out of his own integrity. This would not have felt good to him, and his natural position would be to rigidify. Then our egos would be like two sumo wrestlers trying to gain control of the ring of experience we were creating together.

I would also be reinforcing his sense of "somebodyness." I would, in effect, have been handing over to another person the power to decide my happiness. This is not healthy for me, nor is it healthy for him. And if he was getting off on the power that I gave him, I would have had to deal with all the negative feelings that come after an attempted manipulation had failed, after I had sold and debased myself to no avail.

So what actually happened that day when I got a dose of imaginary truth serum? There was a merging, a kind of interpersonal aikido that started with absolute truth. There was no sumo match of egos, just a kind of playful flow. There was, at the end of it, pure recognition between the two of us of our own humanity. And beyond that, even though neither of us would have been able to articulate it, was a strong feeling that we were both the same. Perhaps playing two sides of the same coin in that moment, but having a same-same experience nonetheless.

This is nothing short of consciousness conversing with itself; we shared a glint of recognition of the God that is us. I dropped my identification with my role of cajoling motorist, and he dropped his identification with his role as police officer. What revealed itself was an easy playfulness.

Now, I'm not saying that this will always be the case. It could easily have gone another way. But so what if it did? Your freedom from identification, your understanding of the connectedness of everything, is not dependent upon other people's reactions. And it most certainly isn't yet another strategy to get what you want.

It's just that when one approaches a situation or person with innocence, then the outcome, whatever it is, is going to feel better for you, no matter what their response.

CRASH LANDING

Last year I got in a serious car accident that was completely my fault. (At this point I'm sure you're all wishing I would ride the bus, but it was actually my first accident in twenty years that was within my control.) I had just done a "rebirthing session" that involved a lot of holotropic breathing, which can put you in a state of altered consciousness. The purpose is to get you to relive the trauma of your own birth, releasing a lot of emotions, after which you feel very blissed out. It is a combination of *pranayama* breathing (a yogic technique) within a Western psychological paradigm.

The end result that day was that I was slightly spaced out. I stopped at a green light to make a left turn. The sun was in my eyes. The cars were coming around a curve, whipping out from under the freeway underpass, which was shaded. I waited until there was an opening and turned left.

A gray Toyota was suddenly on me. The driver must have been speeding, because suddenly he was just there.

I had that moment where everything slows down and future, present, and past bleed together.

Oh no, I thought, *he's going to hit me. No, no, no.*

In the suspended animation of that moment I could see the young driver's terrified face, contorted into a grimace as he struggled to veer out of my path and slow his car down.

Oh my God. I thought as the two cars collided head-on in the inhuman grind of metal and glass, *he's hitting me. No, no, no.*

The cars spun in lazy slow motion with bumpers interlocked, like two dancing hippos in a cumbersome waltz.

Oh my God, he hit me! Shit! I can't believe he just hit me!

And then silence as we skidded to a stop.

Stillness.

I wasn't hurt. I scrambled out of the car as steam jetted out of the radiator, and rushed to the other driver

"Oh my God," I said. "Are you hurt? Are you okay?"

"I . . . I think I'm okay. Are you okay?"The young man, no older than twenty, was shaken but unhurt. I helped him out of his car and we walked to the corner, leaving our cars where they were.

"I'm sorry," I said. "I didn't even see you."

"That's okay. We're both okay. . . ."

We were both relieved to be unhurt and also, I think, to be in a civil exchange. As we swapped registration, license, and insurance information, not a single accusatory or recriminatory word was spoken. Miraculously, his car was drivable. Mine, the sitting target, turned out to be totaled.

Later, as I waited for the tow truck, I began to think about what a metaphor this accident was. Like so much of life, there is the sense of "this can't/shouldn't be happening" immediately followed by a frantic effort to change the course of events, usually followed by regret, recrimination, and self-blame. All this was going on during the course of my accident. In my case it actually took five minutes to even accept the fact that the accident had happened. My head clanged with *No, no, no! Shit, shit, shit!*

Then, after the eventual acceptance, came thoughts of "if only." *If only I'd paid more attention. If only he hadn't been speeding. If only I'd waited to make the turn*. The mind becomes a chorus of recrimination and wishful thinking about what might have been.

Then came the inevitable anxious thoughts about the future: *This is going to raise my insurance. My beautiful old car—I'll never find one like it. What am I going to drive? I have a thousand-dollar deductible on my insurance. Where's that money going to come from?*

I was already inventing a future hell that was pure imagination. But what was my reality? I was sitting outside in the sun, unhurt, after a pretty major crash. Was I feeling gratitude for this narrow escape? No. Was I thankful that I could even walk and talk? No. The mind had already begun its litany of problems that were going to be created as a result of this crash.

All I could see was that my undrivable car was sitting in the road and life was whizzing by me. I was stuck. I was unhappy. I wasn't having fun.

BREAKDOWN

The car, symbol of freedom, mobility and status, will, like all physical objects, break down. Someday you will undoubtedly be sitting by the side of the road with a flat tire or a steaming radiator or even a completely totaled vehicle. When your ship of freedom and music taking you to your next event has been grounded on the rocks of mechanical failure, it can cause a deep sense of annoyance, panic, and even dread. It can also be dangerous, especially for women traveling alone.

We are very identified with our automobiles as a source of freedom. The auto industry has made a fortune linking cars with lifestyle advertising. You are what you drive. It's your statement to the world: "I have arrived." It's a way of telling people who you are and where you fit in the food chain. You drive a hybrid and are environmentally aware. You drive a Mercedes and have a lot of money. You drive a convertible and thus value fun. A female friend told me about trying to set up an acquaintance with a male friend of hers. The woman's first question was: "What does he drive?"

I am not immune to this. I favor old Saab convertibles (before they changed their style, removing their quirkiness), and after I totaled my last car, when I went to the body shop to remove its license plate and all the junk in the trunk, I had a surprisingly poignant moment. It was around this car that I'd danced to the *Moulin Rouge* soundtrack with a woman with whom I'd fallen madly in love. Numerous trips were taken up the Pacific Coast Highway to Santa Barbara with the top down, going to the beach with friends. That car was red and fun, and there was a sense of loss when it went to the junkyard.

But when you identify with what you drive, it becomes another false suit that obscures who you really are. And the more you are identified, the more you will suffer when your source of identification breaks down, because it is *you* that has, in some sense, broken down. As cars whip by you in the flow of life, you are stranded, helpless, out of it. But the truth is that when you attach your happiness to the impermanent, you are writing your own prescription for suffering. The impermanent will always whip by you, even if it's happening in slow motion. Even if it's on the level of stars collapsing and planets dying, everything is impermanent except the vertical experience of right now, which remains fresh and alive and free for as long as you live.

What, you may be asking, does that last sentence really mean?

It's the core of these teachings. In this case, if you are free from identifying with your car, something that might define you as "you," something that will pass, then your only reality consists of your direct experience right now in this moment. What's happening in the room you're in? Is there a breeze? Sunlight streaming through a window? What are the noises? Any sirens in the distance? Traffic? A television from the next apartment? What do you see, hear, touch, and smell? This becomes your reality, drop by drop, and your experience of it is permanent, for now never ends and never changes, no matter what is happening on the surface.

This is true even when sitting in the sun by the side of the road. My happiness was never closer to me than in that moment.

I'm not saying that you won't love your new car when you've worked hard and saved and finally splurged. Go ahead and love it until it gets the proverbial first ding and loses that pristine quality reserved for new cars. But why wait for that? The car will be scrap metal some day. Accept the impermanent as what it is, a fact of life. See more deeply into what is eternal, which is only this moment.

So the event or thought or feeling that happened four sentences ago is as dead as a corpse in a grave. As useless as my totaled car.

Again: flowing, unattached, free, this moment is all that there is, all that is real, all that is livable. The past is not livable. The future is not livable. Only right now is livable.

So in that now you're driving your shiny new car. A fantastic moment. Enjoy it! But know that the car is as ephemeral as the moment. The car is not eternal, so don't bother hanging your happiness on it. Nor do you want to hang your happiness on that particular moment. It's already gone, seamlessly replaced by another moment, which is alway fresh.

And if we don't drop our identification with our cars, what's the alternative? Being more attached to them? Being chained down? What's the result of that? Unhappiness. A lack of freedom. A sense of loss or anxiety when they are threatened or disappear.

So when your car breaks down, know that a lot of these projections will be running through your mind. Lots of thoughts. Lots of identifications. Just witness them.

MY CAR'S BETTER THAN YOUR CAR

The game is not about becoming somebody;
it's about becoming nobody.
—RAM DASS

There is another disadvantage to being identified with what you drive. The more identified you are, the more you will notice that you treat people differently depending upon what *they* drive. Comparison is inevitable. Your identification, the price you have put on your own beingness, has obscured to you other people's worth and humanity. This has a subtly alienating effect that results in a kind of internal hardening. It is extremely separating and results in a taking mentality rather than a giving one, even when apparently there isn't anything to gain. To be in this state is to be in a form of "What can this person do for me?"

It plays out like this:

There's a car. A new Mercedes. A successful and powerful person must be driving it. I will treat that person well and allow him or her to merge because that person is successful and powerful. So I am intimidated. Or I am envious. Or on an unconscious level I think that I might be able to get something from that person, so I will respect him or her. I am simply in obeisance to a primitive "alpha dog" conditioning. I am, to borrow parlance from the business world, "managing upward," that is, treating people differently depending upon their level of perceived power in the world.

Or I see a car. A dented 1989 Honda hatchback, driven by a Hispanic day worker. Not a person very high up on the socioeconomic food chain in our society. Not an *important* person, so I pretend not to see him or her at all and don't let that person merge.

Or perhaps in some twisted way I resent the Mercedes, so I create some story about filthy rich capitalists and I cut that person off or treat him or her differently because of that story.

In all cases I have created separation.

The alternative, of course, is to see and treat everybody equally. And in doing so you realize that you are seeing the nondual reality. Stripped of all your identifications with self, ego, material possessions, ideas of success or failure, and the ever-nagging story of the future, of getting where you're going so you can finally "be," you realize the truth that every step on your journey is an opportunity to have a same-same experience with everybody you encounter.

GENEROSITY, FLOW, AND THE HORN

Illusion produces rest and motion
Illumination destroys liking and disliking.
—SENG-TSAN

When driving, try to stay in a state of flow. This means you are not in opposition to what is happening around you. When the twin steeds of pride and ego are running the show behind the wheel, flow is impossible. Your attitude on the road and thus your driving experience are affected by how much you are identified with your small self and with what you drive. If "nobody is home," in the best sense of the phrase, driving becomes deeply impersonal; it is possible to stay in a feeling of connected flow no matter what is happening outside the screen of your windshield.

This may look like many different things. One way to drive is with the intention to never cause another driver to unnecessarily use the brakes to avoid you. This means you are treating people with generosity behind the wheel. If a driver is trying to merge, you wave that person in with a smile. If you're in an intersection and another driver needs to make a left turn, you let him or her go first. If you see a pedestrian step off the curb, you brake and let the person cross.

Why, you ask, should you do this when everybody else is driving and trying to get ahead at all costs? I ask it of myself, who likes to drive fast. Try it as an experiment. See how it feels to offer generosity to another driver, to drive with an open heart, looking for opportunities to give and be helpful, rather than opportunities to grab and take for your own. Now switch back to driving like "it's me, me, me—it's all about me." Cut people off, don't let them merge—drive like a complete jerk. Finally, go back to generosity again. Give it all away.

How do the two modes feel internally? Which causes a clutch to the gut? Which makes you feel relaxed and good about the world? Which adds to stress and which relieves it? Which makes you feel disconnected and which connected? Play with the different modes of being and the answer becomes obvious.

Notice, too, that you don't really get to where you're going any later. But you do get there much more relaxed.

This form of kindness has the most integrity because it is anonymous; you will not benefit from it except in the way that you feel. Nobody's going to give you money or accolades or your own TV show. The most someone else might do is wave thanks and smile. But this is huge. If the other person is awake, your kindness might be passed on to another driver, who might, in turn, pass that along.

And if you are at the mercy of another driver's selfishness or carelessness, notice how that feels. Notice the quick surge of rage. Of competition. Of frustration.

Here's the hard truth: if you don't drive with generosity, the person causing that rage is *you*. You're just passing it on to the next person, who will say, "The hell with it," and pass it on to the next. The web of connectivity is unveiled in the flow of infinite decisions made every second by every driver in your city. It is like the famous "butterfly effect" theory of what causes hurricanes. If one traces through a nearly infinite number of factors, ranging from high pressure in one country to a storm over the ocean, until one gets back to the original act that traggered all the rest, it might well be the flapping of a butterfly's wings two thousand miles away.

Are your actions on the road like a butterfly's wings? What will you pass on? What will you personalize? What will you hold as a grudge? Will you be the raging person who causes pain and suffering, or the smiling one who softens somebody else's day? The decision is ours, every day.

And could it be possible that ten thousand interactions may pass between people of our city and we might actually receive that gift back from a complete stranger? Somebody who was the recipient of your original peace and generosity ten thousand times removed?

Maybe, maybe not.

But there is no doubt that when kindness is meted out, many times that kindness is passed on. And in this way, the interconnectedness of everything makes itself apparent.

A friend of mine named Nancy told me a story about her and her girlfriend, whom we'll call Katya, driving on the freeway. Katya was driving fast and merged into a lane, tapping another car, which was also driving fast and merging into the same lane. According to Nancy, it wasn't really anybody's fault—it was just an accident. The two cars pulled over and Katya and the other woman got out, assessing the damage, which was minimal. This didn't stop the two women from exchanging heated words, accusing each other of almost having caused an accident. The other woman, wearing jeans and a scarf around her head, was extremely hostile, and Katya responded in kind. They both got back in their cars and slammed the doors shut, getting back on the highway.

"What a total bitch," Katya fumed.

After about a hundred yards the other woman pulled in front of Katya and slammed on the brakes, furiously gesturing for her to pull over. With a combination of anger and trepidation, Katya pulled over. The woman got out of her car and stormed over to Katya's, angrily motioning to her to roll down the window.

"Can't you see? Can't you see that I've got cancer? the woman shouted at Katya before ripping the scarf off her head, revealing a scalp made bald by chemotherapy. Then she burst into tears.

When Nancy told me the story, she said it had been only then that she noticed the scarf on the woman's head and the thinness of her body. Nancy was mortified and instantly empathetic. She felt terrible. The story brought tears to my eyes, and I wish I could say there had been a moment of immediate understanding and regret between the two women.

But Katya shouted at the woman, "Well, no wonder you have cancer! Look at how you treat people!"

The other woman stared at Katya for a moment and then silently walked away, got in her car, and drove off. Nancy felt terrible, but

Katya was so incensed that she didn't see how hurtful she was being. Nancy said that even after she cooled down, Katya didn't see the other woman's reality until after it was spelled out for her. So she missed a moment of forgiveness and understanding with this stranger. She missed that moment of powerful healing that happens when you pull back from a painful situation and crack wide open, saying, "Oh my God, I'm sorry. I'm so sorry," letting the light of your own humanity show.

And the other woman? After this exchange, how could she not feel that the world was a harder place? The fragility and vulnerability that illness brings make the world seem sharp and dangerous enough. Illness makes you feel like you inhabit a parallel universe separate from the world that is blithely barreling along. No doubt the woman went home with that feeling further amplified.

I'm not picking on Katya; we have all been deeply unconscious in our lives. We have all acted thoughtlessly. We've all been rude and inconsiderate. But consider the situation you are in when you don't know what is going on with the other driver. Would you give the finger to somebody who had just lost his father? Would you honk at a person who had just caught her husband in bed with another woman? Probably not, but it could well be the reality of the person who inadvertently cut you off.

I remember driving down Topanga Canyon in Los Angeles one glorious day. In front of me was an SUV that was crawling down the mountain. You need to drive slowly down this canyon, because it's steep and curvy, but this was ridiculous. What the hell was the driver doing? Cars were backed up behind me. At this rate it would take an hour to get down to the Pacific Coast Highway. I was just about ready to blast the horn when I saw a tiny little hand reach up from the seat of the SUV. It was a baby. The driver was driving so gently because he or she didn't want to upset the baby was petrified of having an accident. But how was I to know?

This is the point. How do any of us know what the other human being in the car next to us is going through?

HONKING AT BUDDHA

The idea that we are all chips of consciousness, that we are already enlightened and just have to realize the truth about ourselves, is the core of the teachings upon which this book is based. So when you drive, try keeping this in mind. See the other person not as a competitor, but as Buddha or Christ.

This can be applied to all aspects of your life. Can you see beyond the shape of the person in front of you to their most noble self? When you look in their eyes, try to see their essence. Distill it down, the way a perfume maker takes a field of flowers and creates a scent, and see if you can see the person's higher self. What do you see? Patience? Steadfastness? Subtlety? Humor? Loyalty? Compassion? When you see people this way, you will accord them the respect that you would a master. Understand that each and every person is this inner master, whether they are revealing it or not.

Would you honk at Christ, telling him to move his skinny ass out of the road? Would you honk at Buddha, telling him to move his fat butt and drive faster? See everybody as an expression of this consciousness, all doing the best they can with what they have, even if their inner master is nowhere to be seen.

So what is the horn for? It's to let other drivers know you are there if you think they haven't seen you and the situation is dangerous. That's it. It's not for expressing impatience or your opinion of another person's driving or to yell at somebody.

Every time you get in the car, you have an opportunity to either pass on light to the world or to drop a pile of your conditioning at their door and say, "Tough luck, deal with it."

Every day you have the choice to transform your car from a things of glass and steel into a sacred temple.

TURN IT DOWN

Noise Versus Sound

Silence is not the absence of sound,
but the absence of self.
—H. W. L. POONJA

While we were sitting in silence at the beginning of a dharma conversation in our tiny meditation center, a car paused at the corner stop sign. The car had a trunkload of speakers and was booming rap music. The bass was so strong, it vibrated the plate-glass windows of the center as though they were the head of a drum. I could feel a tickle in my sternum that was not unpleasant. I smiled, marveling that mere sound could move windows, never mind a bone in the center of my being.

After a moment the car moved on, accentuating the silence by its absence. I opened my eyes and began the dharma conversation, commenting on how interesting my experience of the noisy car had been. How the sound arose out of the silence and fell back into the silence, not unlike thoughts in our own heads. How there was nothing to do but to witness the arising and watch it, like all phenomena, inevitably fall away.

Robert (not his real name) started to speak. He was agitated and talked about the urge to rush out and confront the "jerk" in the car who was being so selfish. And then he said he felt immediate shame for the impulse.

"Yes, yes," I joked, "let's all run out with the veins popping out of our heads, shouting, 'Shut up! Can't you see we're trying to be spiritual here?' "

Everybody laughed, but we all recognized how Robert felt. How often is the noise in our head so much louder than anything happening around us? The raging voice inside saying, "Shut up!" followed by a chaser of adrenaline as visions of revenge against the "noisy jerks" dance in our mind. There is a famous quote: The mind makes a wonderful servant but a terrible master.

With the right awareness, you can be relaxed in the noisiest of situations. But if the mind is running the show and you are identifying with every thought, you can be in the quietest desert and suffer mightily.

Phenomena will always arise in the form of sound. In cities it's usually the background noise of traffic and everyday life, punctuated by blaring sirens and honking horns. Jackhammers, construction, garbage trucks, television, boom boxes, screaming fights of neighbors—, all add to the decibel count. Even as I write these words, my apartment building is being painted, providing a symphony of scraping, drilling, and shouting workers. Car doors slam shut. A truck is backing up, piercing the morning with its warning beep. A person in a nearby apartment is attempting to learn the trumpet, without much success.

What would turn these sounds into suffering? Quite simply the belief that the sounds shouldn't exist combined with the desire that the situation should be different. In short, nonacceptance. The driver of the car should turn down the stereo, the workers should stop shouting, and on and on. The insertion of the little self into the equation of life is what causes the suffering. *How is it affecting me? How do I feel about it? What should I do?* But silence is an inside job. And acceptance of external noise is the first step to internal peace.

The great nondual teacher H. W. L. Poonja famously said: "Silence is not the absence of sound, but the absence of self." To what was he referring? What did he mean by the absence of self? And how can the self disappear? Isn't it always with us?

Poonja meant that if we are quiet on the inside, it doesn't matter what's happening on the outside. We could be in Times Square during rush hour and still experience internal silence. The absence of self is the absence of the ego-mind: always identified, commenting, self-referencing, and concerned with its own survival (and by survival, I mean the fulfillment of the needs, wants, and desires of the small self). When the internal monologue, random thoughts, and craziness are raging, obliterating your experience of now, then it is difficult to experience quite under even the most perfect of circumstances. But when we are internally peaceful and quiet, then the outside world becomes largely irrelevant to our equanimity.

Does this mean we need to eliminate our ego, our mind, and our thoughts? As I've mentioned, it is unnecessary to eliminate your internal monologue in order to experience the stillness from which everything springs. Your mind may never become silent. Mush you therefore give up on freedom and peace? Absolutely not.

I have come to look at the noisy, repetitive monologues of the mind as a babbling brook. Sometimes, given a certain stimulus, the brook becomes a raging river. Other times it subsides to a trickle. Ultimately neither state is necessary to experience peace or freedom. What is necessary is to no longer *identify* with the internal noise of every passing thought. Quite simply, you no longer feed the story or neurotic thought with your attention.

In this way not only do you escape the subsequent tunnel vision of being self-absorbed, but you don't even enter the tunnel. You see it as part of a larger context: the mountain, the sky, and the road leading up to the tunnel.

Look at it as if you are standing in front of a bookshelf. You may be reading a particular book cover, perhaps even focused on reading a particular book. But that doesn't mean the rest of the bookshelf disappears. The whole universe is still there, already merged with your awareness. If you're reading the book on your personality or addictions, don't try to transcend it. Dive in fully. Own the feelings it brings up as part of you and know that it too is consciousness. It comes along, but it is not the only book on the shelf. All it takes is a slight flick of attention to be reading another book.

I would also like to clarify that when I talk about dropping identification with your internal noise I'm not talking about eradicating personality. Poonja isn't suggesting you become a silent and detached cipher or lose your individuality. These teachings are impersonal but not detached. When you lose your identification with the "noisy" aspects of your personality, your personality actually becomes more distinct. You cease to care what people think because you understand that the personality—a result of genetic and environmental conditioning—rests on a foundation of deeper awareness. So your relationship with your own personality becomes looser and more relaxed. As you become comfortable in your own skin and the skin of your own personality, you just let things fly. In doing so you experience less constriction and more freedom. You are also more fun to be around.

Up until this point I have been discussing how to approach internal noise. But this method is also appropriate for external sound. Even the language we assign can be indicative. What is our interpretation? Is it noise (pejorative, irritating, stressful) or is it merely a neutral sound?

I know somebody who gets anxious at the sound of a street sweeper. I was surprised because I've always found the swishing sound inherently soothing. I am fond of them because they remind me of big Tonka toys that are cleaning up my world. But they always make her wonder if she is going to get a ticket for parking on the wrong side of the street, even though she now parks her car in a garage!

With external noise, avoidance is impossible: where does one go where there is absolutely no sound? Think about it—even nature has "noise." I once went on a silent retreat by myself up to the White Lotus Foundation in Santa Barbara. It was back in the early days of my exposure to these teachings, and I was looking forward to deep silence. But it was spring at White Lotus. A beautiful time in nature, right? Sure, except for the frogs. Every night the frogs came out and created a cadence as loud as a garbage truck. I didn't sleep one minute that first night, and my mind reacted. *This shouldn't be happening! I'm on a silent retreat and nature is keeping me awake!*

Then I snapped out of it. What was I to do? Rage against nature? That would be ridiculous, right? Almost as ridiculous as raging against noisy people, who are just another manifestation of nature. The next morning I drove to a drugstore and bought earplugs.

The only response to uncontrollable noise is acceptance. This doesn't mean that you don't nicely ask the neighbor to lower the stereo; it just means that the noise doesn't own and control you.

Most noise is actually the *controllable* external noise we impose on ourselves. We get in the car and switch on the radio. We get home and turn on the television. Even on a hike with a friend in nature, we talk, talk, and talk, obliterating any silence that could be created. We avoid any time alone when we might be quiet. So another aspect of dealing with noise is cultivating a love of aloneness, stillness, and silence, when you actually have the choice as to how much external sound you let in your life.

It is in silence that we discover our bond to the universe, because it is from silence that the whole spectacle of the universe arises. When in silence, we do not limit our experience of the silent awareness underlying everything by noisily trying to name it, categorize it, or quantify it. In fact, in silence we have our best chance to experience consciousness because the mind's limitations and madness are made so evident. When we are quiet it is easier for the nondual experience to arise because silence is what we fundamentally are beneath all the activity of our mind and the business of life. We thus bring ourselves into resonance with the silent tone of the universe, the silence we will return to upon our death.

WHEN YOU ARE THE NOISE

Any intelligent fool can make things bigger, more complex, and more violent. It takes a touch of genius—and a lot of courage—to move in the opposite direction.

—E. F. SCHUMACHER

A close friend of mine is a talented musician. Ann has a beautiful voice and is occasionally used for commercials or as a backup vocalist in well-known bands. At one point she was putting together her own demo reel and sometimes sang in her small studio apartment during the day, composing her songs. Above her lived a woman who had made it her mission in life to get Ann evicted. The woman called the police, organized eviction petitions, and complained to the management all the time, even when Ann was out of the country and couldn't possibly have been making any noise.

Now, I happen to think that Ann sings like an angel. But for this woman it was obviously torture. She made Ann's life a living hell, until Ann was afraid to open her mouth in her own home. Meanwhile, when the woman walked across her apartment, her heavy step often woke Ann up.

Ann fought with the woman constantly, unable to keep from being pulled into a conflict. During one of the confrontations, Ann found out the woman used to be an amateur opera singer. This was a revelation. She was obviously working out some issues dealing with her failed musical aspirations. Ann used to come to me filled with rage and indignation, telling me the details of the latest round, the latest letter written, and the latest heated exchange. When I suggested that she move, she said that it wasn't her fault and that she wasn't going to be bullied out of her own home. It was so unfair!

In between bouts of indignation she also felt that if she could get to a point of spiritual understanding, she would be able to transform the situation. Being the dedicated yogini that she was, she would be able to understand the woman's vindictiveness and somehow transcend it.

In trying to transform the situation, she reminded me of the story of the young student who went to study with a master. He traveled a great distance, and when he reached the town of the master, he rented a room over what he later found out was a motorcycle repair shop. He suffered for weeks trying to meditate with the sound of engines roaring underneath him. He tried everything—talking to the managers of the repair shop, wearing earplugs, and so on. Finally he went to his master nearly in tears.

"I have failed in my spiritual task," he cried. "I can't meditate in that place."

"Why don't you move?" his master asked.

For the young student this was a revelation. Being spiritual didn't depend upon conquering the noisy situation, which was creating suffering for him. It meant being flexible enough to see when a situation was untenable and then simply moving away from it.

How often do we try to make something work that isn't working with the idea that if we were just spiritual enough, this job, this relationship, this home, this noisy neighborhood would be fine? We set up our lives as a kind of spiritual gauntlet, a daily tribulation to be conquered through prayer, meditation, and self-sacrifice. But this type of self-abuse is entirely mental and is more about controlling the self than anything. Sometimes the only solution is the one the old master espoused: "Why don't you move?"

And so it came to be with Ann, albeit involuntarily. The day came when the management, having had a meeting with the woman (organized at a time when Ann was out of town), had enough of the woman's tenacious campaign. They sent Ann a letter telling her to "cease and desist" all singing or she was going to be evicted. It dragged on a couple more months, and then she was finally evicted. But before she left Ann came to an important realization for her: stifling who she is wasn't a way to become more spiritual.

Her whole essence, the very fabric of her being—indeed, her dharma in life—was to express herself through song. To have that stifled for any reason was to stifle her deepest self. Why was she fighting to stay in a place that didn't support who she was? A place that was trying to control her natural expression of life? A nondual sage once said: "When you are living in your joyful realization, it doesn't matter the circumstances." And this is true. But it is not meant to taken as a challenge, a fight to the death, with enlightenment being the prize.

Of course there's another side to this also. There are times when it may be right to stay and fight—for ourselves and society. But this is a choice in life. Nothing is being done *to* us, as much as it sometimes feels it is. So it's worth asking what we are fighting for.

It all depends on your perspective. In a larger sense, anytime we try to control noise we are trying to extinguish some form of life that is expressing itself. For it is in noise that life and creativity are usually given voice. So why not have gratitude for that life? And for our own life, because our own ability to hear sound, in all its wondrous and awful permutations, means *we are alive*.

I have a friend who lives in an apartment building. Upstairs lives a schizophrenic given to the most unbelievable screaming and swearing tirades I've ever heard. The first time I experienced it, I thought somebody was being murdered. Beside her lives an old lady with two constantly yapping dogs. Across the hallway lives a woman with a pet potbellied pig who is always running around the garden being chased by dogs, with the pig's owner yelling, "Cuddles, come here, you bad pig." The level of noise in this apartment building is phenomenal. When I mentioned it to my friend, she just shrugged and said that it rarely bothered her. She wasn't adding her own internal noise to the external noise.

The point isn't to eliminate noise by going to a monastery or the desert or some mountain retreat in order to feel the stillness from which everything emanates. We can tune in to that silence anywhere at any time. This is done by dropping our ideas of what should be, our indignation at what shouldn't be, and our expectation that what is should change. When we try to control noise, we are contracted, irritated, upset. When we let the noise flow through us without trying to battle it, we are relaxed, accepting, and free.

The silence is always here even when we are making the noise.

I once went snowshoeing in Idaho, deep in a 350-square-mile wilderness area, traipsing up a mountain in five feet of snow. Elk foraged among the trees; I was alone and miles from the nearest road. *Crunch, crunch, crunch,* I trudged up the mountain. When I paused to catch my breath, after the blood stopped pounding in my head, I was greeted by the most profound silence I'd ever experienced.

Not a sound came from the snow-muffled landscape.

It was so quiet, the silence felt like it actually had a sound—like a whooshing or ringing in my ears. In a state of wonder, I stood in silence for twenty minutes and then resumed hiking, creating sound, *crunch, crunch, crunch*. It was then I realized I was walking through a perfect metaphor most of the time we carry our noise with us, in the form of mind. This is what Poonja meant when he said silence isn't the absence of sound, it's the absence of self.

And if audio irritation can't be avoided, what about the irritation that arises as a result of being irritated? As Robert said that night about the car booming rap music, "I'm an evolved, spiritual person. I shouldn't be feeling like I need to scream at somebody who's playing their stereo loud." And yet this too can become a play of mind, which reacts to sound and then creates a self-recriminating story about reacting and not being "spiritual."This is very tricky. It doesn't feel like a story because it's about your spirituality. But the mind has no compunction about using even spiritual yearning to obscure the moment and put you to sleep. You can drown in a steady stream of self-recriminating thoughts that you believe are more real because they're "spiritual." But they are just thoughts.

Recently a close friend of mine hosted a silent retreat at her house. The house, spacious and beautiful, with hardwood floors and spiritual artifacts from around the world, also has stunning mountain views. It was a perfect place to hold a silent retreat except, apparently, for one thing. My friend has a dog named Bushie, a mutt of great and eccentric personality, who just so happens to snore. During the meditations the large living room would be silent enough to hear the fountain burbling in the courtyard, when suddenly a deep snoring would begin to emanate from the corner. It was greeted at first by silence, as everybody tried to maintain the silence of the moment.

Snoooorrrrrre. It sounded like an old man clearing phlegm from his throat. More silence. More snores.

Then came the first giggle. Bushie continued unabated throughout the meditation. As some people tried unsuccessfully to suppress their giggles, like trying not to laugh in church, other people grew more irritated.

During the dharma discussion that followed, the reaction was entirely about Bushie's snoring. Some people were amused. Others were deeply irritated and felt the dog should be locked in the bedroom. Others weren't affected one way or another. One person was so upset, she was thinking about leaving the retreat.

Because the retreat was *supposed* to be silent, some people had a hard time. To say something as natural as a dog snoring is inappropriate because we're being "spiritual" here misses the point. It's all spiritual—not just at a certain time or place, not only with certain people, but in every moment and every encounter. Drop all ideas of the way it *should* be.

NOW AND SOUND

That for which we find words is something already dead in our hearts. There is always a kind of contempt in speaking.

—NIETZSCHE

What is the reality of now and its relationship to noise? For example, what are you doing right now as you read these words? If you are fully absorbed right now in reading, notice now your awareness of external sounds fades. Now pick a sound and focus on it. It can be a bird, traffic, wind, the creak of your building, the sound of voices in the distance. See how the sound grows in your awareness and my words fade in their vibrancy as your focus is split.

Now bring your full attention to the sound. Take a moment and stop reading. Really dive into the sound with your full attention, focusing your whole being on nothing but the sound.

Sit very still and listen.

Notice that when you are engaged in active listening, the sound can fully bring you back into the present moment. Far from being a source of annoyance, sound can be used as a way to play lightly with your attention and awareness. It can become a tool for becoming *more* aware in the present—even during a dharma conversation on a silent retreat when that darn dog shouldn't be snoring!

The point is that sound arises. And annoyance at this sound arises. And even thoughts that this annoyance shouldn't be happening arise. But so what? It's impermanent. All of it—the sound, the annoyance, the annoyance at the annoyance—will fall back into the silence from which everything arises.

The tag line for the movie *Aliens* was "In space, nobody can hear you scream." It's funny to think of that line when contemplating the vast silence of space compared to our noisy little planet. But in the same way our planet sits in a universe of silence, we too rest in a perpetual bed of stillness that is always available even in the worst cacophony. Like tuning a radio, you can direct your awareness to either the stillness or the noise. It doesn't really matter; it is all consciousness.

The real question here is the realtionship of mind to the arising phenomenon of sound—which in itself is a question of the relationship of our small self to the rest of consciousness. Mind has been compared by sages to a ball of snow that one throws in the ocean. The ball of snow is ego-mind and the ocean is consciousness. The ball of snow is nothing but frozen water but might think of itself as different from the water. It appears to have its own nature—solid versus liquid, more cold versus less cold, white versus blue or green. But once thrown in the ocean, it again becomes liquid because actually it is nothing but water, merging with its essential nature. There is only water in various states. In the same way, there is only consciousness in various states. Keep this perspective and enjoy the silence that is here.

The less you pay attention to your internal noise, the more you are able to feel the silent consciousness that permeates everything. Even inanimate objects take on the pulsation of silence. When sitting quietly in meditation with a group of people with the same intent, the silence gets so thick you can cut it. Very sweet.

We are like the Buddhist mandalas, the intricate and beautiful sand designs that take months to create and then are ceremoniously swept away. Time marches through our lives like an ancient master, scattering the sands of our existence back to silence.

But like the sun that doesn't stop shining just because clouds are in front of it, this silence is happening all the time, even in the loudest, most annoying, and most quotidian of circumstances.

BLISS AT KINKO'S

All my days I have been raised among the Sages and I found nothing better for oneself than silence.

—ETHICS OF THE FATHERS 1:17

The other day I was in Kinko's waiting in line to pay for something. It was the classic Kinko's moment, almost Soviet in the slowness of the line:

Machines hummed and whirred, ticking out paper copies.

A woman robotically stapled papers together.

A man carried manuscripts across the room, shoes scuffing the carpet.

A woman argued fiercely into a cell phone.

The large clock on the wall flicked by the seconds.

The smell of toner made it seem like a morgue for paper.

The line stood frozen as the cashier disappeared.

I released my impatience, shrugging it off like a heavy overcoat on a hot day. I suddenly felt cool and light, and the sounds and activity humming around me seemed more like a symphony than disparate and obnoxious noise.

I relaxed even more deeply, and my whole field of vision shifted. The entire room suddenly felt like an integrated mechanism, harmonious and perfect. It was as if somebody had removed the back of a finely tuned watch, revealing its normally hidden movement. Binding all the activity was the vibrancy of consciousness: silent, palpable, subtle, and as smooth as my own heartbeat, which I could feel as part of the whole.

It was *samadhi* at Kinko's.

That was the thought, at once profound and hilarious. And with the thought the moment passed. The woman in front of me finished her lengthy explanation of the task she wanted Kinko's to perform. She moved, and I was confronted with the bored, slack face of a person who wanted to be anywhere else. As we spoke I tried to engage her with my eyes. I tried to get back the mystical experience that had made me feel so connected to everything and everybody around me and to the silence that ran through it all.

But it was gone.

And I was in a new now with my fully loaded agenda, which never works.

The noisy surface of the present moment is ever changing and never twice the same. All the manifestations of consciousness are rubbing up against each other in an endless dance of creation and destruction—consciousness polishing itself, or entertaining itself.

But under the surface is the still pool of silence that is never changing and never less than whole. Although the surface of now changes constantly and is indeed never twice the same, the present moment remains steady in an eternal and vibrant now, now, now. No matter what the external noise is.

In Kinko's I had a mystical moment. Then it was gone. The next moment I was with the bored clerk. Not so mystical, but very ordinary and fine in its ordinariness.

Not every moment is a peak experience or an unblended mystical moment of connection. No one I've met is experiencing the mystical silence of being 100 percent of the time. But it is in the apparent differences in your states of consciousness that the mystical is highlighted. If life was all mystical, it would be difficult to see it as such.

The apparent dichotomies of existence, while all part of the whole, point out the different states of being within this whole. Up defines down. In defines out. Light defines darkness. Sound defines silence. In this way, the mystical punctuates the seemingly mundane, but both are infused with consciousness and in deep connected harmony.

THE PAST POKER HAND IS DEAD

"Do not search for the truth, only cease to cherish opinions.

—SENG-TSAN

I play poker every other week and have been doing so for four years with the same group of friends. Call it a different kind of *sangha* (spiritual community), but it can be one nonetheless, like any gathering of people.

Poker is an amazing and sometimes painful way to see your shortcomings. It is also a decent metaphor for our inherent characteristics. If you are risk-averse in life, so you will be at the poker table. If you are idealistic in life, seeing only what you want to see, so you will be when you play poker, much to the detriment of your wallet. Greed in life makes you overreach at the game. Whining about your life makes you a sore loser. Impatience makes you play bad cards instead of waiting for good cards. Staying in the story of the last hand prevents you from playing well in the current hand.

In short, poker is a game where seeing what is versus what we want to be is rewarded with hard cold cash.

One night we were playing Hardbody, a five-card, one-draw, roll-your-own, high-low game that our group invented. It is a supremely exciting game to play, with high stakes, lots of bluffing, and pure game theory. And you can go high or low, so you have a better chance of staying in a hand.

After the draw, I had a full house, three queens and two nines—a monster hand. We began to roll out our hands, one card at a time. After each card there was a bet, and I bet it to the hilt. After four cards were rolled, there were only two people left in the hand.

I had two queens and two nines showing, with one queen still to be rolled. He had one queen and three sixes showing. We were both going high. He was a substitute that night, had never played Hardbody, and was betting very heavily.

But I was going to win. I had a full house. My full house (three queens and two nines) was going to beat his three sixes and two queens.

Or maybe he was insanely bluffing four sixes.

Did he have four sixes? He had drawn two cards. The odds were about twenty-three to one, very high that he didn't. I decided he had the lower full house.

Those of you who play poker will see a problem here. I had three queens. He had one queen showing. That makes all the queens in the deck. He wasn't representing a full house, because there were no more queens. He was representing four sixes, which beats a full house.

Does he have four sixes? The thought crossed my mind as I stared at him, even though in my narrow seeing I didn't recognize that he couldn't have had a full house.

His hands were shaking. It was a huge pot. I considered whether I should go low, take half of it. *Nah, Take the whole pot,* the voice in my head said. *No way your "queens over boat" can lose.*

I had started the hand a sure winner. I was going to ride it out.

We made our bets.

He turned over his last card. A six. Four of a kind.

Impossibly, I had lost with a huge full house.

Afterward I thought about this hand long and hard. It is the perfect metaphor for the constantly changing nature of reality.

At the beginning I was certain I had the winning hand. I would have bet the farm! But all the information I needed to change course by the end of the hand was there: the four queens showing; the eager betting of my opponent despite his newness to the game, which made any bluffing unlikely; his shaking hands belying a huge hand.

Because I wasn't being mindful of the present I didn't see how reality had changed in just a matter of seconds.

If I had taken a moment of silence there, just paused for a moment and stopped listening to the voice in my head, which was seeing what it wanted to see, I might have seen through it, past the intensity, the money, and the desire, to the reality that was there, hovering right in front of me in that moment.

It always pays to pause before an important decision or before saying anything rash. Come fully into the moment of what you are about to do. Feel it fully. Don't be operating the way I was, too busy living in the past minute, back when I was certain I had the winning hand.

If you are stuck in the past, the present will run you over. In poker and in life.

I bring this up because it is related to the phenomenon of spiritual materialism, which has a similar dynamic to my poker experience of hanging on to the past.

I once engaged in a dharma conversation with a person who was constantly seeking to reexperience a single moment of bliss she had had several years before. She yearned for that moment when her mind had stopped completely and she was at peace in what she called a "super-glide flow moment." But her way of trying to retrieve it was to go into her *memory* of the experience. This would give her a temporary feeling of peace, but it would disassociate her from the now, which ironically is the only gateway back into that selfless state of bliss.

There is nothing to do, nowhere to go, nobody to see. It is as if you are hanging from a bar on a boiling hot day suspended a foot above a cool swimming pool. All you have to do is relax and you will fall into who you are, into what already exists—the refreshing and always innocent now.

This is true whether you are in silence or in noise.

So many spiritual teachings talk about practicing to get to wakefulness or enlightenment. (I avoid that word, as it comes with the baggage of being in fully realized awakened awareness 24/7, all the time, with no slips. I haven't met anybody who is fully realized, and who needs that pressure anyway?) But the whole idea of practice, whether in the form of chanting, meditation, or trance dancing, in order to become enlightened in the future is suspect. Whether the practice is enjoyable or incredibly byzantine, it may work, it may be fun, but it isn't necessary. The only time you can actually be awake is right now! You can't wake up in the future, so what are you practicing for?

It's like saying you're going to practice being human. Wait—you *already* are human.

There is no room for yearning about the past ecstatic moment or hoping wakefulness will arrive in the future after more practice. Right now is the only opportunity for wakefulness.

One time when I was hiking in Machu Picchu, Peru, I snuck over to the neighboring mountain, Huayna Picchu, and climbed to the top with a friend, despite the fact that the mountain was closed to hikers due to erosion of the trails that made it a dangerous and difficult climb. But at the top we looked down on Machu Picchu from a new angle, with the ancient ruins on one side and the rain forest on the other. A rainbow emerged from the clouds, painting a bridge between the forest and the ruins.

It was a stunning view, but the best part was the two butterflies we saw. The rain forest produces huge butterflies, the size of birds. And out of the mist flew a pair of violet and red beauties that were straight out of a magical kingdom. They enchanted us for an hour, just by flying from tree to tree. It was definitely a "peak experience."

Later that day, in the town of Aguas Calientes, which lies at the bottom of the mountain, I saw a man selling the same species of butterfly. They were dead, pinned in a square box, colorful but inert. I stared a long time at those dead butterflies, almost tempted to buy one to take back as a reminder of what I'd experienced. But I knew it was useless.

Trying to grasp past ecstatic experiences is like capturing butterflies, killing them with formaldehyde, and pinning them behind glass. It gives you a shadow of the real experience while deafening the vibrant silence that is animating this moment.

So accept the mystical one moment and the ordinary the next. Accept annoying noise one moment and nourishing silence the next. Accept it all as it comes, because if you don't, *you miss your life*.

From ordinary noise to mystical silence, each moment brings its own gift, perfect exactly the way it is.

SPEAK, DON'T SPEAK

The unspoken word is capital. We can invest it or we can squander it.

—MARK TWAIN

Often in life there are situations where silence is the only response. To even respond is to engage, and sometimes engagement of any sort is not the peaceful solution. To engage with somebody who is screaming or unreasonable or threatening violence may be adding fuel to the fire. Resistance may be what that person is looking for, whcih then gives him or her the opportunity to turn up the volume. In such cases it is better to say nothing.

The art of aikido takes this idea to a physical level. The principal idea of aikido is a nondual one. If we are all manifestations of God, then we are all sacred. If we are all sacred, how can we hurt another person? How can we punch anyone in the face? In aikido, you flow with the other person's energy, merging and dancing with it, before letting it flow past you. When you are pushed, instead of pushing in return, which would create deadlock and conflict, you relax back. You create receptivity and a vacuum, and your so-called opponent falls forward, driven by the momentum of his or her own aggression.

This is true on the level of silence and action. It exists on the level of the individual as well as between nations. Leaders such as Martin Luther King Jr., Nelson Mandela, or Gandhi all met the brutality of the world with an example of peace and nonviolence.

One of the tools of peace is silence. When confronted by aggression or harsh words, silence is often the only response. Silence allows the antagonist's own voice to ring in the air, to be heard by all. Thus no violence is done to return the violence coming your way. The conflict is dissipated rather than agitated.

The fourteenth-century Persian poet Hafiz wrote: "Is not most talking a crazed defense of a crumbling fort?" And isn't the "fort" the ego?

Think of the last time you were in a huge argument—how the voices got louder, the positions entrenched themselves, and in the end there were hard feelings on both sides. Does anyone ever really win such an argument? How many times has a fight raged about something and, even a day later, you can't remember what it was about? The emotions that were so strongly felt disappear like steam churning out of a factory and evaporating on a cold winter day. And even if you have "won" and bludgeoned acquiescence from your opponent, the aftertaste is bitter. A piece of pain has been passed on and embedded in the other person's heart, where it can take root and fester, only to be passed on in the next go-round. And so you win the battle and lose the war.

I was at a small dinner gathering, shortly before the start of the second Gulf War. The subject turned to our government's plans to attack Iraq, and two people at the gathering put forth the idea that the United States government was responsible for the September 11 attacks—that we had hijacked our own planes and attacked the Pentagon and World Trade Center in order to create enough public opinion to attack Iraq. Every logical argument was met with a combination of derision and accusations of naiveté. A plane didn't crash into the Pentagon; it was a bomb. U.S. fighter pilots shot down the plane that went down in Pennsylvania. No terrorists were on the planes that hit the World Trade Center. And the absolute lie about how four hundred Jews didn't report to work in the World Trade Center that day was given as an example of a Jewish conspiracy.

On and on it went, each claim more outrageous than the next. I found myself trying reason, responding with facts, but to no avail. Voices were raised, and insults were traded. After a while I realized I was actually in the rarefied company of conspiracy theorists. They didn't want the facts; their minds were already made up. It was like arguing with somebody about religious beliefs. And any further escalation would just create more personal animosity. At that point I just made a joke and ended the discussion. I stopped responding and fell into silence. Shortly after dessert I left.

Through peaceful silence, the cycle has an opportunity to be broken, whether on the level of family, community, or nations. But even if it isn't broken, it is equally beneficial to save your energy by avoiding the brick wall of intractable conflict. There is a fine line between a productive exchange of ideas and interpersonal war. Often the debate is not about the topic at all, but rather is an incarnation of conditioning that is simply re-creating embattled family dynamics. Raising one's voice rarely works because it is like tossing gasoline on the fire of another person's suffering.

As Gandhi said: "An eye for an eye leaves the whole world blind." So it's worth asking ourselves if what we are engaged in is creating more harm than good. If it is, and it almost always is, shouldn't we put down our own personal eye gougers and free ourselves from the need to be right? Letting go of trying to control other people's opinions creates much personal liberty. This is different from not ever having a discussion or voicing your own opinion. It just means that you let go of trying to forcibly change another person's mind.

I heard a story about a therapist who found himself at a dinner party with a person who was very derisive about the idea of psychotherapy.

"A psychiatrist is just a paid friend!" the guy said with a sneer. "Who would hire someone to listen to them talk about their problems?"

The therapist took a moment to try to explain what a good therapist does: providing insights someone might not otherwise have, calling a person on his or her issues, exposing patterns of behavior, and so on, but the insulting partygoer didn't want to hear it.

"A paid friend," he repeated. "Pathetic."

The therapist just shrugged.

"What's good for some people isn't right for everyone," he said. "Probably wouldn't be the thing for you."

The guy relaxed, they spoke about some other things, then went their separate ways. The next day my friend got a call from the man he had met at the party.

"I've been thinking about what you said, about getting good insights I might not otherwise have and learning about patterns of behavior. I'm thinking I might want to come in and talk to you, see what your therapy thing is all about."

The man wound up being the therapist's patient—and that moment was the beginning of a journey of personal growth. The therapist's ability to be detached from the person, to offer his truth without feeling judged by the response, let the other guy feel comfortable enough to ultimately change his deeply entrenched views.

Perhaps you want to make a difference in people's lives. Perhaps you feel you are right. But this wise therapist didn't need success in every encounter in order to feel validated. He didn't need to make a difference every time he opened his mouth. If he didn't reach everyone, then so be it. And in this case, not needing to make a difference made the biggest difference in the world.

RECEPTIVITY

The deepest hunger of the human soul is to be understood. The deepest hunger of the human body is for air. If you can listen to another person, in depth, until they feel understood, it's the equivalent of giving them air.

—STEVEN COVEY

Being quiet and listening is a form of receptivity. When you truly listen, you can forget yourself completely, and you are free. If you cannot forget yourself, if you are constantly in the mode of self-reflection *(what do I think about it),* you can never be free and can never truly listen. How many times do we just pretend to listen, nodding but thinking about something else? Or stand there formulating our response while waiting for the other person to stop talking so that we can start?

The satirist Fran Lebowitz writes, "The opposite of talking isn't listening. The opposite of talking is waiting." She's right for many of us much of the time: when we're waiting, we're not listening.

By allowing the yin qualities of receptivity and silence (instead of volubility) to take hold, you actually have a better chance of seeing reality clearly without the projection of mind shaping what it is you want to see. In your generosity to another person, you also get to take a break from your self.

We spend much of our time in a constant state of noise, information, and entertainment, which we immediately regurgitate and claim as our own. We absorb other people's opinions in newspapers, on television, and in books. We talk and talk but are rarely silent. We give voice to our thoughts, believing them to be unique. But most of these thoughts are not even original. And so the external noise we experience continues unabated in our heads, and we in turn continue to chatter, adding to the general cacophony.

By deeply listening we take a break from the nonstop regurgitation of information. We digest when listening. In silence, we realize our true nature is much deeper than our surface thoughts.

NATURE'S SANCTUARY

It's worth asking where you are directing your awareness. What stories are you telling yourself about sound? How does one tune into the underlying silence in the middle of the worst cacophony?

Nature is essentially silent in the way that H. W. L. Poonja defined silence, as the absence of self, not the absence of sound. A frog, a deer, or a dog is essentially quiet inside, no matter how much noise it is making. There are no neurotic thoughts in an animal because it is fully present in the moment. It is not thinking about the future or regretting the past. For an animal the future never arrives except as a never-ending series of *now*.

Nature just *is*.

And even to the unobservant, nature is everywhere, existing as a reminder of the silence that pervades everything. It is essential, unlike the mind activity floating on top of it, which is nonessential. It is important to be aware of the difference between the essential and nonessential; there is no way to make the nonessential essential. They are what they are, and in the end the essential silence holds all the noise and sound rising out of it.

So right now, in this moment, where is the essential in your life? Where is nature, the sweetest manifestation of this essential silence? Is it your pet, dozing on the couch next to you? Is it the tree rustling outside your window? The plant on your desk? The ant trudging up the wall?

Perhaps you are in a cell, devoid of sunshine and of any other life but your own. Perhaps there isn't a window nearby. Yet even here, the silence of nature abounds.

We talk about nature as if it is separate from us. We must preserve nature or exploit it or go out and "be in nature." We forget that we are animals too and thus are an intrinsic part of nature. The same intelligence that animates the natural world beats in our own hearts, fills our own lungs, and drives our own instinct for life. We are not separate from nature but one with it, and to do battle with it is to do battle with ourselves. To destroy it is to destroy ourselves. And to live in harmony with it is to live in harmony with ourselves.

Nature is here in the very air that you are breathing; every breath you take can bring you closer to the essential and further from the nonessential.

To "be in nature" simply means just merging your awareness with nature's profound silence. So right now allow your attention to fully fall on the little bit of nature in your presence, even if it's just the smallest bit, like the houseplant that needs watering. Even if it's "just" the air that you breathe. The breath that you take in so unconsciously is probably the best and first place to connect with silence. The mind isn't drawing it. Your natural self is making it happen, which is why so many meditations start with a concentration on breath.

Take a moment here, right now, to bring your awareness to the powerful silence and stillness inherent in your breath. Sit comfortably. Bring your attention to your breath. Experience yourself as a part of nature: unconscious, without thought, as if you are being breathed and not doing the breathing. Again, this silent aspect of nature is available at all times to you because *you are nature*.

Shut your eyes and really feel this for a moment.

So often in the rush of our "civilized" lives of mind and ambition and doing, we forget our animal nature, which is relaxed, present, alert, and nondoing. This is not laziness, which feels lethargic and dull on the inside. This is a natural, animalistic nondoing, which engenders alertness and presence. In it you are not sluggish on the inside, but actually energetic, radiating energy.

Just watch any other animal in the world to get a sense of this still alertness. Silent, watchful, awake to the moment, it is not in the noise of mind and ego, but connected to infinite nature through its own nature.

The same is always available for humans. We only need to remember it for it to be so.

Understand that external sound is a reflection of this nature and becomes noise only because of the interpretation we put on it.

If we are not self-reflecting in the infinite mirrors of our mind, then noise is simply sound, another phenomenon that arises in and falls away to the silence that informs everything.

KEEPING UP WITH THE JONESES

Awaken from Status Envy

If you realize that you have enough, you are truly rich.

—THE TAO

A couple spends $30,000 on a birthday party for their six-year-old son, including elephant rides and expensive catering. Another gives their teenager a Mercedes for her sixteenth birthday. In a society where more is better, how much is enough?

After the unprecedented abundance and consumerism of the late nineties, during which people tried to fill a bottomless void with material possessions and experience, the average family is now experiencing uncertain economic times. In America, the gap between the ultrarich and the working poor is larger than it has been at any time since the Gilded Age of the late 1800s—the middle class is disappearing. According to the Economic Policy Institute, the top 1 percent of the U.S. population controls 38 percent of the wealth, while the bottom 80 percent holds only 17 percent. And the top .01 percent—a mere 13,000 families—have as much income as the 20 million poorest households, with incomes 300 times those of average families.

The new concentration of income at the top is a key reason that the United States, for all its economic achievements, has more poverty and lower life expectancy than any other Western nation. To put it another way, the share of wealth that has accrued to the top 1 percent has roughly doubled over the past thirty years and is now about as large as the share of the bottom 40 percent of the population.

Again, 1 percent of the families control as much wealth as the bottom 40 percent!

What accounts for the major disconnect between the extremely wealthy and those who are merely trying to become extremely wealthy? What makes people greedily acquire more than they need while others around them struggle or even starve?

MORE, MORE, MORE

Part of this disconnect is a result of our billion-dollar advertising industry that relentlessly hypes us: if we buy this object, we will have access to happiness as represented by a certain lifestyle, one involving beautiful people and possessions.

The deluge of advertising is now like an IV, a constant drip right into the vein of existence. Recently they've put video on the small screen at Bank of America ATMs, lest you spend a moment alone without being told to buy something. The commercial-saturated, science-fiction worlds depicted in the movies *Blade Runner* and *Minority Report* have arrived. Go to a movie and you will see not only previews, which, of course, are commercials for upcoming movies, but also actual commercials for products, clumsily tied into the movie business. Does anybody even question the fact that we are paying $10 for the privilege of seeing more commercials?

Advertising is ubiquitous, like the air we breathe. But this air cultivates sickness and a permanent sense of deficiency and competition; it drives a wedge into the heart of the country.

As Salman Rushdie writes: "The commercials soothed America's pain, its head pain, its gas pain, its heartache, its loneliness, the pain of babyhood and old age, of being a parent and of being a child, the pain of manhood and women's pain, the pain of success and that of failure, the good pain of the athlete and the bad pain of the guilty, the anguish of loneliness and of ignorance, the needle-sharp torment of the cities and the dull, mad ache of the empty plains, the pain of wanting without knowing what was wanted, the agony of the howling void within each watching, semi-conscious self. No wonder advertising was popular. It made things better. It showed you the road. It wasn't part of the problem. It solved things."

It is impossible to talk about status envy, which is a symptom, without talking about the disease, which is the relentless hype to buy more and more. We are swimming in commercialism and fed a massive daily dose of conditioning. It saps our freedom and increases our sense of an isolated identity. Our sense of self becomes, without our permission, defined by our possessions; we judge and parse each other in this paradigm, and in doing so we travel further from the recognition of our connection to each other. Separated by the walls of money and possessions, we believe these walls to be true, forgetting that all is consciousness.

In the end, we work ourselves to death trying to keep up with the consumption. According to the International Labor Organization, Americans now work 1,978 hours annually, nine weeks more than Western Europeans. The United States as a society took all of its increase in labor productivity in the past thirty years in the form of money and stuff instead of time. The harmful effects of working more hours are leading to stress that causes heart disease and a weakened immune system. Fast food and a lack of exercise have led to an epidemic of obesity and diabetes. Many parents complain that they do not have enough time to spend with their children, much less become involved in their community. The weight and worry of debt and bankruptcies exhaust many Americans. By contrast, over the past thirty years Europeans have made a choice to live simpler, more balanced lives and work fewer hours. Western Europeans average five to six weeks of paid vacation a year; we average two.

Why have we made this choice?

ADVERTISING AS PORNOGRAPHY

I have often stopped by a newsstand and stood frozen, stupefied by the plethora of glossy images depicting the "good life." Magazines such as *Maxim, Gear,* and the honestly named *Stuff* scream out at me. Invariably the accumulation of material things is accompanied by a supermodel promising, by association, to fulfill my every sexual fantasy, just as soon as I buy enough stuff. The content of such publications used to be separate from the advertising. Now the content *is* the advertising.

The problem is what I call the numbing effect. A magazine such as *Stuff* excites us to believe we do not have enough. In the same way that sexual pornography extravagantly points out—with its huge penises and inflated breasts that could be used as life preservers—what might be "missing" in your partner, material pornography points out what is "missing" in your life. It screams that you can't be happy, or hope to get the girl of your dreams unless you own this gadget, this car, or this house, laid out in a gleaming come-on from the pages of a magazine.

Why not just create a centerfold of the latest gadget you can't live without? You could list the things the gadget likes to do in its spare time, what its favorite movies are, and so on. I'm only being half facetious; the centerfolds selling us stuff already exist. Thus the stuff becomes a symbol of happiness, rather than happiness itself, a proxy for power, rather than the personal power within. We are also taught by the media to focus on the rich and famous, becoming addicted to hearing their every movement, how they live, what they wear, what they have. They are our gods and we worship them, and in doing so we lose connection with the simple and free pleasures of life right in front of us.

As with all external sources of happiness, from drugs to sex, we become numb to the effects of acquiring; eventually we wind up needing a little bit more to get off each time, until we are addicted to a kind of material version of crack cocaine.

The habit of acquiring does seem to solve things for the moment, relieving anxiety and obliterating thoughts of our own demise. Having a lot is a way to try to protect oneself against death or uncertainty or impermanence. We collect things as a way of saying *I am here* and *I exist*.

But just like a drug, it is only as good as its last hit.

POOR AT FIFTY MILLION

Desires achieved increase thirst like salt water.

—MILAREPA

Once we are ensnared in the habit of acquiring as a way to achieve happiness, it is difficult to break. No matter how much is actually purchased, if the dynamic is still locked in place, there is always more that is available, another high to attain and another person to outspend. There's a similarily between shopping and casual sex: the desire, the chase, the catch, the high, and then the feeling of emptiness. Shopping has turned into a form of leisure and pleasure; it's what people do on weekends. And what you have is equated to what you know, as in being in the know about the finer things in life. But accompanying this dynamic are feelings of envy, greed, and even *Schadenfreude*. The final result is a feeling of separation and emptiness, a sense of being a hungry ghost asking, "Is this all there is?"

And it doesn't matter how much a person makes; it's the dynamic that's important. Lewis Lapham conducted a study of Americans of different incomes, asking them how much they would need to be genuinely happy. The answer was consistent no matter how much they were making. Virtually all interviewed told him that they would really be happy if they were earning twice as much as they do now. Those making $50,000 said they could be really happy at $100,000, those making $100,000 said $200,000, and those making $1 million said $2 million.

This was the result in spite of the large body of research on well-being that shows that wealth above middle-class comfort makes little difference to our happiness. According to Tim Wilson, psychologist at the University of Virginia, "We don't realize how quickly we will adapt to a pleasurable event and make it the backdrop of our lives. When any event occurs to us we make it ordinary. And through becoming ordinary, we lose our pleasure. We don't know we adapt and fail to incorporate that into our decisions. So we then move on to the next thing and make the same mistake again."

This makes the obvious point that happiness is only possible in the present moment, no matter what the income.

A friend told me a story of a friend of his who made $50 million in the Internet bubble. He now has three houses, access to a private jet, a private chef, several luxury cars, and so on. He told my friend he feels like he is at the bottom of his level—he is the "poorest" of the group of billionaires that he hangs out with, and works sixteen-hour days in order to move up. He has lost sight of his wealth relative compared to 99.9999 percent of the people on the planet and can see only his deficiencies to compared the remaining .0001 percent! He is, quite frankly, trading in his life in order to keep up with the Jonesres. It is a "big" life, with big expenses and complications and a large environmental tab to go with it. And he wants it to be bigger in a world where, according a study by the World Health Organization, 170 million children are malnourished and 17 million die as a result every year. The world over, 80 percent of people live in substandard housing, 70 percent are unable to read, and 50 percent suffer from malnutrition. Here in America, 37 percent of our children (27 million) live in low-income families. And 16 percent of children (over 11 million) live in poverty.

In 1986 America still had more high schools than shopping centers. Less than fifteen years later, we have more than twice as many malls in America as high schools. Regarding college, we spend more on shoes, jewelry, and watches ($80 billion) than we do on higher education ($65 billion).

AUTOMATIC BUY IT

Never keep up with the Joneses; drag them down to your level. It's cheaper.

—QUENTIN CRISP

The statistics can give one a sense of what is going on, but not the real impact. For that one must actually venture out to the world of direct experience. I was in New York recently walking on Madison Avenue on the Upper East Side with a pregnant friend. We stopped in an upscale baby boutique, and I encountered a woman who was marching through the store with a personal shopper and two salespeople in tow. The razor-thin woman had a ring with a diamond the size of a robin's egg. Her face had the slightly surprised look of someone not unfamiliar with Botox and plastic surgery. She brushed by us as if we weren't there, pointing at various items while chanting, almost like a mantra: "I'll take this, . . . I'll take this . . . I'll take two of these . . . and I'll take four of these." Her minions could barely keep up with the stream of "I'll take." My friend and I left the store empty-handed as the pile by the cash register grew larger and larger.

Later in the afternoon, after my friend went off to a meeting, I continued to walk around the neighborhood, following people. Two women, one with red hair, the other wearing a fur, were talking about a necklace glittering with diamonds they saw in the window of a boutique.

"See the line?" one said. "Not too low. It would be stunning with the Chanel."

"Mmm," the other one murmured. "You think so? It's not too much?"

"No. It's tasteful. Elegant. Just right. And I have other clients with this store, so it would only run about three hundred."

I was standing right next to them and couldn't help but stare. They were both expensively dressed, but one was clearly a client, with the other one being a stylist or personal shopper. I thought: *What is it with people who need other people to shop with them? And who are these people who can contemplate a $300,000 purchase with the same attitude most people have buying a pair of pants at the Gap? Isn't there a better use that the money can be put to? Save a village? Give out ten college educations to poor students?* Apparently all these questions were written on my face.

"Can I help you?" the professional shopper asked me, glaring at me as though I might be dangerous, or at least dangerous to her commission. The other woman looked at me as if she understood what I was thinking.

"I don't think I'm in the right economic bracket," I said lightly, moving down the street.

I spent the rest of the afternoon drifting around the neighborhood, observing the denizens of this rarefied world the way a naturalist might observe a rare species of birds. I watched six people spend tens of thousands of dollars on clothing, jewelry, and art without blinking an eye. They spent like there was no tomorrow. The thing that was most clear was that, except for the $300,000 necklace, most of the spending was automatic. It was in the line of "I'll take that."

What really struck me, however, was that the purchasers did not seem happy. They seemed disconnected, almost automatic in their acquisitiveness. There was an underlying feeling of anxiety, a heaviness, as each item got piled on. Here was another object to be insured, cared for, and protected against theft or loss. The fleeting hit was no longer even getting them high, but was merely holding them in place, propping them up against the reality of their emptiness.

Even though they lived what some might think an enviable life, I found that after an initial wave of envy at their freedom to buy anything without thinking about the price, I suddenly felt a wave of compassion. It was like they were on a horrible internal Neverending treadmill.

We come into the world naked and we go out of the world naked. So why do we spend our precious life accumulating stuff in between? Why do we literally trade our life for material possessions? Why isn't our time on the planet, the one immutable and nonnegotiable number, more important? In the land of plenty, why do most people feel as though they don't have enough?

SPIRITUAL HUNGER

A good thing, not as good as nothing.
—ZEN KOAN

At the core of this consumerism is a kind of spiritual hunger, even when we don't know it. It is like a person who has a lot of sex without knowing that what he or she is looking for is love. We become overly identified with external definitions of self, belying an internal emptiness. Into this emptiness we pour possessions and experiences, attempting to ameliorate our loneliness and separation. And the less connected we are with our true selves, the less aware we are of our interior landscape, the more we pile on the material possessions. It's a way of saying "I'm important." For some people it never ends, as the houses get bigger and bigger, but often the bigger the house, the smaller the internal spaciousness of the person inhabiting it. How much house do we really need?

This way of being is worse than pouring water into a bucket with no bottom. The very process of trying to fill oneself up with external possessions leaves one feeling empty and lonelier than ever.

The other day I wandered into Fred Segal, a store in Los Angeles, because I had a gift certificate. A pretty salesperson was hovering close enough that I could smell her perfume. I was looking at a suede jacket, until I saw the price: $2,100.

"Wow, expensive," I said, quickly putting the jacket back.

"Yes," she said with a warm smile. "But think of all the compliments you'll get for years to come."

I smiled back at her and left, getting a glimpse of her approach to selling overpriced clothing to people with too much money and too little self-worth. Anybody who's tried the "shopping cure" understands this. The warmth and value generated by the friendly salesperson (your best friend for as long as the transaction lasts) evaporate shortly after you leave the store. The hit of feeling important, powerful, and in the flow of life is just that, a hit. It wears off like any other high. We are left with the possessions—cars, clothes, houses—hanging on our personal identity like garments on a corpse. Maybe we even do get compliments on it. But does this capture who you really are, any more than any other identification—education, career, income?

Not only is the belief that we will feel better about ourselves by somehow climbing the consumer ladder just plain false, but the deeper truth is that any identification with this small self is going to create unhappiness and a lack of freedom. Tether yourself with any identification, whether it is "rich Malibu housewife," "Catholic priest," "spiritual healer," "software salesperson," "school janitor," or any other label, and you are limiting your reality. You are forgetting the consciousness, the clear, creative awareness that gives birth to all happiness and freedom.

Although there are plenty of opportunities to lose ourselves in the trance of identification, nowhere is it more prevalent than our relationship to material possessions and to other people and *their* material possessions. The pursuit results in comparison and judgment of others while perpetuating a sense of something lacking in ourselves.

In short, status envy.

Underneath this status envy is a spiritual desire for wholeness, for connection, for peace. Ironically, these yearnings can't be fulfilled from the outside in, but they can be fulfilled from the inside out. And it doesn't cost a cent. Connection and wholeness are as close as the present moment. Forget the story that you don't have everything you need to be happy. Once you stop believing that lie, then you can relax with what is free and most precious: the sunshine on your face, a walk in nature, the warmth of a friendship, the love of family, the joy of relationship, the peacefulness of meditation, a swim in a cool lake or ocean. None of which costs money.

Spiritual yearning can't be satiated with material possessions.

But it can be fulfilled by a sense of being in the now—free, full, and whole.

HOW DO YOU COMPARE?

Don't count the teeth in someone else's mouth.

—SAYINGS OF THE FATHERS, 4:30

Comparison, the building block of status envy, takes place in both overt and subtle ways. It could be as petty as two women talking about the fashion style of another woman, as in "What was she thinking?" If an attractive man walking with a woman passes other women, maybe they will glance at him and then immediately try to determine what the other woman is doing right in terms of hair style, makeup, and clothing, internally judging.

This type of comparison is simply human nature—we all do it sometimes. But for some people it is a constant hum of competition and envy; just walking down the street is a living hell. Notice that whenever we are in judgment, it is usually an externalization of some inner monologue. We are treating other people in the same way, usually unconsciously, that we treat ourself. The conditioning is automatic.

There is no need to stop this reflexive conditioning; simply becoming aware of it will break it up. Just watch the thoughts as they come up, as you compare your circumstances to another person's: *I wish I were better-looking. I wish I had that car. I wish I had that girl.*

Feel the feelings the thoughts engender: the anxiety, the loneliness, the anger. After a while you will begin to see that the thoughts have nothing to do with your circumstances. They have nothing to do with anything external. They are a product of your own habitual conditioning and are not a product of love. The loving thought would be *I'm happy for that person.*

How weird does that sound to you, to be happy for a stranger's good fortune instead of comparing yourself to him or her? We are not taught this in our society. We look, we compare, and we compete, separating the world into winners and losers. We feel isolated and bitter if we feel we don't measure up. As Gore Vidal once observed: "It is not enough to succeed. Others must fail." This type of thinking and behavior can crop up around absolutely anything.

Another form of subtle status envy is when experiences are accumulated and displayed as assiduously as any material possession. It's the "You simply must go to Belize" *(we're rich)* and "Last night we ate at XYZ" (*we're rich and somebody)* and "Madonna's concert was amazing" *(we're rich and connected enough to get good tickets, what's wrong with you?)*. All the subtle ways of comparing, judging, and competing reinforce the feeling of an isolated identity in need of constant external affirmation.

It also makes other feel bad. You don't actually garner the admiration you're looking for, but rather impart a sense of deficiency in the people you're one-upping. Your insecurity is feeding on their insecurity to try to make yourself feel better. The hit doesn't last very long for you, but other people might feel its effect for quite a while. They walk away from the exchange feeling drained. You walk away feeling alienated without quite knowing why.

Again, this is just human nature and conditioning. Simply observe it in yourself when it arises, and pull your awareness into the moment. Avoid having "an experience." An experience can be captured and filed away, pulled out as an accouterment to ego. *Experiencing* makes everything a communion, which ensures it's happening in the moment.

As Nisargadatta Maharaj wrote in *I Am That:*

> *You need not gather any more [experience], rather you must go beyond experience. . . . To believe that you depend on things and people for happiness is due to ignorance of your true nature; to know that you need nothing to be happy, except self-knowledge, is wisdom.*

Comparison breeds the concepts of inferiority and superiority. When you don't compare, inferiority and superiority disappear. Don't look to other people to find out who you are, because there is always somebody who is more beautiful, more talented, stronger, more intelligent, or happier. Or less so in some or all of these ways. What difference does it make to your happiness?

Rather, look to see if you are fulfilling your own existence in the truest way you know how. How do you do that? By focusing internally instead of externally. For instance, if I sit here and compare the writing of this book to other writers, I will become paralyzed. If I start thinking about what I have to offer, what hasn't been said before by more articulate people, and so on, I will never finish the book. The only thing I can do is my best, working on it moment by moment.

Realize that all comparisons and aims and ideals and goals and systems of improvement and betterment are lies. Drop the idea of self-improvement. Who and what is being improved? Right now, in this very moment, you cannot be improved, no matter what thoughts are running through your head.

The French philosopher René Descartes had it exactly backward. It's not "I think, therefore I am." It's actually "I am, therefore I think." You are not your thoughts. You exist first and think second.

You are consciousness itself. Personality is given by conditioning and is imposed or reinforced by whatever society we are born into. What choice did you have? Existence is given by simply being; it is there before the conditioning is set. There is nothing to do. There is nothing to add for deep happiness, no matter what our conditioning tells us every single day. And the only thing to subtract to experience deep freedom is to stop believing the conditioning.

Society will always move against simple, nonstriving existence because society doesn't want people who are absolutely dedicated to freedom from their own conditioning. Society wants obedience to its vested interests, which is to keep the engine of commerce running.

Even though we already *are,* we are told what to *be* by advertising and conditioning. Then we strive and compete with our fellow humans to accumulate as much as we can so that we can judge ourselves and others to see how we're doing.

But we can lighten our load by not identifying with the externals.

THE MATERIAL WORLD

Egocentricity is that constant concern with how I feel, what I think, what I'm doing, what I want—looking at what is and seeing it as inadequate.

—CHERI HUBER

An integral part of this external persona is the material possessions one gathers—the cars, the clothes, the watches, and all the rest. I'm not saying that possessions are bad in and of themselves. It is one's relationship to them that is important. And even if one has an easy relationship with material possessions, notice how much energy they take to maintain and protect.

Materialism feeds the presentational self. The presentational self is one step removed from the natural core self, which is *still* not your true nature. In fact, the less connected you are to yourself, the more possessions are needed to front a presentational self. Psychologists would call comfort with the presentational self, as opposed to comfort with the core self, a case of textbook narcissism.

Emptiness needs to be filled by externals. A rich interior life has very few needs.

Recently I was introduced to a man named Edward, who happened to be the brother of a famous man. The woman introducing me casually mentioned that Edward was the famous man's brother, as in: "This is Edward. His brother is so-and-so."

Edward is a close friend of the woman, so if he didn't want to be introduced in this way, I'm sure he would have privately told her. But he said nothing. I began to muse why she introduced him this way and why he allowed it. It's another way in which people cloak themselves in social finery. She knew Edward, who was the brother of this famous man; Edward knew that others were aware he was the actual brother of the famous man. It gave them both a boost, a way of establishing immediate social currency.

Notice all the ways in which we clothe ourselves in presentation. In countless subtle and unsubtle ways we identify and categorize ourselves in relation to other people. And so we tell ourselves the story of who we are. And then we tell this story to the world. In turn, we figure out other people by their externals and judge if they are worthy. We might as well send our possessions to have a conversation. My Bill Blass suit could talk to your Donna Karan dress and report whether or not it was interesting. No need for the actual people to show up!

When you allow yourself to be defined by possessions, you are practicing a form of self-objectification. You have woven a dream of your own presentation, and then you have to try to live up to it. The clothing becomes armor: the mansion becomes a prison. Nobody gets to know who you are because you have become "somebody." And if you have become "somebody," you lose the ability to just hang out because the persona needs constant attending. You become concerned with how the persona is doing, whether or not there is any slippage. Eventually, because you always react to situations through this persona, you experience mechanical reactions rather than heartfelt responses to life. Ultimately, holding up this presentation results in exhaustion so deep, it's as if the very marrow of your bones has turned to dust. And when you look at other people by that yardstick, you put both of you in the same prison, interacting with each other in the same narrow way.

How limited this is! It's like trying to comprehend the vastness of the ocean from a glass of water.

Persona, however, can be hard to shake when it's a result of familial conditioning. One time in our dharma conversations, Seth was talking about how he felt he was carrying his father around on his shoulders. His father was a very successful and brilliant man. Seth felt he was becoming his father, almost by osmosis. He felt he had to present a certain aura of success. Seth wanted to get back to his "integrated self," who he really was, his "real" personality. I joked, "Why bother? That's not who you are either." A persona is usually just a weird permutation of conditioning, who you think you should be in the world. It is similar to your ordinary small self, telling you who you think you are in the world.

Both the persona and the small self evaporate under a single question: "Who am I?" The answer is that all of us are consciousness itself, layered under all our misperceptions of duality. Ken Wilber put it well when he asked us to look at reality as though it were waves on the sea: all have different sizes and shapes, each absolutely unique in the way it rises and falls, with different rhythms and volumes, some catching the light, some not, yet all are water. Our senses give things their separateness; it is how we negotiate this reality. It is not that we are all one thing, with no differentiation. It's that we are "not-two."

In this "not-two" knowledge we experience the discrete world without feeling a sense of separation from it. In this "not-two" knowledge any persona we've cultivated falls away because we don't need it.

Yet I understood what Seth was saying, and I empathized with him. We all have our conditioning that is handed down. It is hard to avoid.

Is there an alternative?

LIVE NAKED

In order to swim one takes off all one's clothes—in order to aspire to the truth one must undress in a far more inward sense, divest oneself of all one's inward clothes, of thoughts, conceptions, selfishness etc. before one is sufficiently naked.

—SØREN KIERKEGAARD

To live in the world nakedly, without the false cloak of presentation, whether it is social, material, or even spiritual, is to be free.

When you live in the world nakedly, you have a chance of seeing reality more clearly because you have removed your own obscuration. When you are naked to the world, you are vulnerable, human, and real. You are not hiding from anything. You are not protected from raw experience, and you simply *feel more* when you drop the presentation.

To be naked is to live simply. To live simply is to be free.

Simplicity means being connected directly to what is in front of you right now, whether it is the most opulent dinner you've ever eaten, a sandwich on a park bench, or only a blank wall and your breath.

Young children live in the world naked. They don't care about the car you drive, the clothes you wear, or whom you know. They just care if you're funny, if you can play, if you're nice. They are interested not in a beautiful house but in a beautiful you. They don't care how many things you have, but how open and available you are.

As I sit here in a coffee shop writing these sentences, a three-year-old girl is running around saying hi to everybody, regardless of who they are. She is neither acquiescent nor rebellious, but innocent and spontaneous, true to her own nature.

Her young mother, patient as a Zen master, follows her, trying to anticipate major calamities. They don't realize it, but they are funnier than a Marx Brothers routine. When the girl toddles over to a pyramid of ceramic coffee mugs and starts to pull it down, her mother catches two before they hit the floor, saying kindly, "That's why we don't do that." The girl smiles and moves on to the next person. She is an indomitable, curly-haired, thirty-pound wrecking ball, inviting everybody out of their separate bubbles and into the infinite now.

And the invitation works. I take it. Even the other writers furiously typing or staring out into the middle distance become engaged.

As I watch this moment of human theater, I see a homeless person trudging by the large windows.

Cars drift by on the shopping street.

The stereo plays Cat Stevens as people traipse in and out of the coffee shop.

The little girl smiles at a crippled poodle, who snarls at her.

Two old men talk about where they can get their hats cleaned and blocked.

A fat man in a white leisure suit and red shirt begins to snore.

Steam hisses from the espresso machine and then gurgles into a cappuccino. The universe suddenly spins and whirls in a perfect dance. I feel a great welling up in my chest, as if my heart were a sponge absorbing and shedding tears at the same time.

Now people are smiling as the man's snores grow louder. The little girl walks over to the snoring man and says, "Wake up!" startling him awake. He rubs his eyes.

She is God, wandering around reminding each of us that we too, even when we are asleep, are also God—God talking to God and saying, "Wake up!"

What else do we need except each precious moment?

There is no me. There is no them. I simply vanish. Feeling heartbreakingly connected, I vanish into all.

VANISHING TO SELF

What is left when we disappear to ourselves? What is left when there is no "I" but just a sense of beingness? Joy and love. And a sweet sense of tenderness for every living being on the planet, especially humans, the only species aware of its own eventual demise. I feel it now very strongly in this café, an unmitigated sense of the infinite.

The heart of a mystical experience, as opposed to a religious one, is this connection to the infinite through something as small and specific as this moment right now. Which means it doesn't always arrive in beautiful places or on spiritual retreat, but is available in the most ordinary places, under the most ordinary circumstances—a café, a train, an office.

But this bliss is not available through the mind; words are incapable of communicating this state. It's like trying to describe the taste of a juicy peach to somebody who has never tasted one. Yet still humans persist in trying to share the ineffable via the blunt instrument of language.

This is particularly true in trying to communicate a mystical experience—it's like grasping for the infinite with finite tools. But even in the apparent duality of language, which instantly creates a speaker and a listener when you open your mouth, it is still possible to vanish. If you can listen without referring back to a listener, speak without self-reflecting as a speaker, then it is possible to disappear under any circumstance—peaceful or intense, boring or stimulating.

Even when the mind is in an "I want" mode, even as covetous thoughts creep in and desire drones in your head, you can be free. Think of these desires as the embers of a fire lit by conditioning long ago, now dying in the corner of your mental hearth. If you dont' pour the gasoline of your attention on those embers, fueling the fire, it is possible to be awake even as the thoughts come up. By relaxing your attention into the now, those embers will eventually burn themselves out until the conditioning is simply dead energy. It won't burn because there isn't any more fuel.

At that moment, as the little girl was exhorting the sleeping man, you will wake up from the trance of desire.

CONTENTMENT VERSUS DESIRE

Fill your bowl to the brim
and it will spill.
Keep sharpening your knife
and it will blunt.
Chase after money and security
and your heart will never unclench.
Care about people's approval
and you will be their prisoner.

—THE TAO

Catherine Ingram says that "contentment is perhaps the most underrated aspect of happiness in our culture." We are told over and over again that contentment is the same as apathy, lack of ambition, or ennui. That all progress is due to a lack of contentment. But it's not. Being content means being grateful for what you have right now, with the operative word being *now*. How happy you are doesn't depend on how much you have. If you live comfortably, and if you're reading this book my guess is that you are living comfortably enough to purchase it, then you have enough. Right now as you read you probably have a roof over your head (be it ever so humble), and you have food in your belly or in the fridge. Right now everything is fine.

Fame, power, glamour, youth, glory, and riches are constantly touted as sources of happiness; we don't even question it anymore. Leading a simple life has no value. Living a quiet life filled with intrinsic humanity is considered boring. People are told to "dream big" and that America is a place where you can "do anything." Not only is the cult of the individual worshiped, it is exacerbated into a frenzy by the media—turn on the TV and you will see people selling products that are supposed to make you rich, happy, and beautiful, like them. And lately, appropriating spirituality itself, the media is selling "contentment" or "peace." Thus you are being sold something that is already yours.

When these desires are thwarted, inchoate anger and a sense that "I'm not enough, no matter what I do" becomes prevalent. Or the reverse happens—all the desires are slaked and there is still hunger. It is a form of national sickness that is the darker underbelly of capitalism. Marx had one thing right: capitalism depends upon ever-expanding markets and an ever-expanding appetite for consumption.

Even many of our religions are consumerist in nature, staking out their territory and competing for a share of followers, telling other religions that there is only "one truth." Or the urge for spirituality is corrupted by New Age hokum about "manifesting" or "creating your own reality" to get the material possessions and lifestyle that you desire, reinforcing the message that you need something external to be happy. But as we have seen all too clearly throughout history, the divide between spirituality and organized religion has widened to the point of incompatibility. Exploitation of the natural and unique human impulse for devotion has led us to nationalism (hatred of other countries) instead of patriotism (love of one's own country), religion (ritualistic services) instead of spirituality (devotion to love). We are worshiping the false idol of consumerism, which is reinforced at every turn.

So it wasn't surprising that after September 11 President Bush said, in effect, "Go shopping." We all know the importance of keeping the economy going, but was this the best response to the worst crisis America has experienced on its land since the bombing of Pearl Harbor? What about sacrifice? What about the very human need to do something with a higher purpose than consumption? It's hard to imagine John F. Kennedy, who spoke the ringing words "Ask not what your country can do for you; ask what you can do for your country," would have said "Go shopping" after the death of even three thousand Americans.

The irony is that so many people displayed remarkable courage and sacrifice in dealing with the crisis of September 11. They risked their lives in order to save others. Hundreds of millions of dollars were donated to the survivors' families. Countless acts of kindness were done by complete strangers as people pulled together in ways that they had perhaps not even imagined before.

But just look at our government's response to the national tragedy of September 11. There was no harnessing of the world's support into a unifying vision. There was no appeal to our true nature of love and kindness. Not even a call to our willingness to sacrifice by cutting our consumption of oil, thus lessening our dependence on the Middle Eastern countries. There was only a call for revenge, a call to get the perpetrators "dead or alive."

Many of our role models, from politicians to pop icons, demonstrate a major disconnect with their quieter, nonacquiring selves and consequently with a planet that is, according to the Union of Concerned Scientists, increasingly on the environmental brink. Instead of seeing through the phantasmagoria of conspicuous consumption, environmental degradation, and mindless stimulation, we aspire to it. We export it to the rest of the world in a cacophony that we call "pop culture" as something other people should aspire to. And they do.

On an international level, the rest of the world is looking at us in the same way less wealthy individuals look at a rich person: with status envy.

THE HEART

The deeper truth is this: *Human beings want to be loving. It is their true nature.*

The great playwright Tennessee Williams once said: "Sometimes we kill our hearts in order not to feel." A daily life focused on striving, on competition, on comparison, can kill our hearts without us even noticing that they are dead. But the true nature of humans yearns to rise above the conditioning that puts them in a state of separation and fear and in competition with each other for a piece of the pie.

Any crisis, whether a terrorist attack, an earthquake, or miners getting trapped in water two hundred feet underground, can bring out the best in people. Unfortunately, it often takes a disaster to bring us into our true nature of connectedness and caring. Many veterans talk about their combat experience in this way. They miss the closeness they felt to the other soldiers in their unit, all of whom were pushed to the limits of courage and fear, in a battle larger than themselves (not necessarily the war, but the struggle for survival). They were bonded to each other in deep ways, their individual fates dependent on each other and starkly illuminated by the presence of death. It is in this heightened reality that sometimes the real reality can be seen—in this case the interconnectedness of the soldiers in their unit.

Unfortunately, this sense of connection doesn't extend to our daily competition with each other for material gain. Is it possible to have this heightened sense of connection without the tragedy?

Possibly, but first we must deal with our own disease of affluenza.

AFFLUENZA

Anyone—regardless of their net worth—who believes that they must be rich, that more is always better, is a self-condemned prisoner of the "golden ghetto."

—JESSIE H. O'NEILL

Over the past two decades the difference in incomes between the wealthy and the average person has increased dramatically. Twenty-five years ago the average CEO made 45 times the salary of the average worker. Now the average CEO earns *450 times* the salary of an average worker every year.

Think about this for a moment. One human being is making 450 times what another human being is making at the same company. This goes beyond any rationalizations about "creating wealth" and "employing people" and "deserving the riches for taking the risks."

This is firmly in the arena of obscene avarice. It is the difference between mansions in Malibu and the tiny shacks the workers in third-world sweatshops live in. The only compassionate solution is an ethical profit-sharing program so that all can reap the benefits of a company's profit making.

And then there are the dishonest CEOs. The looting is astonishing. Enron's Kenneth Lay stole $81.5 million in loan advances. Tyco's Dennis Kozlowski reportedly received $135 million in forgiven loans, real-estate payments, and bogus charitable expenses. WorldCom's Bernie Ebbers stashed away loans of $408 million, and Adelphia's John Rigas and sons cooked the books for $2.3 billion in off-balance-sheet loans. Their gluttony has left thousands of workers jobless and with their hard-earned pensions wiped out.

Again, how much is enough?

In the face of such greed, it might seem easy to rationalize stealing office supplies—the "hey, everybody's doing it" defense. But whether you're looting the company pension or getting freebies from a friend at the company store, the dynamic of theft is the same. No matter what level we occupy in an organization, we are all faced with tests of our own integrity, even if it's on the level of not overbilling a customer. Whether or not you're going to slide down the slippery slope is up to you.

Simply defined, affluenza is a dysfunctional relationship with money or wealth, or the pursuit of it. Globally it is a backup in the flow of money, resulting in a polarization of the classes and a loss of economic and emotional balance.

Among the symptoms of affluenza Jessie O'Neill has defined in her book *The Golden Ghetto* are:

An inability to delay gratification or tolerate frustration
A false sense of entitlement
Low self-esteem
Low self-worth
Loss of self-confidence

Preoccupation with externals
Depression, self-absorption
High regard for outer self, low regard for inner self
Survivor's guilt, shame
Sudden-wealth syndrome, sudden-poverty syndrome
Workaholism
Other compulsive-addictive behaviors, such as rampant materialism and consumerism

The psychological dynamics of greed, arrogance, and a sense of entitlement go far beyond people providing themselves with security and luxury. Neil Gabler, a senior fellow at the University of Southern California, claims the larcenous CEOs had a different motive. They coveted beyond all else, making a grand display of their wealth.

"This was showmanship," says Gabler. "They wanted to be Masters of the Universe."

These are extreme cases of affluenza, yet it wouldn't be hard to identify this dynamic in each of us at times, even if it's just the purchase of a lottery ticket, believing that it would change our lives for the best if we could just have that money.

A friend of mine, a very successful screenwriter, once said that the money didn't change him; it changed the people around him. He still had to get up every day and be himself, wrestle with the writing, and deal with the loneliness of the lifestyle. Other people were more impressed with the success that he had achieved than he was.

In the immortal words of the first Master of the Universe, King Solomon, in Ecclesiastes: "I denied myself nothing my eyes desired. I refused my heart no pleasure. . . . Yet when I surveyed all that my hands had done and what I had toiled to achieve, everything was *hevel havalim*—vanity of vanities—a meaningless chasing after the wind."

What is sacrificed on the altar of consumption? What did Christ mean when he said it is easier for a camel to pass through the eye of a needle than for a rich man to enter the kingdom of heaven? He meant that in a lifetime of acquiring you sacrifice something important: humility, simplicity, a lack of ego. In a lifetime of pushing, demanding, and conquering you become entrenched in the idea that it's all *you*. You are engaged in a lifetime of ego inflation and becoming a *somebody*.

Or, as Lily Tomlin once said: "The trouble with the rat race is that even if you win, you're still a rat."

Most Americans cling to this myth of unlimited success. Like people buying lottery tickets, they think that someday they'll be millionaries. In fact, 19 percent of Americans already believe themselves to be in the top I percent of earners. A further 20 percent think they will end up there within their lifetimes. Even though it's impossible that 39 percent of our population will rise to be in the top 1 percent of earners, it's part of our nation's optimism and core self-image. And part of the mirage used to justify everything from tax cuts for the rich to cutting affirmative action. But what is the reality? What has the ordinary citizen really won? Americans have less free time, more stress, and eleven thousand homicides a year (compare this to other Western industrialized countries such as Germany, France, and Canada, where homicides number in the low hundreds). Last year Americans, who make up only 5 percent of the world's population, used nearly a third of its resources and produced almost half of its hazardous waste. Add overwork, the erosion of family and community, skyrocketing debt, and the growing gap between rich and poor, and it's easy to understand why the American dream comes at a steep personal and planetary cost.

An acquaintance of mine is a lawyer trying to make partner. Melinda is also a mom who is buried in seventy- or eighty-hour workweeks and will be for the next six years, at which point her daughter will be seven. She is missing irreplaceable years with her daughter and growing old before her time, withering from lack of sunlight and exercise.

When I asked her why she doesn't live more simply and cut back—work half time, only make a hundred thousand dollars a year—she shrugged.

"When I make partner, I'll be set," she said.

But she won't. She'll still be working too many hours, albeit for more money.

Meanwhile she is literally trading her life for that dream.

GRATITUDE VERSUS DEFICIENCY

Beyond ambition,
Beyond attainment,
Is home.
Contentment,
Without content;
Peace,
Uncaused.

—A. H. ALMAAS

When a sense of deficiency is activated, it cannot be appeased by acquiring; it can only be assuaged by gratitude. If one has a rich interior life, one need very little on the outside. But in fact I am not even arguing for needing very little on the outside; after all, this is America, and we have a *lot*. Good places to live, good food to eat, movies to see, television, books, security, wonderful parks to visit . . . by any standards (except those of affluenza) our average welder is much richer today than the average king was three hundred years ago. It's a better life. As Bill Maher says, anyone born in America in this generation has won the geohistorical Powerball lotto. And yet we strive as if it weren't enough.

We know that after a certain point, it's all about ego, which is actually about insecurity—trying to outdo each other in competition rather than work together in cooperation.

I had a theory that I ran by a female friend recently. I said that what men did, they did for women. They acquired money and things and became powerful to impress and thus acquire women. It was a biological imperative. Men pursue power, which gives them access to beautiful women. Women pursue beauty (in themselves) to pursue powerful men. Thus any solution would have to encapsulate a change in values promulgated by women. If women didn't care about the size of their house or diamond engagement ring, then men wouldn't feel the need to overkill the mastodon.

My friend strongly disagreed. She said it was true up to a point, after which, for most women who are psychologically integrated, the money becomes irrelevant. She claims that it's all about men and their ability to stand up in the company of other men. Or, as she indelicately put it, it's a case of "my dick is bigger than yours."

Okay, so our social and biological conditioning is strong in many different ways that prevent us from being happy with what we have, which is the only way to be happy. How do we unhook from the dynamic of acquiring?

The best way to combat it is to bring our attention to gratitude for what we have. There are all sorts of ways to remind ourselves of how blessed we are. One of them is to volunteer, whether informally or formally.

A friend told me a story of a man who was bored with everything. He had made a lot of money and had everything he needed. He had no family to leave his wealth to, and after he sold his company he had no responsibilities. He traveled all over the world, consumed the best of everything, dated supermodels, and drank champagne in the best clubs in Paris. His whole demeanor was "been there, done that," and he really had been there and done that.

Nothing moved him until he met a woman working with Cambodian orphans. For some reason he was overwhelmed with empathy for their plight, and after much negotiation he adopted two, a brother and a sister, out of an orphanage. Now, this man didn't start an organization or volunteer in any formal way. But in a very real way, he saved these children's lives, giving them an opportunity they never would have had. But what he got from the action was a renewed zest for life. He has stopped feeling entitled and always trying to be entertained, and is no longer bored. Life is plenty entertaining!

Do something for those less fortunate than yourself; it creates connection and appreciation and empathy. Know that in any given moment, when thoughts such as *This isn't enough* or *I want that* arise, they can be counteracted by an act of generosity. Perhaps even a smile or a kind word will create generosity from the inside and put you back into a direct experience of life, reversing the energy of trying to fill yourself up from the outside. It will remind you of *what is,* that we are fortunate and blessed. The rest of the world is struggling for food, and we live in a place where we're impressed by how it's served and what kind of car we drive to the restaurant. It's all about perspective.

If you are fortunate enough to be very wealthy, think about how you want to spend those riches. And remember what the definition of *wealthy* is. Are you stuck in Lewis Latham's cycle of always needing twice as much? Or are you aware of Bill Maher's insight that you've already won the geohistorical Powerball lotto?

The different ways to be in the world of wealth can be summarized in the way in which two millionaires deal with it. One is a management consultant who, when he went to Kenya, was struck by the plight of the wildlife as well as the poverty of the people living among them and poaching them out of desperation. He decided to take his money, buy a nearby game reserve, train the Kenyans to make clothing with environmental messages, build sustainable rammed earth housing and a factory for his workers, and employ the men to guard against poachers. He created a sustainable system that saved wildlife and provided for people's needs. The program is now being replicated in different parts of the world.

Our second millionaire is a huge Hollywood producer. One night I went to the movies with a friend and a young man sat in front of me, throwing his jacket over three seats, saving them. This producer came in and sat on the aisle seat. He had the young man, who was his assistant, sit two seats over, reserving the middle seat for space between them. The theater filled up. A woman came up and asked if anybody was sitting in the middle seat. The producer's assistant said yes. During the movie the producer kept his assistant busy with trips to the concession stand for drinks and food. The third seat was never filled.

Two people with similar amounts of money, each choosing to relate to the world in a different way. The money didn't make the difference; the attitude toward it did.

This choice is true in each of us, no matter how much money we have. It all depends on the way we relate to ourselves and our world—most of which is a manifestation of the thoughts happening in our head.

HIJACKED BY DESIRE

A wise woman who was traveling in the mountains found a precious stone in a stream. The next day she met another traveler who was hungry, and the wise woman opened her bag to share her food. The hungry traveler saw the precious stone and asked the woman to give it to him. She did so without hesitation.

The traveler left, rejoicing in his good fortune. He knew the stone was worth enough to give him security for a lifetime. But a few days later he came back to return the stone to the wise woman.

"I've been thinking," he said. "I know how valuable the stone is, but I give it back in the hope that you can give me something even more precious. Give me what you have within you that enabled you to give me the stone."

I live in an apartment in Santa Monica, California, south of Montana Street. North of Montana home prices range from $1 million to $6 million. The other day I took a walk down the tree-shaded streets and crossed Montana, moving from my neighborhood of nice apartments into a neighborhood of beautiful homes.

As I passed these houses with their perfectly manicured lawns, quaint little picket fences, and flourishing bougainvillea, I found that desire was arising in me. I fantasized about living in this house or that house. A kind of yearning arose, and suddenly my lot in life didn't seem like it was enough. I wanted that house and the car in the driveway. And come to think of it, I wanted the beautiful woman coming out of her house walking the yellow Labrador, straight out of an advertisement promising the good life. I felt this desire come up until it was a kind of palpable ache, filling my awareness for the few moments it lasted.

And so I effectively ruined a lovely walk.

Instead of reveling in the sight of the bougainvillea, I wanted to own it. Instead of gratitude for what I have, which is a beautiful apartment four blocks from the beach, I was caught momentarily in what was missing.

But what was I missing in that moment? I was walking down the same street, breathing the same air, bathed by the same gentle California sun. I didn't own any of the houses, but so what? It was only in telling myself that I would be happier in the house that I was actually creating my misery. There I was, walking down the street on a beautiful afternoon and not slaving away in some office trying to pay for an expensive house, and yet it was I who felt the lack.

What are you to do when you catch yourself experiencing this affluenza? When you find yourself wanting more? Striving to prove yourself instead of enjoying what you have?

Well, you could beat yourself up for not being spiritual enough. Take yourself out back for a good scourging and a cup of cold gruel to wash it down.

Or you could smile at yourself and remember that you're human, that the culture works this way . . . and be pleased that in this moment you've remembered what's truly important.

The same goes for other people. You see people striving and you can judge them and realize that they are hollow, callow bastards with no sense of real value. Or you can know that they're caught in the same web of humanity that we all are. And you can get to know them for who they are.

When I was young and working in Newport, Rhode Island, for the summer, I was a sommelier in a restaurant owned by a wealthy restaurateur named David Ray. David had purchased an eighty-five-foot wooden sailboat from David Rockefeller called, appropriately enough. *Nirvana.*

I didn't even know what the word meant at the time, but I knew it was a stunning boat. It came with a full-time captain who used to take any interested staff members out for sails every few days. We did that all summer long. I had been sailing my whole life, and near the end of the summer, when the captain asked me if I wanted to help deliver the boat up to Camden, Maine, I jumped at the chance. We set off with two young women, just the four of us on this magnificent boat. We sailed in shifts, and I ended up sailing the 2–6 a.m. shift with a beautiful woman named Lori.

As we sailed the boat through the rosy-fingered dawn, out of sight of land, every sail up, spray dancing off the bow with myself at the wheel, I marveled that I had spent more time that summer on this boat than the owner. As the sun came up, whales breached just off our bow.

I never once thought, *Wow, I wish I owned this two-million-dollar boat.* It never occurred to me that I needed anything else to be happy in that moment.

It was an extraordinary moment, but the same is true of ordinary life. When we drop the story of "not enough," we can directly and truly the simple wonders of life. Every moment in this realization is a peak experience, allowing, as Catherine Ingram likes to say, the ordinary to become extraordinary.

So see the sumptuousness in each vibrant moment, rather than in the accumulation of possessions and experiences. When you want to feel rich, to feel sated, focus your awareness on whatever is in front of you: a flower, a piece of trash, the rhythmic slosh of windshield wipers on a rainy day.

Notice how in this awareness the whole world takes on a beautiful luster.

The radical truth is that in this very moment nothing needs to be added and nothing needs to be changed.

You have enough.

There is nothing to envy.

As H. W. L. Poonja famously said, "This freedom is our birthright."

WALKING DOWN A DARK ALLEY

Awareness and Violence

> The mind is its own place, and in itself
> Can make a heaven of hell, a hell of heaven.
> —JOHN MILTON

The man cocked the gun. It was the loudest sound in the world.

"Give me your fuckin' jacket," he shouted. The veins were popping out on his hand, which was shaking.

I hurriedly started unbuttoning my coat in the cold Boston winter. A car turned down the empty street. I stared in disbelief—it was a police car. The man tucked the gun in his shirt, stepped back in the alley, and sprinted away, disappearing as quickly as he had appeared. The police never caught him.

Violence is like that, fast, random, and on some level inexplicable. One minute you're walking down the street; the next minute you're being mugged or worse. In a blink, it's over, leaving you shaking with rage, hatred, and pain.

Violence also leaves us with many ethical and spiritual questions. Should we practice nonviolence? Or should we fight and protect ourselves? We will take a look at both options in this chapter.

It is also frequently difficult to determine if the threat of violence is real or imaginary, especially in the jittery world we live in.

There is an old story about a man who kept mistaking a rope for a snake. If everywhere you turn you see snakes for ropes, you're doomed to live in fear. However, if you see a snake and mistake it for a rope, you could be bitten and die. This is the razor's edge of living in a big city, differentiating between real and imaginary dangers. If we err on the side of paranoia, we can become virtual prisoners in our own minds, never leaving the house. But if we don't clearly assess the danger, we could die.

Either way, whether the violence is real or in our imagination, being in a state of wakefulness is the best response. When awake, one is able to see reality more clearly and see potential danger immediately, avoiding certain neighborhoods and situations. When awake, you also have a better chance of seeing through the mind's confabulations and paranoia and making the right choice for yourself in the moment, whether it is to run, fight, or talk.

Recently, a few blocks from my house, a homeless woman was ranting and raving. The police had her cornered and their guns were drawn. She was brandishing a screwdriver and the police shot her. Was she a snake or a rope? In the police officers' minds, she was obviously the latter—dangerous and unstable. To the larger community, the police had overreacted. This situation has played out over and over in cities from New York to Los Angeles.

And yet even as I write this, in front of my apartment, eight police cars have descended on an old man in a dilapidated twenty-year-old Volvo. The man is screaming as six cops handcuff him. It looks like horrible overkill from my window, so I go down and see what's happening. The old man, clearly demented, was driving with no license and registration and had been chased for fifteen minutes by a police officer without pulling over. It looked like overkill until you saw on a street level the care the police were taking not to hurt the man, who refused to sit in the back of the squad car. And it certainly doesn't seem like overkill when you take into consideration that three weeks ago ten people were killed by another confused old man who drove his car into the local farmer's market.

Often it is hard to tell what is dangerous, so we evaluate situations in our head every time we walk out the front door. Is that person dangerous? Is this neighborhood safe? We constantly judge other people, putting them into an "okay" or "dangerous" category, with the latest menace being all things Muslim.

The threat of violence can provoke overreactions in individuals as well as nations. One of the goals of terrorism is to get the larger, dominant group to overreact, thus winning the public relations war. On a more personal level, one of the results of crime is to make us afraid, reactive, and less generous, whether the individual situation warrants it or not.

But the risks that rivet attention and raise anxiety levels are the unfamiliar ones, not necessarily the most dangerous. According to George M. Gray, a risk analysis expert at Harvard University, fear spikes when a new or highly publicized risk appears. For example, in 2002 five Americans died in anthrax attacks, in which letters were sent containing the deadly germ. For months people everywhere were afraid to open their mail. When a few shark attacks were in the news, people shunned the ocean. And when recently child abduction was in the headlines, parents refused to let their children go to the playground, even though studies were showing that child abduction statistics were actually down during that period.

By contrast, roughly 925 people are fatally electrocuted at home annually, but in 2001 there was no sudden rise in the number of those unwilling to plug in the toaster.

There can also be a danger in reacting to the perception of risk, as opposed to the real thing. After September 11 people stopped flying and instead took long trips by car. But the risk of dying in a car accident, as every American has been told a hundred times, is far greater than the risk of dying in a terrorist attack.

"The problem with being afraid," Mr. Gray said, "is if it makes you do things that actually increase the risk."

Again, it comes down to discerning the snake from the rope. This is particularly difficult after we have been attacked.

Are we experiencing reality in these moments or living in the reality of our own heads? The proverbial cliché of a white person crossing the street when he or she sees a black male is a good example. Is the reality of the moment being taken into consideration? For example, is the man acting strangely or eyeballing the other person? Or is the action of crossing the street just the result of a thought programmed in by years of conditioning? Such thought's can perhaps obscure the real danger of a threat that doesn't fit our conditioned seeing—like getting hit by a bus while rushing to cross that street.

Wakefulness, on the other hand, allows you to see trouble before it happens, allowing you to move out of its way or intervene in a helpful way. It means not going into a situation with any preconceived notions, able to react flexibly to whatever is happening.

THE SNAKE AND THE ROPE

I once arrived at the Los Angeles airport after a long flight. I had awoken in Toledo, Spain, at five in the morning and then taken a four-hour car ride to Madrid, where I caught a nine-hour flight to New York. Then I had a three-hour delay before flying six hours into Los Angeles. In short, I was exhausted.

I needed to get a cab home but had no American currency. I went to an ATM machine that was right next to baggage claim and slipped my card in. I was vaguely aware, in my exhaustion, of two men walking out of the bustling crowd and standing in line behind me. I proceeded with my transaction without looking up.

"You . . . I watch you," I heard a man off to my right say. I glanced over. He was short and dark and leaning against a luggage cart. He had an unidentifiable accent and was talking not to me but to the men behind me. Let's call him Sam.

"You're a dishonest man. I watch you," Sam said to the men.

"You mind your own business," said one of the men behind me. "I'm not messin' with you."

"Come away from there." Sam persisted. "I know what you do. You're a thief."

Now he had my attention. I turned around, waiting for my cash to eject, and I saw two black men. The one in a yellow Adidas track suit and lots of gold jewelry we'll call Jamal; the other man, wearing jeans and a tight white T-shirt, we'll call Carl.

Jamal and Carl didn't seem particularly threatening to me, but both did seem to have a slight gang-banger attitude, although I couldn't tell if it was real or wannabe.

"What's up, guys?" I smiled at them. They both nodded.

"Nothin'," said Jamal. I decided to let it go. I didn't feel like I was in any danger in broad daylight in the bustling terminal. I went back to my transaction.

"You go away now," Sam kept insisting to Jamal and Carl.

"Don't be playin' me, motherfucker," Carl snapped, his tone suddenly ugly. "Motherfuckin' bean eater. I'll fuck you up."

Now suddenly I was wide awake. I stuffed my wallet in my pocket. I heard the two men behind me talking.

"Go back to Mexico, wetback. Fuckin' bean eater," Carl continued his screed.

I grabbed my cash and card and jammed them in the other pocket. I glanced at Sam, a short man with a mustache, who actually looked more like he might be Pakistani than Hispanic. He stood there calmly, steadily watching the two men. I walked over to Sam as he continued to watch as Jamal fumbled in his wallet, looking for his ATM card. Carl glared at us, occasionally offering to rearrange our facial structure.

Now this is where I thought I *knew* what was going on. Sam was watching the two men to see if they actually had an ATM card. If they didn't, then their motives for being in line were suspect. I admired his Good Samaritan tenacity.

"What's going on here?" I asked Sam.

"This man, he hurts my customers." Sam said in his ambiguous accent. I immediately assumed he was watching out for the greater good, his hand on his cell phone to call 911. Meanwhile Jamal, fumbling for his ATM card couldn't seem to come up with it. My eyes narrowed suspiciously: just as I suspected, he didn't have a card. He was some kind of scam artist or money snatcher.

"Fuck this shit," Carl said, sliding away, leaving his cohort still looking in his wallet.

"They take money from you as you get it out of the machine?" I asked my rotund vigilante. Sam nodded in response. Jamal finally produced a card out of his yellow track suit. He held it up and smiled at us.

"Thank you for watching out for me," I said to Sam. He nodded as I walked toward baggage claim, considering myself lucky.

This is where I find out I didn't know what's going on, at all.

After waiting for a few minutes, Jamal came over to the baggage carousel, accompanied by Sam, hauling his luggage carrier. They stood next to me and amicably waited for luggage.

"Excuse me," I said. "I'm confused. Can you tell me what just happened back there?"

"He is my customer," Sam said. I looked at Jamal in his yellow track suit.

"My driver," Jamal yawned, still looking menacing, but now in a wealthy rapper kind of way.

"So you don't know that other guy, the guy that was being so rude?" Jamal shook his head, uninterested.

"But this makes no sense. . . . You were talking to him. I thought you were together."

"Nah."

"But why would he try to rob us? You? I mean, we don't exactly seem like pushovers. At least you don't."

"It's cool." Jamal hovered above me at the height of boredom. He wasn't about to give me anything. Perhaps he was embarrassed by the whole episode, but I felt like there was a reason he wasn't communicating, as if there was some other web of social protocol that I couldn't penetrate.

"I see him before. He's a bad man," Sam offered.

"So you weren't helping me out?" I asked.

"Not really. I watch my customers."

I glanced at the tall kid in the yellow track suit. I didn't understand his reticence. Who was he? Why wouldn't he just tell me what was going on? What he thought about the event that had just transpired? What was he was thinking now?

A red Nike bag dropped down the chute.

"That's it." Jamal pointed to the bag. "Red bag."

Sam scrambled for the bag and put it on the cart. I nodded at the two men.

"Thank you for your help," I said to Sam. "You know, warning me at the ATM."

"I help my customer," Sam said.

"Later," said his charge.

I watched as they wandered away, the one pushing the cart, the other whipping out an impossibly small cell phone.

This short interaction has so many lessons in it. I was not, in my fatigue, awake to the situation. I didn't even sense what was happening until it was called to my attention in the most obvious way. If somebody had wanted to take advantage of me, I would have been an easy target.

In a study of criminal behavior, a videotape of ten different women was shown to fifteen convicted rapists. They all chose the same two women they would attack, citing their distracted demeanor and lack of presence, confidence, and directness in their walk. In short, a lack of wakefulness.

If you're not in a "be here now" state of mind, you might not be here later. Literally.

I marveled at how, coming out of my travel-weary stupor into the moment, I had completely misapprehended the situation. I was so asleep at the wheel that it felt like waking up from a nap into the middle of an ongoing play. The actors were there. The set was in place. But I had no idea what the story was and what was going on. In my fog, I wasn't reading the situation correctly. One minute, given the information I had, I saw the man as a gang member, a threat, a predator to be closely monitored. Then, with a little more information, in the next minute, I saw him as a wealthy and successful entertainer using his hood "vibe" to maintain the necessities of street cred.

And if I had stayed with him a little bit longer? I might have found out who he really was.

What had changed? What was going on with my perceptual abilities? On the one hand, nothing—I was responding to the information as it was released to me. On the other hand, I was not getting all the information because I was asleep in the moment. In order for my mind to try to catch up to what was going on, it began padding my direct experience with a story of what *I thought* was happening. It filled in the blanks about who Carl and Jamal were and what they were doing. My mind lumped them together even though the driver had been talking about only one of them when he had said, "That man is a bad man." In a state of incomplete comprehension, I just assumed that the driver was having a language problem and that both the men were gang-bangers.

Where did this entire projected story come from? Certainly not from a clear seeing of my direct experience of reality. I can't even say it came from an honest emotion like fear. I wasn't actually afraid. My response came out of my own tangled bundle of conditioning and thought. My mind was filling in everything, working overtime, trying to make sense of my direct experience.

I was seeing a snake where there was only a rope.

This happens a lot. The mind is a faulty lens—it often jumps to conclusions based on what it has been conditioned to see and not on what is. With every direct occurrence of life we bring all of our subjective experience and judgments. The result is often a work of fiction, not reality.

A STONE'S THROW FROM THE STONE AGE

In this world hate never yet dispelled hate. Only love dispels hate.
This is the law, ancient and inexhaustible.
—BUDDHA

Much of our conditioning is primal and instinctual. We are, after all, still animals, with very basic needs and desires. We have biological hardwiring that can be triggered into a fight or flight response in a split second.

I am reminded of a time I was visiting my cousin in Orlando, Florida, when we were both in our twenties. He took me to a night-club filled with rednecks and women with big hair, all of whom were drinking hard. Afterward, as we approached our car, a black man sprinted by, running for his life. He was being chased by six beefy white guys who were shouting and carrying two-by-fours from the parking lot, which was under construction. As they cornered the man, my cousin, Michael, jumped out of the car. I tried to grab his arm to tell him not to get involved, but it was too late.

"What are we doing here?" Michael said, jumping in the middle of the fracas. "Are we back in the stone age? Are you going to club him like you were the Flintstones?"

"This nigger stole my girlfriend's bracelet," shouted the largest man, moving forward, veins popping out of his neck. The black man cringed against the wall, but my cousin stood firmly between them. He looked the big guy in the eye.

"Okay. So what if he did? Let's just say he did. Are you going to change your entire life? What if you seriously hurt him? What if you kill him? And then you go to jail and your life is ruined. What is the point of that? All for a bracelet. Is it really worth it?"

Silence as the men absorbed this. They were enraged with hurt ego and pride. Their racist conditioning was running full steam. But there was no denying that my cousin had a point. Sirens started to squeal in the distance.

"There are the police," Michael said, calmly nodding, looking the big man in the eye. "It's not worth it, is it?"

"No," the man agreed. "He ain't worth it."

With that, the men dispersed. The black man stood up. Michael turned to him. "Did you take the bracelet?"

The man looked at the ground.

"I didn't take nothing."

With that, the man took off running.

"I think he took it." Michael smiled at me as he got back in the car.

It was an amazing demonstration of wakefulness in a dangerous situation. But no spirituality was applied. It was about meeting the moment in a way that could be heard and understood by all the participants, without lecture or judgment. It also appealed to the men's higher nature, which wasn't apparent but is often available, even the most dire circumstances.

MOMENTARY MADNESS

Many times violence erupts out of a momentary madness between two normally well-meaning people, stressed beyond their edge.

I have a friend who has a Staffordshire terrier named Finkle. He's solid muscle and looks like a complete killer but is actually a gentle, flatulent character who is scared of the rain. He has a big head and the poignant face of a canine Hamlet.

One afternoon I was walking Finkle with his owner, Jennifer, and her eleven-year-old son, Oliver, in a suburb of London. Finkle strained against the leash as a mutt came up to say hi. I turned my head for a moment, and quick as a wink I was presiding over a hellacious dogfight—Hamlet had turned into Hannibal.

Finkle clamped onto the other dog's neck and mangled him to the ground. I had to squeeze Finkle's snout and work the other dog's skin free, inch by inch, in order to separate them. It took five minutes, with lots of cursing, tossing of water and the owner getting bitten by his own dog.

After the dogs were separated, then the people got involved. The owner had a full-on meltdown and threatened to kill Finkle, who frankly couldn't have looked more pleased with himself.

"My dog's not a fighter, he's a lover!" the big man screamed at me. "That dog's a bloody maniac. He's a killer!"

"He hasn't killed anybody *here,*" protested my friend.

"My bloody hand's going to fall off and my dog's going to die," the man continued screaming. "Then I'm going to sue!!"

"Your dog's fine," I said as calmly as possible. "I'm very sorry about all this, but I'm more concerned with your hand."

The man's hand was indeed bleeding, and a small crowd hand gathered on the sidewalk. Everybody seemed to know everybody else.

"Actually," a scruffy guy said to the hysterical guy, pointing at me, "he could take a gun and kill your dog. His dog is on a leash, yours is not. That's the law."

"The law!" the injured man roared. "This is Hampstead Gardens. All the dogs here are socialized! This dog is a killer!"

"Jim, are you saying that because this is Hampstead Gardens, we don't have laws here?" the scruffy man said, plowing forward, either not seeing or caring that the man was enraged.

"Stay out of it, Roy, and mind your own damn business." The enraged and injured Jim started pushing Roy around. I almost thought they were going to get in a fight. On and on it went. About forty people showed up, including the constable, who had heard that a child had been attacked. Pretty much the whole town showed up.

"That dog should be put down," huffed a woman with a crisp English accent.

"Actually, dogs are allowed one free bite," chimed in another.

"Staffies are the most misunderstood dog on the planet," said a woman sympathetically.

"They're killers. You never know when they're going to turn."

Egged on by the crowd, Jim continued to accelerate in his aggression, anger, and pain. Then he punched the wooden sign that welcomed people to peaceful Hampstead Gardens, and started in on me again.

"You shouldn't walk him here in town." Jim shook his bloody hand at me. "I've seen him here before causing trouble."

"Actually," I said, borrowing the line in *The Pink Panther* when Peter Sellers asks the guy if his dog bites, "it's not my dog."

"I don't care! If my dog dies, I'll kill your dog myself!"

"No you won't," eleven year-old Oliver shouted, upset. "Finkle's a good dog!"

I simply stared at the man, who seemed like a decent guy riled beyond his limits.

"Your dog is going to be fine," I said gently. "I promise you, I saw him up close and I know this is upsetting, but your dog is uninjured."

The anger melted off Jim's face.

"Do you think so?" he asked, suddenly hopeful and worried at the same time. "Do you really think so?"

Jim was more worried about his dog than his own blood dripping on the sidewalk.

"Yes," my friend Jennifer chimed in. "Believe me, we totally understand your reaction. We are all dog people—we all love our dogs, and if anything happened to my dog, I would just go insane."

"Oh, I know," Jim said. "I've had my Blackie for eleven years. He would die for me. I just don't know what I would do without him."

All of a sudden he had tears in his eyes. The pain, the anger, and the threats all stemmed from a simple love of his dog. We all got a bit emotional.

"You'll have many more years with him," I said. "Now let's get that hand looked at."

We walked with Jim to the local doctor, who was eighty years old and couldn't hear a thing. While the good country doctor treated the man's wound, Jim continued to be actually more worried about his dog (who really was unhurt) than his hand. As he got the tetanus shot from the shaking hand of the doctor, Jim, suddenly vulnerable said, "I hope I don't faint. I hate needles."

People kept drifting in, saying they'd heard he'd lost a finger.

"They'll probably have me dead by nightfall," Jim quipped, beginning to feel better. Jennifer rambled on about how Finkle normally never had problems with other animals.

"What about the bull Finkle attacked?" Oliver interrupted her.

Apparently Finkle had clamped himself onto a bull's testicles a couple of years earlier. Poor bull went crazy until it ran directly into a pond to get Finkle off his balls.

Children, always in service to the truth.

When we got Finkle home, he skulked around looking extremely guilty for his actions. His big noble head was bowed, and his expressive eyes were wet with what looked like remorse. He was so gentle with people, but he had lost a battle with his inbred nature.

In *Hamlet* there are the lines:

> *So, oft it chances in particular men,*
> *That for some vicious mole of nature in them,*
> *As, in their birth wherein they are not guilty,*
> *Since nature cannot choose his origin.*

The same could be said for Jim, momentarily enraged by the potential loss of his beloved dog. Normally a gentle man, he had in that moment reverted to a vicious nature that he couldn't help, that he hadn't chosen, that was an innate reaction. Pumped up on adrenaline, he had become almost animalistic, but even in that he was innocent.

When you encounter somebody in that moment of madness there is nothing to do but not add fuel to the fire. Wait for the storm to pass and try to take care of them in all of their pain and fury.

To do otherwise would be not be accepting the situation. Nor would it be accepting the reality of provoked personality in all of its fight or flight reactivity.

It would be like expecting Finkle not to be Finkle.

FLYING WITH TERRORISTS

It is better to be violent if there is violence in our hearts, than to put on the cloak of non-violence to cover impotence.

—GANDHI

Sometimes the lens of perception is clear and the person has enough fortitude to actually act on their perceptions, even when faced with ridicule or the idea that they are being hysterical.

The always intense actor James Woods had the opportunity to see reality clearly a month before the terrorist attacks on New York's World Trade Center. The fifty-four-year-old actor was questioned by the FBI following his report that while on a commercial flight from Boston's Logan Airport to Los Angeles one month prior to the attack, he may have shared the first-class section with the same box-cutter-wielding terrorists responsible for hijacking American Airlines flight 11.

According to Woods, he was on a flight back to L.A after visiting his mother in Boston. He was alone in the first-class section except for four Middle Eastern men who, in Woods' estimation, were behaving bizarrely. The actor noticed that they never ate or drank, never spoke to the flight crew, and addressed each other in hushed tones. For the majority of the cross-country flight the men sat and stared straight ahead, stone-faced.

After picking up on the group's odd demeanor and tense body language, Woods actually mentioned it to a flight attendant, who dismissed it. Woods then reported it to airline authorities on the ground, who didn't seem to want to pursue it.

After the attack, Woods again called authorities—this time the

FBI—to report his experience. This time, in less than twenty-four hours, federal agents arrived on his doorstep to examine every detail of his story. Although the agents didn't share any information of their investigation with the actor, out of the thousands of tips they received they treated Woods' tale extremely seriously. The four men are now believed to have been enacting a trial run of their suicide assault on New York.

An actor's craft is based on instinct, empathy, and observation of human behavior. The craft of acting is also an exercise in being present and responding to what is happening in the moment. Actors are extremely sensitive, and Woods saw things in the men that the other people didn't see. He was more awake in that moment, more in tune with how these four men made him *feel,* than the other people who came in contact with the men. His early warning system was switched on rather than switched off. Because he knew what he was feeling, he was able to ascertain a truth that other people missed, namely, that these men didn't quite add up.

If you can identify a particular feeling in the moment and excavate it up to the surface, you will certainly come to a truth that might have otherwise remained hidden. This can only happen when paying attention to *feelings arising in the moment rather than ignoring them. Or relying solely on the mind's interpretation of what's happening.*

It is not a matter of spiritually tuning out, but rather *tuning in*, whether to violence or love. It can also save your life.

FEAR OF FEARING

The violence done us by others is often less painful than that which we do to ourselves.

—FRANÇOIS DE LA ROUCHEFOUCAULD

Gavin de Becker's book *The Gift of Fear: Survival Signals That Protect Us from Violence* talks about the lifesaving and necessary uses of fear and how, as a whole, our society is losing our pure animal instinct, overridden as we are by political correctness or an inability to see reality clearly. Fear is a useful emotion and one that should be accessed and listened to in the moment, without the mind coming in and explaining it away.

In the book de Becker tells the story of a woman who was raped at gunpoint in her apartment. Afterward the man got up, got dressed, and said she should stay where she was while he left. He said he wasn't going to hurt her. On the way out of the room he closed the window. Intuitively, without logically putting it together, the woman got up and followed her attacker down the hall. The rapist turned right into the kitchen, and she turned left into the dining room. She heard him opening drawers in her kitchen, rattling through knives. She stepped out her front door and ran, stark naked, across the hall to the safety of her neighbors.

Later, when she was interviewed by de Becker, she couldn't put her finger on why, for the first time during the ordeal, she felt terrified when the rapist got up to leave the room. She had been through a terrible three-hour ordeal, yet during all that time she hadn't approached the level of fear she felt as he walked out of the room. She all of a sudden knew he was lying and that he was going to kill her.

After coaxing her through an interview process, de Becker helped the woman realize that the tiny detail of the man closing the window was what made her afraid. It was too small a detail for her cognitive mind to process in the moment, but her instincts took over, revealing themselves with the alarm bells of fear. Way before she put it together that he shut the window (while supposedly on the way out of the apartment) in order to muffle the sounds he would make while killing her, her intuitive emotional self felt afraid. Before her mind realized that he was in the kitchen looking for a knife, a quieter way to do the job, her fear commanded her to action. She said it was as if something deep and instinctual within her took over and galvanized her into the risky movement of following him out the door. Her mind had nothing to do with it; it was emotional.

Emotions should not be ignored just because you are on a "spiritual path." So many spiritual teachings talk about detachment from emotions as being a goal. People interpret this as a higher state, free from the vicissitudes of feelings, one in which rational thought replaces blind emotion. But these teachings don't have any such strictures. You don't become dispassionate the more awake you are; you actually become more passionate. You are engaged, not disengaged. To be disengaged is to ignore what is happening in favor of what you think should be happening or would like to be happening. It is actually an attempt to control what is going on, namely, the feeling of uncomfortable feelings.

When confronted by danger, this disengagement can cost you your life.

BRIDGE THE GAP

My best friend is from Johannesburg, South Africa—currently one of the murder capitals of the world and the most dangerous city on the planet. When I visited last year, I noticed that security is still taken very seriously—most homes are surrounded by high fences topped with razor wire. While decreasing in frequency, carjackings, invasions of the homes of the white upper class, and murderous takeovers of farms are still realities.

My friend's mother, Maja, still lives in the large family home there with her husband, David, and their old and crotchety family dog, Bernice, a cranky Belgian shepherd of capricious temper.

In the middle of the night they were all woken up by four robbers, one of whom was a teenager. All of the men had guns, and Maja and David were shoved into seats at a small table in the kitchen. One of the men held an automatic pistol at Maja's head and said he was going to kill them if they moved. The other three men began to ransack the house looking for a nonexistent safe.

"There's no safe in this house," Maja protested to the man.

"Shut up!" he shouted. "I will kill you both if you move."

They stayed like that for almost an hour, as the house was torn apart, room by room. Finally the other three men came into the kitchen, angry and frustrated that their search had failed. One of them was carrying an iron, which he plugged into the wall. He turned it on high. The other men watched him, including the wide-eyed boy, who must have been about sixteen.

"We are done fooling around," said the man. "You will tell us where the safe is or you will get burned."

"We've told you, there is no safe," Maja said.

The man picked up the iron, checking how hot it was. It was three in the morning, and the house was on a large lot in a neighborhood surrounded by high walls and thick gardens. It was a desperate situation involving desperate men, and nobody would hear a thing. Maja stared at the leader's profile.

"Is there no other way we can speak to each other?" Maja asked, filled with a sudden empathy for the men. "Is this the only way?"

But the man holding the gun didn't respond, didn't even turn his head.

Later somebody said to Maja that she was suffering from a version of the Stockholm syndrome, where you identify with your captors as a way to survive, most famously illustrated by the Patty Hearst case.

They couldn't have been more wrong.

To call Maja's spontaneous feeling of empathy based on her deep understanding of the country, the social and economic influences with which she was so familiar, and the intuition of her own experience is to dismiss not only their humanity, but hers. She felt the reality of the moment was so heightened, so raw and stripped down, that it focused her attention completely in the present, where she saw the whole picture. The result was she felt compassion.

"Please, please," David implored, watching the iron heat up. "Please don't hurt my wife."

"Shut up."

They sat like that in silence, the iron heating up to a red glow.

"Can I recite a psalm?" David asked the man holding the iron. The man shrugged, licked his finger, and touched the bottom of the iron. A slight sizzle.

In quiet voices David and Maja began reciting the twenty-third Psalm.

"The Lord is my shepherd, I shall not want. He makes me lie down in green pastures, he leads me beside quiet waters," David and Maja murmured. "Even though I walk through the valley of the shadow of death, I will fear no evil, for you are with me; your rod and staff comfort me. You prepare a table before me in the presence of my enemies. You anoint my head with oil; my cup overflows. Surely goodness and love will follow me all the days of my life, and I will dwell in the house of the lord forever."

Unfazed by the psalm, the man held the red-hot iron close to Maja's face.

"Where is the safe?"

"You really need to be thinking about the example you are setting for this young boy. You can burn us, but you will get nothing except what will lie on your own conscience and the memory of this boy, who will have learned brutality from you." Maja stared at the man, filled with intensity. He paused, staring back across the great divide of education, privilege, and a loving family.

At this exact moment Bernice came into the room. Normally she would bark and growl at anything unfamiliar. But this time it was love at first sight. She went up to the robber who was holding the iron in one hand and the gun in the other. She licked the hand holding the gun. She licked him like she was greeting her master back from a long trip.

"Stop that, you stupid dog," Maja said. "Don't lick him, he's robbing us."

But Bernice just kept on licking the man's hand. David began to laugh, and so did the teenage boy. Maja started laughing too, and so did the rest of the robbers. The dog went on licking his hand, and when she stopped, he stroked her head.

"There is no safe. Take whatever else you want," Maja said. "But there is no safe."

Still petting the dog, the robber put down the iron. He unplugged it, nodding.

"We go now." With that the men got up and left the house as silently as they had come, leaving the people in the kitchen unharmed.

When asked how one keeps a dharmic perspective in the face of violence, there is almost no better example than this story. It would be easy to dismiss the men as animals, willing to torture an unarmed couple for their money. But that would be reductionist. The men are men and have emotions—fear, anger, sadness, and joy—just like the rest of us. They also are the products of severe conditioning: poverty, brutality, hopelessness, and generations of racism under the apartheid system.

But somehow this desperate situation was turned around. There was the calming and centering effect of reciting the Twenty-third Psalm. Then came the humanizing warmth of an old dog, wandering into the picture in all its innocence. The dog, like the sun itself, gave love without a thought to the worthiness of the recipient.

But the real thing that turned the situation around was Maja's response. Treating them as humans and not monsters, she asked them if there wasn't another way to meet. She questioned their behavior in front of the boy and asked them to connect themselves to the larger picture of teaching a child an unspeakable lesson in human brutality. She asked them to take responsibility for themselves and their actions.

Now, I'm not saying this scene could not have played out with a different ending. The robbers could have laughed at the dog, burned the people with the iron, and then killed them. The dog could have bounded in and bit the guy, and Maja and David could have taken the opportunity to overpower the criminals. No one knows how these volatile situations will play out. The truth is that we have no control over them. We only have control over ourselves. But if you are aware, present in your moment, then you can pick from a variety of responses and try to do the best you can do in any given situation.

In this case the right (and possibly only) response of making a connection was used.

People will often rise to the level of dignity with which they are treated. And although Maja's response was a challenging thing to say to a robber getting ready to torture them for information, the metamessage was "I am human, you are human, and the boy is human. I acknowledge that and see that within you, even as you prepare to act inhumanely."

There is a Sanskrit word, *namaste,* which communicates "I bow to the divine in you." In a sense, when you are asking a person who is acting inhumanely to touch the part of themselves that is still human, then you are saying *namaste*.

The teacher Joel Goldsmith talks about how every person is begging to be recognized as Christ consciousness. The beggar, the thief and the murderer, are all screaming out to be recognized. The Buddhists call this concept "sleeping Buddha," meaning everybody embodies Buddha nature, which is love itself, but some of us are not yet awake to it. They are sleeping Buddhas, waiting to be woken up to their own inherent divinity, no matter what they are doing. In that moment Maja woke them up to the deeper reality that they were all connected.

Maja asked the robbers to reach in and acquire something much more important than what was in the imaginary safe, namely, their own humanity. Indeed, the very idea of looking for the safe becomes a metaphor for what the robbers were yearning for in a deeper way: the "safe" they think money can buy. The truth is there is no safety, even for the wealthy, as they were themselves demonstrating. But they could only see the money—until Bernice woke them up some more, which led to Maja's quip. "Don't lick them, they're robbing us." Her quip cut right through to an absurd truth that was funny and appreciated by everybody in the room. It bridged the gap between themselves and the robbers by pointing out how the dog wasn't playing along with everybody's assigned role of robber and victim. How could you press a hot iron against another person's tender flesh in the light of the humor and humanity of the moment?

The great Indian poet Rabindranath Tagore once said, "The burden of the self is lightened when I laugh at myself."

I'm convinced that laughter provides a moment of pure enlightenment; it is a wordless Zen koan. It is impossible to think and laugh at the same time. Time disappears. All the wonderful teachers I have listened to, including the Dalai Lama, Catherine Ingram, H. W. L. Poonja, and Thich Nhat Hanh, have displayed a great sense of humor. Listening to tapes of Poonjas dharma talks, or *satsang,* one is struck by how much laughter is pealing forth. (*Sat* means "divine" or "truth," and *sang* is short for *sangha,* which means "community" or "association." "Truth community" is my favorite definition of *satsang*—a group of people gathered together to remind each other of the truth.)

During a good laugh, the brain is "snapped out" of its trance and popped into the truth of NOW. It is literally a call to wakefulness and made it possible for Maja to bridge the gap with the would-be torturing robbers.

GOOD AND EVIL

It was the best of times, it was the worst of times, it was the age of wisdom, it was the age of foolishness, it was the epoch of belief, it was the epoch of incredulity, it was the season of Light, it was the season of Darkness, it was the spring of hope, it was the winter of despair . . . —in short, the period was so far like the present period.

—CHARLES DICKENS

It is tempting to start any sentence dealing with violence with the qualifier "In these difficult times . . ." Every generation believes it to be facing the worst time in humankind's history, but as Dickens' quote implies, the times we live in are no more or less violent than at any point in the past.

In spite of terrorist attacks, wars, and flareups in various parts of the world, we are still living in relatively peaceful times when compared with the rest of history. This may sound radical not long after the events of September 11 so completely changed our lives, but actually the world has grown less barbaric rather than more.

Still, the questions about good and evil remain. What is evil? Does evil really exist in the world?

At first glance it seems like this is a ridiculous question. Apparently evil acts are perpetuated every day. Murder, rape, outbreaks of genocide, and pedophilia are in the news all the time, as are stories about the degradation of the air, water, and land in exchange for short-term profiteering, and even the raping of toddlers in Africa by men infected by AIDS, who believe they will be cured by having sex with a virgin, no matter what the age. Every form of madness, violence, and debasement that has ever been imagined is happening all the time, even as you read these words. Different beliefs cause misery around the world in the name of customs or religion, from the killing of female babies in India because parents don't want to pay the eventual dowry to the entrenched position of the Catholic Church (no stranger to the concept of good and evil) against birth control, which causes unspeakable environmental and human suffering as the planet gets more and more crowded. And if the robbers who invaded the home of Maja and David had indeed tortured them, wouldn't they have been evil?

But what is the mind of somebody who takes the life of another person? I am always amused by the verdict not guilty by reason of insanity. Isn't somebody who kills another human being by definition at least temporarily insane? I know it's meant to delineate whether a person understand what he or she is doing is illegal, or knew what he or she was doing at all, but that always seems like putting a pretty fine point on it. What sane, well-adjusted person would murder another person?

The fact is that almost all of the perpetrators of evil are also victims. Alice Miller writes in her classic *For Your Own Good: Hidden Cruelty in Child-Rearing and the Roots of Violence* that the perpetrators are usually passing the hot potato of conditioning on to the next person.

In a chilling passage she describes the abuse of a four-year-old boy, who was beaten regularly and locked in a closet for days at a time without food or water. He wasn't allowed to express his emotions, and there wasn't a single other human being from whom he received empathy. At the end of the paragraph, your heart is breaking for the young boy. Then you turn the page and learn that it is a description of Adolph Hitler's childhood, a childhood that foreshadowed the concentration camps.

In the book Miller goes on to describe what she calls the "poisonous pedagogy" of child-rearing techniques in prewar Germany. Children were routinely beaten to keep them in line, robbing them of their sense of autonomy and safety. They were taught in a totalitarian manner to obey the father and not to question authority. They were manipulated, bribed, broken, and controlled. In short, the entire country was primed to be good little followers—obedient and unquestioning.

Miller looked into the childhoods of all the leaders in Hitler's Third Reich, from Göring to Goebbels to Himmler. They all suffered the same unspeakable childhoods filled with violence, control, and sadism. Miller's central thesis was if Hitler had stayed a failed artist and gone on to inflict his pain on five children, the Holocaust would never have happened. He wouldn't have re-created his childhood imprisonment and deprivation in the form concentration camps. And when you couple his psychological background with thousands of years of institutionalized anti-Semitic conditioning, the Holocaust almost seems inevitable. Like countless other unspeakable acts by madmen, it is a matter of individual conditioning played out on the massive stage of history.

Others will argue that human nature itself is intrinsic and intractable. Nurture is no match for nature. Rehabilitation often fails to cure violent criminals; identical twins raised separately exhibit uncanny similarities; reading bedtime stories to children has little effect on their intelligence aptitude. Some believe that violent behavior is all about survival on an instinctive, animalistic level.

But after taking into account biological abnormalities, what explains "evil" actions? What makes people behave so viciously? Is it not the warping of the personality by various aspects of environment?

My point in bringing this up is to stake this radical claim:

"Evil" doesn't exist.

I am not debating that there are deeply unconscious people who cause massive amounts of pain and brutality. What I am saying is that it just isn't useful to categorize the world in terms of good and evil. It creates a duality of *us* versus *them*. It is dehumanizing, and anytime you dehumanize another human being, it becomes allowable to treat that person as subhuman. Whenever you dehumanize another human being, a part of your own humanity dies. This in turn creates more unconscious behavior. Ironically, it creates more "evil."

As Carl Jung said: "Every part of the personality you do not love will become hostile to you. And if it becomes hostile to you, it will inevitably become hostile to others."

Let's take it one step further and say that every part of *everybody else's* personality you do not love will become hostile to you. They will become hostile to you even if they don't actually do anything. Why? When you meet somebody who really bugs you, someone whom you instantly dislike, that person is usually some reflection of yourself that you have not dealt with. You have internalized what it is you don't like about yourself and then labeled it evil or sick or bad or wrong. In banishing that part of yourself, you dehumanize anyone else who displays it. You won't look at the other person, and you won't look at yourself. It's easier that way. But that shadow part of you continues to lurk, unexamined, unloved, and unforgiving. Eventually it will keep on surfacing, creating havoc and suffering, until it is integrated.

Most of the people behaving horribly have been horribly warped themselves, their actions created by a perverted version of love in their childhood. So what is the point of labeling them as evil? They could easily be us, given the right circumstances. The die is cast at a very young age. If put through enough pain, any of us would warp in similar ways. Any of us has the capacity for cruelty, just as any of us has the capacity to be the love of Buddha or Christ.

This is not to excuse others' behavior or to say that sometimes other people undergoing the very same pressure aren't able to rise above it and become self-actualized. (Often this depends upon their genetic resiliency or whether there was an empathetic person to whom they could confide their pain.)

It is only to say that with enough understanding you will see the whole picture; you will see their suffering, and by extension the suffering they cause others, with compassion.

Still, what is there to do when confronted with real-life deranged violence? Is nonviolence the only spiritual response, or should you protect yourself?

RESPONSE TO VIOLENCE

It is better to do nothing than to do what is wrong. For whatever you do, you do to yourself.

—BUDDHA

Somebody once asked the Dalai Lama, "Why didn't you fight back against the Chinese?"

The Dalai Lama paused and then said, "Well, war is obsolete, you know." After a few moments, he continued, "Of course the mind can rationalize fighting back . . . but the heart, the heart would never understand. Then you would be divided in yourself, the heart and the mind, and the war would be inside you."

America is a place that glorifies violence. Our nation was born in bloodshed and built on the brutality of slavery. There are more guns than adults in America, and every day twenty thousand guns enter the stream of commerce. America's murder rate is ten times that of other Western nations. Our armed robbery rate is one hundred times higher than Japan's. All of our movies venerate the hero who can save the day using violence. On a national level, our solutions tend more and more to be violent rather than diplomatic.

We know violence in this country. It is part of our culture that exacts a daily toll in human life, productivity, and emotional well-being.

Still, given all this, it is still a choice. We always praise the courage of people who use violence to solve problems. But what about the courage to be peaceful? Peace is always seen as a passive thing, but peace can be very active. It takes courage to promote peace, both individually and on the level of society. In a macho world (as opposed to a truly masculine one), promoting peace is seen as effete or impotent or cowardly. But tell this to the followers of Martin Luther King Jr. or Gandhi, who were faced with vicious dogs, fire hoses, and murder and still maintained their conviction that nonviolence was the only solution. Peace takes more than an incredible amount of self-control and restraint in order to not react; it takes true courage.

Still, there are many different perspectives when we look down the barrel of violence. In those circumstances, it doesn't matter if you are creating duality by calling the person evil or if you're taking the larger view that they are asleep or running their conditioning. What matters is that they are threatening your ability and right to simply exist. And sometimes, no matter what you do, how awake you are, or how compassionate you feel, you will still be killed.

If a crazy or drunken human being is lurching down the street, foaming at the mouth, looking for a fight, then the obvious thing to do is to get out of the way. But what if the deranged person chases you and corners you? What if the person bears down on you intending to snuff out your life? What if it comes down to kill or be killed? In that moment, when all concepts and principles are under siege, what do you do?

BRIDGE THE GAP, PART 2

One time my brother was walking down the street to his neighborhood Laundromat. It was dark and fairly late, and he was carrying a laundry bag filled with dirty clothes. A man with a knife slid out of the shadows and shoved him against the wall.

"Give me your wallet," the man said, eyes red-rimmed, hands twitching nervously, flashing the large blade.

My brother handed over the wallet. The man, checking the wallet and pulling out several large bills, got very close to my brother.

"Now empty your pockets,"

My brother emptied his pockets, handing over a bunch of quarters with other loose bills. My brother could smell alcohol on the mugger's breath, but his twitchiness was more like that of a tweaker or crackhead. The knife was dangerously close to his heart, and my brother suddenly felt concerned. What was the robber going to do after he had the money? He wasn't wearing a mask and so my brother could easily identify him. What if he didn't want to leave a witness?

"Can I keep some quarters for the washing machine?" my brother suddenly blurted out.

"What?" The mugger looked at him like he was crazy.

"Quarters. The change machine's always broken, and I need some clean clothes for tomorrow."

A long moment passed as the mugger looked at him.

"It's a hassle finding quarters at night in this neighborhood," my brother continued.

"Yeah." The mugger dropped some quarters in my brother's hand. "Do your laundry."

With that, the mugger took off running down the street and disappeared down the alley.

When I asked my brother why he asked the mugger for his quarters back, he couldn't really say. It just came out. But what happened in that long moment when he and the mugger exchanged looks? I would venture to say that the mugger saw my brother as a human being for the first time in the exchange—a human being on his way to do laundry, perhaps something the man could identify with. It created a moment of humanity between the two men, breaking down the identification of the two roles, one of "mugger," the other of "victim." It may well have saved his life.

Another way to deal with impending violence is to manipulate the situation. A female friend of mine once went to a rave. It was filled with lots of people on Ecstasy, and anywhere there are very open and vulnerable people, there will be predators. As my friend went out to her car to leave, a man grabbed her and shoved her against his car, groping her.

"You want it, don't you, bitch," he said, opening his car door. "Get in."

"You know, I was watching you inside," my friend said. "I think you're fuckin' hot. Let me just grab my purse and I'll come with you."

The guy was so surprised he loosened his grip. She jerked away and ran back inside.

When dealing with violence, first, of course, you try to avoid it before it happens. Wakefulness is the only tool for this. Second, if it's upon you, you try to remove yourself from the situation by whatever means necessary, paying no attention to your reactive ego saying things like "A real man would fight" or "I shouldn't lie." No. The important thing is to get away and survive. If it is impossible to escape, then you try to reach out and communicate, bridging the gap the way Maja and my brother did. Often this can be effective. You are, after all, dealing with another human being, not a monster.

And still, what if you are awake and have managed to avoid obviously dangerous situations and have tried to bridge the gap but still find violence bearing down on you, intractable and non-negotiable?

Then you are faced with an individual decision, and protecting yourself is a reaction you might choose. But if this is the case, if you choose to protect yourself against somebody who is intent on harming you, try to do so without hate in your heart. Try to do the minimum necessary to extract yourself from the situation and stop the other person in a way that's as impersonal as possible.

It won't always be pretty.

REALITY

Fight or surrender can be outlined in two stories, both of which could have had any number of different outcomes.

One is about a personal trainer, a strong guy who got caught in a robbery at a 7-Eleven. The robber stuck a gun to his head, grabbing his wallet. He told him to get on his knees. The trainer was afraid they were going to shoot him and contemplated rushing the guy, but obeyed his command. It was the most terrifying moment in his life, but the robbery ended with the robber killing nobody. The trainer survived, shaken but unhurt.

Now for another story, a similar robbery in a 7-Eleven, with eight victims who got robbed by two men at gunpoint. At the end of the robbery they start tying people's hands behind their backs and make them lie on the floor. One victim looks at the robbers and knows what's going to unfold. Why tie the hands of eight victims unless you are afraid they'll fight back when you start to shoot them? This man notices that when one of the robbers ties the hands of the people lying on the floor, he sets aside his shotgun. This victim can't take it—he is too afraid. When the robber goes to tie the hands of the person next to him, he grabs the shotgun and shoots one of the robbers. The other robber runs away. Later, the police reveal that these criminals are guilty of killing all their prior victims.

This victim saved his life and the lives of all the others in the 7-Eleven.

Now, could he have grabbed the gun and disarmed the men without hurting them? Ideally. But maybe he would have been shot. The point is, we weren't there. We can't judge that situation. But we can assume that if he had done nothing, he would have died.

To say that nonviolence is the only answer all the time is to be as asleep as somebody who uses violence to solve every problem. This is a profoundly individual choice, and only when we are in the situation can we know what we will do and what is the right thing to do for ourselves.

Much violence can't be negotiated with. Remember in *Schindler's List* how arbitrary the violence was? One woman tried to help the Nazis by offering architectural advice as they built barracks, and they had her shot in the head for being "an educated Jew" and then went on to implement her suggestions over her dead body. Others fought back and died, some kept their heads down and died . . . there was no formula for surviving that horror, no one trick that worked. Sometimes violence is like that.

But if you are trapped in the idea that violence should only be met with violence, then you could well be one of the people who get shot with their own gun in their home.

I know a man who was obsessed with security in his home; he owned guns, had a sophisticated security system, dogs, everything. One day in the middle of the night his alarm went off and his dogs, locked in his bedroom, started to go crazy at the door. The man grabbed his shotgun, put his wife in their panic room (which was a converted bathroom, I swear to God), and ran to the top of his stairs. He was fumbling with his shotgun shells, dropping them as he tried to get them loaded in time to almost shoot . . . the Brentwood patrol officer who was standing in his front door, which had been blown open by the wind. Fortunately the home owner didn't fire. And neither did the patrol officer, whose gun was also out of its holster.

This man, a friend of a friend, got lucky. He was so obsessed with meeting violence with violence that he created his own violent reality. This is often the case, that violence or intentions of violence will attract the very thing from which you're trying to protect yourself. For this reason a gun kept in the home is twenty-two times more likely to kill a family member or a friend than it is to be used against an intruder. And ten children are killed by guns in the United States every day, on average.

This is not to say the other reality is also a possibility. We can be so obsessed with "being peace" that we bring violence on ourselves. I have another friend named Donald who was very involved in the '60s and '70s with the peace movement. He became extremely involved with racial issues and spent lots of time going into the inner city for meetings.

One night he parked his car in a bad part of town and started to walk to the meeting. He found himself surrounded by a group of black kids taunting him: "What you doing here, white boy?" They didn't wait for an answer and began to viciously beat him up. Donald put his hands up in supplication, saying, "I come in peace" over and over as he was beaten.

Just as he was about to lose consciousness and things were going to get really ugly, the crowd of kids broke up. A member of Donald's group, an African American local of the neighborhood, was there, spraying Mace into the crowd and shouting for people to back off. My friend was saved.

As the local leader helped Donald to the meeting, he asked him what happened. Donald told him that he had engaged in nonviolence, that he held no anger toward these kids; it was all about their cultural situation, and he had the strength to love them even as they beat him.

The guy looked at Donald like he was an idiot.

"I told you when we started working together—you're a white guy coming to this neighborhood for meetings at night, you gotta carry mace. You don't listen!"

Donald was so caught up in the theory of nonviolence that he couldn't accept the reality that was right in front of him. What help would he be to racial issues in the country if he got himself killed? His "nonviolence" was actually a form of self-aggrandizement and denial. It prevented him from seeing reality clearly and doing the simple thing: not traveling alone in the neighborhood.

We do not live in a perfect world. Violence exists. Denying its reality will not protect us any more than insisting that we must always be violent in order to protect ourselves. Every situation is different, and every person is different. It would be arrogant for me to say what is right for you in a given situation.

Also, this book is attempting to deal with reality in a practical way. The main point is that if we are too bound to any form of reaction, violent or nonviolent, then our options vanish. The challenge is to read each situation with as much honesty as possible and then do our best.

It's important to remember that a violent person is undergoing a kind of craziness. Such a person is deeply unconscious, perhaps even fully asleep, and his or her behavior has nothing to do with you except that you happened to be there. But if you respond with violence, you too will go a little crazy. It may be the price of survival.

On the deepest level, filled with Buddha or Christ consciousness, it is actually possible to feel compassion for violent people in their suffering. Christ's words on the cross, "Forgive them for they know not what they do," are applicable here. This truly can be applied to anybody who is perpetrating aggressive violence against another person for no reason or for reasons of personal gain. Even if you are not going to turn the other cheek, try not to harden your heart against the person.

If you feel you must fight in order save your life, then know you will be doing violence to yourself as well as another human being. There may be anger and hatred that will arise in the moment of conflict. Don't judge your feelings. Feel them fully, and they will pass when they are ready.

But understand that there is no free ride. By protecting yourself in a violent way, there is always the phenomenon that the military calls "blowback." Blowback is the unexpected negative consequences of our actions. There are countless examples of it happening on an international scale, the latest being the United States arming Afghanistan with training and weapons in its conflict against Russia and then having them used against us a decade later, or the weapons we supplied to Iraq when they were our allies in the eighties during the war against Iran and which now, if you are to believe our government, were being used to threaten the world.

PERSONAL BLOWBACK

There is a kind of a rush born of violence. I have felt it myself. It is an unfettering of one's psyche from the constraints of civilization. Initially it feels *good* to be free from the concepts of crime and punishment, it feels *good* to not care what people think, to revert back to our primordial nature of kill or be killed.

Perpetuating a violent act creates a momentary enlivening of the spirit, fleeting but potent. What starts out as a call to war, whether on the level of nations trumpeting it with excitement and parades or the unleashing of an individual's animalistic nature, initially feels very good indeed. It gets the blood rushing, gives purpose to empty lives, breaks down a frustrating and ambiguous world into black and white, and engenders a feeling of togetherness. But this momentary enlivening comes at a great cost. It leaves a hangover that shatters everything that touches it.

This is the phenomenon of personal blowback.

The use of violence will have an effect on you that will be unexpected. It might ripple through your psyche for years to come. You might have nightmares or post-traumatic stress disorder. You might develop an unexpected taste for violence. Recall the famous scene in *Lawrence of Arabia* when Lawrence is being interviewed by a British officer about the war he led in the desert, and he says he wasn't afraid of violence, he was afraid how much he *liked it*. You might kill your assailant and have to deal with the guilt of another person's death on your hands. In doing violence against another human being, you do very real damage against yourself, against your own tender-heartedness. The war, as the Dalai Lama said, might end up in your own heart, and the damage you might sustain from that may take years to unravel.

Perhaps, ultimately, this is better than being a victim. Maybe you will recover more quickly for having fought. But in doing so have you compromised something in yourself? Have you compromised your own peaceful nature and become a violent person? Have you been moved off your core intrinsic values?

Maybe we are meant to struggle with these issues. Maybe that's what being human is all about. None of us really knows how we will react when confronted with a life-and-death situation.

Again, in that moment, you may not have a choice in order to survive.

But there is no free ride.

FORGIVENESS

Freedom is not worth having if it does not include the freedom to make mistakes.

—GANDHI

One of the most powerful stories about the Vietnam War that I ever heard was about an American soldier who killed a Vietnamese soldier with a bayonet in hand-to-hand combat. It was a life-or-death situation in close quarters. In the Vietnamese soldier's pocket the American found a picture of the soldier, his wife, and, in the arms of his wife, a four-year-old girl who was obviously their daughter. The American soldier kept the photo.

The war ended, and for years the man felt guilt and sadness about the man he had killed. The photo humanized the Vietnamese man as just another man who had a family, who loved and was loved. It ate away at the American soldier, as he had his own children. What had happened to the poor little girl whom he had deprived of a father?

Finally in the mid-nineties he decided he had to find out and so began a two-year odyssey in search of the little girl in the picture. After many dead ends, he found the girl living in a village in Vietnam. When he went there with a framed version of the picture, he encountered the little girl, who was now thirty-five. They hugged, and both burst into tears. The picture was extremely important to the woman, who had very few of her father and mother together. The soldier asked the woman for her forgiveness, and she gave it to him. Thirty years had passed, and these small players and victims in a global game had finally come together and healed this old wound.

It is through forgiveness that we are made whole again after a violent conflict. Forgiveness is serum for the bite, the antidote to the toxicity of violence. It starts out with self-forgiveness, a compassion for one's own unconsciousness at the time of the misdeed, whether it is as extreme as violence or as minor as rudeness. Forgiving yourself for the violence you have committed allows you to progress to the stage of forgiving others for the violence they have done to you.

It also releases you from the straitjacket of perfectionism and having to be right. With self-forgiveness you can accept that you are human, that you will make mistakes, that you will behave badly, and that there is still a possibility to move beyond the violence of self-hatred into the wholeness of self-love.

This in turn allows you to ask the wronged party for forgiveness. If you sincerely ask for forgiveness, you retrieve your own innocence, no matter if the other person forgives you or not (and must people will, if it's sincerely requested). Just in asking, you let go of the past.

If somebody asks you for *your* forgiveness, this is another opportunity for great healing. Without forgiveness you are bound to the other person by your own anger. You are still in the story about the past. You are stuck.

This is not to say that you should forgive before you are ready, before you have processed all the emotions of rage and lust for revenge. But all healing is actually just a path forward toward forgiveness. It is in finally and deeply forgiving that you can release the connection with the other person. You can once again walk freely in the world: free to love, free to come out of the story, free to be vulnerable again.

Aba Gayle, the mother of Catherine Gayle, who was stabbed to death, found just such forgiveness. For eight years after her daughter's murder she lived in a dark netherworld of hate and carefully hidden rage. Outside she presented a calm façade for her family and other children because she didn't want to burden them. Inside she was seething with a lust for revenge.

Her daughter's murderer, Douglas Mickey, was caught, tried, convicted, and sentenced to death in 1982. She was told she would feel better once the execution took place, but the thought brought no relief for her. Eventually Aba began a long spiritual journey by learning to meditate, followed by intense reading in many spiritual traditions. She slowly began to lose inner rage.

Twelve years after her daughter's murder, she saw in a newspaper that Douglas Mickey was going to be executed. It later turned out to be incorrect, but she suddenly felt like she needed to write him a letter and forgive him. When he received the letter, he responded and requested a visit. After all this time and with much trepidation, she finally met the man who had murdered her daughter. She cried, he cried, and they cried together. He asked her forgiveness, telling her he would gladly exchange his life to prevent what had happened that night. She found that he wasn't a monster, but a human being suffering with his own demons.

She then decided to devote her life to ministering to those on death row and formed an organization to do just that. As she writes:

> *I knew when I dropped the letter in the mailbox I must spend the rest of my life demonstrating that killing is not necessary and that violence only begets more violence. What I learned is healing and grace can be achieved by anyone under any circumstance through the miracle of forgiveness. This may have appeared to be a new paradigm to me as I began this healing journey, but it is actually the universal truth that has been given to all people through sacred teachings such as those expressed by Jesus Christ, the Buddha and other enlightened beings. Love and forgiveness is the way to make our world a kind and safe place.*

This is from a person who is talking about the murderer of her daughter. She ends with a quote from *The Course in Miracles:* "The essence of our being is love. And every action is either love or a call for help."

When you think about violence as perverted love, it is indeed a call for help. It comes from a place deep inside the perpetrator, one that is not immediately apparent due to their lack of wakefulness.

But over time, perspective is gained.

GIVE IT TIME

Those who cannot remember the past
are condemned to repeat it.
—GEORGE SANTAYANA

Both these stories had time to help soften feelings and perspective. And their personal stories are in the connected to larger historical movements. In this way the personal becomes political.

In retrospect, what was the Vietnam War actually about? Stopping communism? A proxy war between two superpowers? The domino theory? Our national pride? Given the distance of time, what was worth the pain of this woman who had grown up without her father? And for the American soldier, who was so young at the time he killed the girl's father, what was worth the pain and guilt he had suffered over the years?

Given what we know about the Vietnam War now, from many different views including those of one of the main architects of the war, Robert McNamara (his book *In Retrospect* is fascinating), most people can't say the war was necessary. But it took time for us to see the truth. Sometimes it takes the long view to see the truth of a situation.

Of course, the other side of the coin is World War II. Few would argue that anything besides war could have stopped Hitler. The Neville Chamberlains of the world, who tried to appease Hitler, were not seeing reality clearly. They were seeing what they hoped to see, in the same way the architects of the Vietnam War were misguided in their perceptions of the world.

The point is that wakefulness means seeing reality clearly. But violence, if is to be used at all, should only be used in the most extreme situations, after every last solution has been exhausted, both on the level of nations and for individuals.

With time, profound changes of heart can occur without the degradation of violence, to both the perpetrator and the victim.

Nelson Mandela, who after nearly thirty years in jail as a political prisoner, didn't become embittered. One of his greatest regrets after being released from Robben Island Prison in 1990 was that he forgot to thank the prison guards. So it came as no surprise that when he was elected president in South Africa's first all-race elections in 1994, the guards were invited to the inaguration and sat on the stage with him. He regularly consulted his former captors about his plans to construct a racially integrated, democratic society. His guards were white, and they had been racist and very hard-core when he went into that prison. Mandela had, in the long course of his imprisonment, through his dignity and intelligence, made friends with them and won them over to his point of view.

This was done not from where he started—a place of violence and radicalism—but from peace and understanding.

This is the gift of perspective that time gives us. The statement "This too shall pass" is true of everything in the world. Nothing lasts forever, not even torture in a dark prison cell. Bitter enemies can become friends, finding out that they shared the same pain and suffering on either side of the struggle.

And over time, how much is left of the original reasons for violence or war? Do you teach people nonviolence by being violent? Do you teach people not to kill by killing? In most national conflicts the anger, fervor, and nationalism don't take long to give way to a hangover of ruined lives, huge debts, and post-traumatic stress syndrome.

Peace that is accessed through love and understanding, rather than war and violence, is a peace that has roots. It is a peace without the hangover.

AFTER IT'S OVER

> We who lived in concentration camps can remember the men who walked through the huts comforting others, giving away their last piece of bread. They may have been few in number, but they offer sufficient proof that everything can be taken from a man but one thing: the last of human freedoms—to choose one's attitude in any given set of circumstances—to choose one's own way.
>
> —VICTOR FRANKL

There is a downside in not choosing or being able to protect yourself. You could get badly and permanently hurt. You could die.

This is the razor's edge of city living. Do you fight? Do you flee? Ultimately it's either a personal decision or a decision that comes down to pure biological impulse and reaction. This fight-or-flight response is deeply ingrained in our animal nature. It is so reactive that one is not to be held responsible for what arises in that moment. Hormones flood the body, and all of a sudden you're swinging away or running for the hills.

I heard a story in Africa about a couple who was on their honeymoon at a game reserve and was attacked by an elephant. The woman ran to a tree and was climbing it when her panicked husband grabbed her and pulled her out of the tree so he could climb it himself. Needless to say, they slept in different quarters for the rest of the honeymoon, and I have no idea if the relationship survived. My point isn't to judge whether this was indicative of his character. It's just to say that when under immediate, dire threat, anything is possible.

But what if you did fight? Or what if you have simply survived a violent attack? What then?

I was with a friend who was physically assaulted for no reason one night. We were standing outside a bar talking quietly when another patron came up and cracked him over the head with a beer bottle and then ran off. I was there—it was a totally random act. My friend, enraged and hurt, jumped in his car and took off down the street. I ran after my friend's car and caught it at a light and jumped in. My friend, normally peaceful, wanted to find this guy and literally run him over with the car.

Luckily for all concerned, the guy disappeared. My friend was angry about this for weeks, which grew into months. He replayed it over and over. What he should have done, how he should have been more alert. He was confused by the guy's motives and wondered if he had offended him in some way. He *hated* this guy, and it grew into a kind of obsession. He took boxing lessons. He wanted to buy a gun, an idea from which he was dissuaded.

It's important to grieve any attack fully. To understand that the emotions of rage, despair, and fear are perfectly natural and must be allowed their expression. This is critical. All psychological literature points to the fact that only with the free expression of emotion does any healing begin. If the emotions are repressed in any way, then the result is quite simply mental illness, no matter how spiritual a person may be. So all the attendant emotions must be felt; this might take a long time or it may take a short time, depending on the person, the severity of the attack, and what kind of love and support the person is given.

But after the emotions are felt and the story is told many times over to many different people, at what point do you stop telling it?

How long it takes can only come from you, nobody else. It will stop when it finally feels right to stop—when the telling of the story becomes free of the original charge and emotion. But at some point it will feel like you're revisiting the original violence upon yourself, as if you are raping or mugging or attacking yourself again and again.

It took my friend almost a year to realize this before he was able to let it go and move on.

At some point, the story will stop and you will no longer identify yourself as a victim. Until then, don't beat yourself up about the telling of the story.

If you are deep in a story of a violent act, know at some point it will stop. Know that after all the denial, anger, bargaining, and depression comes eventual acceptance. You will let it go; it will pass like all phenomena.

And also know the deeper truth. In the face of violence, no matter how severe, there is a part of you that, as Catherine Ingram has said, is untouched and unsoiled by the experience.

Know that they didn't get the true you, that your true nature of pure awareness is still clear, clean, and untouched by the experience.

LESS IS MORE

There are only two forces in the world, the sword and the spirit. In the long run, the sword will be always conquered by the spirit.

—NAPOLEON BONAPARTE

I have a friend named Rick who told me that when he was a young man he often got in fights. Rick never started a fight, but for some reason he was always a target. Rick was skinny and funny, with a mouth on him that he couldn't muzzle in the face of injustice. He also had a certain charm with the opposite sex that made other men jealous. There was a time when Rick couldn't walk into a bar without somebody starting in on him. Then in his twenties Rick began to practice martial arts. Since then he hasn't had a problem with violence.

Rick thinks one reason he was picked on is that perpetrators can smell fear. They move like any predator preying on the weak. But the other part is that Rick stopped overreacting. He had grown up in a violent household and could smell violence a mile away. He was very sensitive and attuned to it. So he would invariably overreact to even the hint of violence because he was afraid. After studying karate for several years, he said he could be in the middle of a potentially violent situation and simply be with it. Not to engage it, but to witness it in a way that didn't pour gasoline on the flames. Instead of fighting for peace, he was peaceful in the middle of violence. This defused situations before they even started.

I was thinking of this in terms of the principle of *ahimsa*, which is the Sanskrit word for "nonviolence". One day in the city I had the perfect opportunity to practice it.

I was walking through the city, approaching an intersection. A lovely woman was standing with her five-year-old daughter, waiting for the light to change. They were a striking pair in their sundresses, with the mother leaning down and making her daughter giggle at a private joke.

As I approached them, a drunken man peeled away from his group of cronies and approached the woman and girl. He was big, dressed in fatigues, slightly unsteady, and possibly homeless. He squatted down at eye level to the little girl and began to make clicking, screeching noises, like the sound of a bizarre rider trying to get a horse to move. The noise pierced the mother's and daughter's laughter like a knife, and both of them stiffened. The man edged a bit closer, grinning, scaring the little girl, who grew silent and clutched her mother's hand. The other people at the corner did nothing except edge away from the man.

Without thinking at all, I decisively stepped in between the man and the women and her daughter. Instead of facing the street, where we were going to cross, I faced the man. I said nothing as he stood up, glaring at me. His breath smelled like beer.

"I may be a Vietnam killer crazy motherfucker," he slurred. "But I know a thing or two about little girls."

He stared me in the eye. It was a truly creepy thing to say, but I don't think he meant to startle the woman and her daughter. I just think he was completely asleep to what he was doing. He was probably deep down attracted by the little girl's innocence and the mother's beauty. They were healthy, a representation of all that is good in the world. This isn't to say that he would have acted on that attraction in an appropriate or harmless way.

"That's good. You have a good day." I said nothing further and just smiled. I didn't move or touch him, having learned my lesson at the bank. He said nothing, staring at me.

"Kick his ass," muttered one of the other men. The drunken man stepped toward me but did nothing else.

We stared at each other, neither of us moving. I could feel his breath on my face, but I did nothing.

After what seemed like a century, the light changed and the woman and her daughter began walking across the street. I turned around and followed. As I passed them the woman whispered, "Thank you," not looking at me. I realized she didn't want to frighten her daughter by making a big deal about it.

"You're welcome," I replied, walking on past her to go feed my meter.

A few minutes later I reached the building where I had my appointment. I took the elevator to the third floor. As I got off I could see the mother and daughter walking down the long hallway, way down at the end. I'll never forget the image of the daughter laughing as they turned the corner.

Ultimately violence begets violence. Our instinct for violence has to be rooted out of our individual hearts, one person at a time.

The dance of light and darkness is constantly playing itself out in infinite ways, both great and small, everywhere you look. From the fields of war to our neighborhood mugger to a local animal shelter, the components of consciousness are there, endlessly informing each other in a dance of banality, indifference, cruelty, love, hope, violence, and despair.

In this awareness, it is ultimately useless to label things as good and evil. For in doing so, some part of you has to close off and die. It is more important to understand the deeper and clearer truth that every time you hurt somebody else, you're hurting yourself. Sometimes, in a matter of life and death, you may not feel like you have a choice. You will choose life.

Some can't make that choice, can't cross the Rubicon of killing another human being. For others it might be simply an ingrained automatic reaction, the anger or fear swamping their awareness, blotting out everything else except survival. But in the end, the violence lands in our own psyche; it seeps into your body on a cellular level and is held as stress, as guilt, as regret. It is usually passed on in some way.

Luckily, most of us in our lives are not put in these life and death situations. In anything short of that situation, nonviolence must be the standard we honor. In this deeper awareness, there is just consciousness—every single person encountered in the moment is a fresh manifestation of God, even if they don't know it. Even if that person has a knife at your throat.

MOVING EN MASSE

Public Transportation

Every day is a journey and the journey itself is home.
—MATSUO BASHO

You're on the subway and somebody steals the seat you were about to sit in. A drunk starts shouting and shoves you, scuffing your precious Pradas. Trains, buses, planes, and subways are places where you stand cheek to jowl with your fellow human and are often a source of deep anxiety, claustrophobia, and even panic attacks.

I have a close friend who is claustrophobic and absolutely hates crowds. When we go to the movies, he has to sit on the aisle. This is not uncommon. Other people find airplanes difficult, filled with bad air and anxious people—no more than a bus with wings that you can't exit without a parachute. For others it's subways that make their palms sweat and their breath shallow. This has been infinitely compounded since the 2001 terrorist attacks. And the effect works both ways. There is a story of a Muslim man who, after September 11, was on a plane and was too afraid to get up to use the bathroom because everybody was either studiously ignoring him or watching him with hostility.

Public transportation is challenging because it removes boundaries between you and your fellow humans. It also removes the illusion of control over your time and space. You have to adhere to external schedules and delays, which can be challenging. And your personal space is easily invaded.

When you're riding the subway in New York, you have no idea what might be coming your way, from a pre-op transsexual hustling money for her operation to a mugger demanding your wallet. In order to cope with this lack of control over our boundaries, we perfect our thousand-yard stare, never making eye contact or even acknowledging the other human beings. We create separation by sealing ourselves within, as if the whole world were an elevator and we all had to face front and avoid looking at anybody.

But is there an alternative other than pretending other people don't exist? Anxiety can be managed only in the present moment, but as that is all that is ever available to us, it is more than enough. In each moment there are opportunities for interaction that can create meaning and connection with each other, greatly lessoning our sense of isolation.

One day I was riding on the New York subway with my friend Helena when a mentally handicapped man carrying a canvas bag walked onto the train. He began to approach people, trying to sell them small porcelain Dalmatians sitting in tiny wicker baskets. They were beyond kitsch; in fact, they were so far into the realm of tacky that nobody wanted one. Everybody avoided eye contact with the man, who grew more dejected with each dismissal. As the man lumbered toward us through this gauntlet of rejection, I began to wonder what I would do. Helena and I, old friends, exchanged glances. She took out her purse.

"What have you got there?" Helena asked.

"Dogs," the man answered, brightening a bit. "I painted the spots on them myself."

"You did? They're beautiful." Helena smiled at the man. He beamed back at us. We now had the attention of the entire subway car.

"Thanks," the man said shyly.

"How much are they?" Helena asked.

"Two dollars each." The man wiped the sweat off his brow and looked at us anxiously.

"I'll take one." Helena said.

"Me too," I joined in, reaching for my wallet.

"Okay," the man said excitedly. "That'll be two dollars. And two dollars . . . four dollars!"

We paid the man. I then looked at the two men in suits next to us and, inspired by Helena, decided to get involved.

"I just know you guys want to buy Dalmatians from this young man," I said pointedly. The men hesitated and then reached for their wallets. The mentally challenged man was positively beaming. I looked across at two hip-looking young women and raised an eyebrow. They laughed and then they too bought a couple Dalmatians. And so it went, down the length of the car, until the man, flush with excitement, sold out. We had created a chain reaction of kindness. Everybody was able to see beyond the material—the sweaty handicapped man and the chintzy porcelain dogs—to a reality that was deeper.

Helena and I took our Dalmatians home. I still have mine, which I keep as a reminder that if you stay awake fully in the moment to what is happening, a natural tenderness toward other people arises.

BE OF THE WORLD

A heretic is a man who sees with his own eyes.

—GOTTHOLD EPHRAIM LESSING

There is an image I had walking down the streets of New York recently. The sidewalks surged and pulsed with human traffic; heads bobbed up and down slightly with each step. I was being jostled, and my elbows were touching other people's as we all struggled to maintain our forward momentum without stepping on anybody's toes.

It was a sunny day, and there was a tremendous amount of energy radiating from the thousands of humans near me, all with their own destinations, lives, and stories, pursuing their own individual goals, both big and small. Everybody was an entire universe of complex thoughts and desires and conditioning, charging off on their mission in life.

But for the moment, walking down the street, the image I had was of individual blood cells flowing through a vein. A blood cell, if it could think, might view itself as an autonomous unit chugging down the main street of an artery, with its own mission to carry its precious load of oxygen and nutrients. It might not feel part of the whole at all. It might even act individually by attacking an invading host. But it is still a part of the larger entity called blood, which exists in and depends upon veins and arteries, which in turn exist in and depend upon the muscle tissue and bone that make up the mind-body organism called a human being.

As I walked down that crowded street I decided to play with my own awareness by relaxing my own agenda. I didn't actually do anything; I simply allowed my mind to stop—stop planning, stop worrying, stop pushing. Rather than trying to control it, I allowed myself to drift with the surge. I suddenly felt connected to the humanity teeming around me. Instead of feeling competition for space and time, I felt in the flow, supported by my fellow humans, drifting down the vein of life with them.

What had actually changed? Nothing. I was still being lightly jostled, but instead of resisting, I was relaxing. Instead of pushing, I was flowing. Instead of competing for space, I was trying to cede it. Only my perspective had changed. And yet that was all that needed to change in order to give me a completely different experience.

This is a key point in public transportation. If you resist, you suffer. If you relax your awareness, you float within the natural flow of life.

RESIST AND SUFFER

For enlightenment to happen the perceiver must turn right around and wake up to the fact that he is face to face with his own nature—that HE IS IT. The spiritual seeker ultimately finds that he was already at the destination, that he himself IS what he had been seeking and he was in fact already home.

—RAMESH S. BALSEKAR

One morning after I got off my flight into Newark airport, I strode outside the airport looking for some transportation into Manhattan. I asked somebody, and he pointed to a row of buses. I rushed over with my bag to the first bus. I was tired and wanted to be on that bus.

"Are you going into Manhattan?" I briskly asked. The driver nodded. "Can I pay you for the ticket?"

"You can pay her over there." The man pointed at a woman in uniform selling tickets.

"Thanks, I'll put my bag on and grab a ticket." The man nodded.

I put my bag in the luggage compartment and walked over to the woman selling the tickets. I bought one. As I turned around, I saw the bus with my bag leaving the curb! I ran over to the bus, which was stopped in traffic, and banged on the door.

"You've got my bag!" I shouted at the driver. He looked at me blankly. "Open the door! You've got my luggage."

The driver smiled with his mouth, but his eyes were blank. He opened the door. "Ticket," he said.

I just stared at him, unsure what was going on. He was husky, with eyes that pooled black underneath a gleaming bald head. Why had he left with my bag? He had watched me put it on the bus and go over to buy a ticket. Was he simply inattentive? Was he running a little scam on the side, stealing luggage?

"Didn't you see me?" I said, handing him the ticket.

"I see you," he said, gesturing to the row of buses behind us. "These buses leave every fifteen minutes. My time was up. I'm on a schedule. But you were in too much of a hurry to think about that."

He was right. I had been in a hurry. I had just jumped on the first bus that was there without even taking the time to find out where it went. I had decided I wanted that bus! I was resisting what was happening, missing the bigger picture. In truth, it didn't matter what bus I was on. Another bus always comes along.

"So you would have left with my luggage? What about the punishment fitting the crime?"

The man smiled at me enigmatically.

"Just keepin' you on your toes." Then he let out a laugh that flashed white teeth against his dark skin.

I grinned, realizing I'd been had. I mean, the bus had barely even left its parking spot. The man was just having a laugh at my expense, watching me hustle after the bus. But the lesson was a valid one. I hadn't been in the flow; I'd been deeply absorbed in my own intention. My heart had been racing, I'd been striving to "make it happen," and in that mind-set the man was no longer human to me, but simply a way to get where I was going. He had seen that and been offended by my attitude. He taught me a miniature lesson.

"You're a real riot," I mock-groused.

"Welcome to New York City." He was still chuckling. "Better wake up if you want to be alive here."

I made my way back to my seat, amused. *Better wake up if you want to be alive here*. That could be the title of this book. Or a motto for living on the planet.

CONTROL IS AN ILLUSION

When traveling via public transportation, the lack of control can be frightening. You are at the mercy of the elements, other people, strange food, different customs—and that's if you just go to New Jersey. (As a former resident, I can make fun of the Turnpike State.) What happens when the illusion of control is shattered? How can we let go of what we think should be happening and open ourselves up to what is happening?

Many times the world reveals itself as not what you perceive.

A couple years ago I met a woman named Emma at a Gabriela Roth dance jam that I go to every Sunday morning. It's called "sweat your prayers" and is an amazing way to reach a nondual state through movement, in this case the five rhythms of flow: flow, staccato, chaos, lyrical, and stillness. It's a form of ecstatic dance, and in addition to being very fun it actually gets you to an extremely connected place with yourself and the hundred or so other people in the room. It's also very intense.

Emma and I had an immediate connection, falling into a dance together that was seamless and charged. Later that night we met for a long walk, and one thing led to another. Over the next week we got involved, carrying over the charge from the dance that started it all.

The only problem was that she lived in Paris and I lived in Los Angeles. And she was leaving at the end of the week.

A month after we said our goodbyes I received an e-mail from Emma saying she was going on a creative retreat in the Armagnac region of France with a teacher named Darrell Calkins and asked if I wanted to go. When I asked her what the retreat was about, Emma was vague but said they were amazing, filled with the most creative and interesting people in the world. I was getting ready to travel in Europe for two weeks, doing research with a director and producer for a script I was working on, and she said I should come to the retreat after and check it out.

And so on a whim I signed up. The two weeks before the retreat were exhilarating and exhausting as the director, producer, and I traveled from Rome to Munich to Prague, interviewing B-movie directors and producers from the sixties. We worked hard, traveled constantly, and played hard. We all got sick in Prague (it might have been the long nights drinking absinthe and checking out the rave scene), and at the end of the two weeks, I was exhausted. I bid my colleagues farewell, and as they headed toward the States I caught a flight to Paris.

Let me set the scene. I was sick. I was tired. I was a bit strung out from spending nights in different hotels in three countries in the past two weeks. I was meeting a woman I barely knew to go on a retreat being led by a man I didn't know at all.

In other words, I was stepping into a situation that was completely unknown. What a relief. When stepping into the unknown, it is sometimes easier to experience wakefulness. One doesn't spend as much time anticipating what might happen. For other people it is easier when they are in their daily routine to relax into wakefulness, but for me, bring on the unknown.

When I got to Charles de Gaulle airport, Emma met me. We hadn't seen each other for over two months, and after hugs and kisses she said we were late and the plane for Bordeaux left from a different terminal. There was a very good chance that we wouldn't make it, and it was the only flight left that night.

We waited and waited for the shuttle to come, with time running out. Each moment we sat there meant we weren't going to catch our plane. We were trapped in one of the hellish aspects of mass transportation: delay.

So we decided to put it in gear and started running.

Now, as I've mentioned before, Thich Nhat Hanh, the Vietnamese Buddhist teacher, will not speed his step to catch an airplane, even when he is thirty feet from the gate. He would rather miss the plane than rush. During his retreats, Thich Nhat Hanh would conduct sunrise strolls in which we would slowly walk one perfect heel-to-toe step at a time, mindful of every pebble under our feet, every breeze on our face. There is no past, there is no future, there is only right now. So what's the hurry?

This is, quite frankly, the best and most peaceful attitude to have when dealing with travel and public transportation.

But this book is called *City Dharma* and is about accepting certain realities of worldly life. So let's say you're not a Buddhist monk. We certainly weren't—we wanted to catch the plane. It doesn't matter. Even when you are going, let's say *really* going, like us running for that plane, you can be awake to each step, feeling the smooth texture of your luggage handle in your hand or the weight of your computer bag on your shoulder, hearing the flight announcements. Quite simply, you are *there,* not in your imagination about the future or recrimination about the past *(should have left earlier, should have planned better).*

After our decision to run for it, in that moment I wasn't thinking about the consequences of missing the plane, which included missing a full day of the retreat. We were just moving fast. But even in going *fast*, you are *being*. It's not so much that you are changing your behavior in these circumstances; you are changing your perspective. In doing so, relaxation arises, and the internal pressure and anxiety are instantly released, even as the sweat drips down your back and you run for your plane.

When we got to the counter to check in, the clerk, officious in an extremely French way, informed us that it was too late to check in.

"But we already have our tickets," I said to Emma, who translated in her impeccable French. It didn't matter to the clerk.

"He says it's impossible," Emma said. "The time has passed for processing tickets."

"But the gate is right over there. It's open. The plane hasn't left. What's impossible about this situation?"

I was tired from traveling all day. Exhilarating as the short race for the plane had been, I was sick, and now I was irritated, certain the man's attitude had everything to do with the fact that we were Americans. In that moment I absolutely hated being at the mercy of public transportation. We went back and forth a few more times, with Emma translating, but the man wasn't going to be budged.

"Tell him he's full of shit," I grumbled.

"I am not full of shit," the man said in a thick French accent. "*You* are full of shit."

"Great. *Now* you speak English," I said, laughing. "I guess that means we're definitely screwed."

"I guess that's just it," Emma said. "What a drag."

And it was a drag. We were going to have to get a hotel at the airport and wait for the next flight, which wasn't until the next day. We had already missed the first few days of the retreat, and now we were going to miss another one. And the person who was meeting us at the airport to take us on the three-hour journey to the château where the retreat was being held had already left to pick us up.

I was torn between my desire to get on the plane and my desire to give up desire—the spiritual seeker's cross to bear. And I was definitely not happy to be thwarted by this petty bureaucrat.

What is the right thing to do when confronted with officiousness that is arbitrary and unfair? I call it the bouncer syndrome. You know, people lording a small bit of situational power over other people who are momentarily stuck in their domain, like flies caught in a spider's web.

Travel for more than a couple of hours using mass transportation and you will almost certainly encounter the bouncer syndrome. For most people this brings up all sorts of argumentative conditioning, myself included. It is like waving a red flag in front of the bull of ego. As I stared at the man, stared at the open gate with the last person *still* boarding, I just nodded. There was no bending this man's will, and any further attempt would debase ourselves and reinforce whatever jollies he was getting from the situation. Like a bully feeds on fear, an officious person feeds on groveling. It is not healthy for either party to agree to play this game; the only thing to do is to accept it and let it go.

"Okay," I said. "Let's go."

"Are you sure?" Emma asked.

"Very sure." I nodded at the smirking clerk, grabbed the bags, and walked away. "There's no arguing with reality."

I try not to argue with reality. If I do, I end up arguing away the moment because I'm in some imagination of what I think the moment should be, rather than what it is. It's only when we accept reality that the moment then becomes livable. We don't waste our energy fighting it. In this acceptance comes great freedom. This is especially true when in the uncontrollable process of traveling.

Some people would argue that all change, good or bad, comes from people having an argument with reality. They don't accept what is, wanting it to be different, usually better. In this way humankind progresses, whether by developing new surgical techniques or inventing cleaner-burning cars. This is often used as a criticism of Eastern philosophy. Those who fully accept the moment have no desire to change it. But then how would anything get done?

In a sense, this is a valid criticism. One answer would be that we would all be much better off if we *did* less, since most of what humankind does is an act of self-destruction or planetary degradation.

However true this is, it is only true up to a point.

What about people who are sincerely working for a better world? What if they can't accept an injustice or want to help somebody? How does this square with accepting the moment?

Unless you get extremely dogmatic here, there is no contradiction. If you are working for a change, you must first see and acknowledge the reality as it is. It's impossible to do otherwise. You must be in the moment and accept it or else you wouldn't know what it is you want to change. Moment by moment, even as you try to effect change, you are wide awake in that moment. In this way you are receptive to the creativity necessary to engender change. This wakefulness is the most effective way to get anything done, because you are accepting all of the bumps in the road and adjusting to them.

It is a creative rather than static way to be in the world.

You work toward change without any attachment to the results. You don't tell yourself a big story if you can't change the reality. You don't get caught up in concepts such as success or failure. You accept the moment's reality, and then in each subsequent moment you accept the new reality, even as it changes under your desire for it to change. You simply *are* in each moment, whether it is in something as sublime as providing food for starving villagers or as ridiculous as arguing with an officious airline clerk.

If you don't go about inducing change in this way, you are doomed to frustration and suffering about what should be. That frustration will surface and actually make you less effective.

Especially in the case of the bouncer syndrome.

With the clerk there was nothing to do but accept the reality that for whatever reason (and it never matters what it is), he wasn't going to help us board. It was inexplicable, because that was his job and he should be helpful. But as long as we stayed focused on that story, trying to budge him, we were stuck.

However, upon accepting the inexplicable reality of his unreasonableness, another reality presented itself—a reality that had remained hidden up to that point.

"Follow me. Just be casual." I whispered to Emma once we were out of the way. I circled back around toward the actual gate.

"Just in the nick of time, it looks like," I said, handing the tickets to the agent.

"Oh . . . yes. We were just going to close the gate." She smiled at us and looked at my huge bag.

"I know this is our responsibility for being so late, but is it possible to get this monster down to baggage claim?"

"No." She shook her head, and my heart fell. "We'll just have to bring it on board."

With that she took our tickets and, as simple as that, we boarded. I saw the officious clerk rushing over to the gate. But it was too late. I waved, and we were on the plane.

As we sat congratulating ourselves and excitedly catching up with each other, I began to muse on the nature of flexibility. The heated words exchanged with the clerk had been unnecessary; sometimes it's hard to know what the right action is. When confronted with a battle of egos, do you make a stand or assume the quality of water and flow around the obstacles? Water always gets where it's going, and in doing so, it eventually wears out whatever obstacles are in its way. When you are like water, you are relaxed and flexible, flowing toward your destination.

When traveling it is best not to try to change reality as it presents itself, but to simply adapt to the constantly changing circumstances. No other quality is more important than this when on the road of life. You will get where you are going—no need to do battle to get there.

Little did I know how much flexibility I would need for the upcoming retreat.

THE CHÂTEAU AT ARMAGNAC

Do not go where the path may lead, go instead where there is no path and leave a trail.

—RALPH WALDO EMERSON

When we landed in Bordeaux, we were met by a young man in a small Honda for the three-hour journey to the château. Emma and I squeezed into the back, and she spoke French as I stared out the window, noisily blowing my nose and clearing my throat. As we drove into the deepening twilight of the French countryside, I could see old stone farmhouses surrounded by orchards.

Occasionally a large château drifted into view. The forests were either fairy-tale woods filled with gnarled trees or acres of timber planted in neat little rows, as if they were pegs in some fantastic board game.

We stopped at a pharmacy, and I loaded up on indecipherable medicine. As we proceeded on in this endless day of planes, trains, and automobiles, I was really feeling sick. When one gets sick or tired, the mind can get a better toehold. I began getting concerned about things not within my control or about things in the future. When the mind is careening, sometimes it's worth it to ask yourself if you're hungry or tired or sick. Know that if you answer yes to any of these, then you will naturally have less buoyancy and resilience to the mind's shenanigans. You are more susceptible to neurotic thought.

In this case, I began to worry about my energy level for the retreat, which was apparently fairly intense, both physically and mentally. Would I have a meaningful experience? Was the guy a charlatan? Would it be a complete waste of time and money? This kind of worry is often exacerbated when traveling to a new place. You don't have as much control. You don't know where you're going or what will happen when you get there. Everything is new, requiring a heightened alertness. It's easy to get caught up in anxiety.

But within each moment of any journey, you do have a choice: neurosis or now. I relaxed and focused on the rows of trees whipping by. Thunderclouds obscured the setting sun. Lightning flashed, and the leaves on the trees flipped up in the wind, revealing their lighter undersides.

Two hours later we turned down a long gravel driveway and came to a stop in front of a large château painted white, with vines crawling up to the roof. As we got out of the car, Emma said that the surrounding land used to produce the grapes for Armagnac, but now the château was used primarily for retreats. A lovely woman came out and introduced herself.

"I'm Isabel." She shook my hand and hugged Emma. "Everybody's in the grand salon. I'll take you to your room, and you can freshen up and meet us there."

We were taken into the château, which was filled with Persian rugs, antiques, and art. As we climbed a stone stairway I heard ringing laughter from some part of the château. We were ushered into an incredible room with a large four-poster bed, French windows overlooking the garden, and a bathroom the size of a living room, complete with a large iron-clawed bathtub. It was a charming room in a beautiful castle that was over four hundred years old.

"This place is amazing!" I jumped on the bed with Emma, and we had a few moments of bouncing around like kids.

We washed up and I took some cough syrup, an antihistamine, and homeopathic flu medicine.

"Shall we go down?" asked Emma, her eyes shining with excitement.

"Let the games begin," I coughed.

Emma, who had been to retreats at the château before, led us down the stairs, through a large dining room, and into the grand salon.

In the salon, the only light was shed by candles. Trippy music that sounded like Mazzy Star played in the background. People lounged around the room in various stages of indolence and undress. Isobel met me at the door and led me through the room to a place on the couch between two men, who immediately snuggled in next to me. "Welcome, welcome," they murmured, resting their heads on my shoulders. As my eyesight adjusted to the dimness of the room, I looked around.

My immediate impression was that I had wandered into an opium den. It wasn't the details, which I wouldn't notice for a few minutes, but the energy of the room—the way people held themselves and looked at me, with either bored indifference or grins that were a bit too bright. I tried to get oriented. Emma was engulfed in a group hug across the room.

"We're so glad you brought him to us," said one man, smearing his body on hers.

"I brought him here to save him," Emma said.

Save me? Save me from what? My mind started racing. *Who is this person, really? I barely know her. Where exactly on the planet am I? Have I wandered into a cult?*

"Which one is Darrell?" I asked one of the men curled up next to me.

"There he is," he said reverentially, pointing at a man with long black hair. The man was wearing a pair of mirrored aviator sunglasses, the kind popular with the late-seventies cocaine crowd. Behind him were two large men who stood with their arms crossed. At his feet were two beautiful women with flowers in their hair, looking up at him adoringly. At the back of the room a man in a baseball cap started asking questions.

"Darrell, what is love? How does it make us feel? Can you tell us what it is? We are all searching for it but never find it." The man kept on talking, not waiting for an answer. "What is it? I want to know what love is. I want to experience love. Unconditional love. Love. Love. I want to love."

Darrell just nodded and didn't say anything. One of the beautiful and scantily clad women at his feet saw me and crawled over on all fours. She offered me her palm. In it was a small red pill. She smiled at me encouragingly.

I took the pill and smiled back, putting it in my shirt pocket.

The man with the baseball cap kept asking his questions about love. Another man, with long, greasy hair, began to laugh hysterically. The two large men behind Darrell frowned at him, but the man's hilarity was uncontrollable.

Darrell just kept nodding.

I was feeling queasy. Maybe it wasn't a cult, but it was definitely some sort of bullshit guru trip. Or the "drug day" on a long retreat. And I was trapped, stuck at least until the morning. Emma was across the room, lounging comfortably in the arms of three people. I tried to get her eye, but she was just staring raptly at Darrell.

A very good-looking man with no shirt and a scarf wrapped around his head like a turban came forward and gave me a flower. On his arm were track marks.

I looked around the room more closely. On the coffee table, which was strewn with wine bottles and empty glasses, were lines of cocaine and a rolled-up dollar bill, along with an ashtray filled with pills of every different shape and size.

"Billy, shut up," shouted one of the burly men behind Darrell. "You're being disruptive. Shut up."

Billy just laughed more hysterically.

"Shut up, Billy!" The man moved from behind Darrell and strode up to Billy, grabbing him by the shoulders. "You will be removed."

"What about love? Where's the love?" the man wearing the Baseball cap protested.

"Shut up, Billy. Shut up."

The man shook Billy's shoulders and then slapped him across the face.

"Hey, hey," I protested, trying to think of a way to reach out to the drug-addled group, of some way to stop Billy from being slapped. Everybody turned and looked at me. Billy stopped laughing. The room fell silent. I racked my brains for something diplomatic, something that would acknowledge that I didn't know what the hell was going on or what kind of process they were in.

"Did you know that in certain parts of the world, there's something called a laughing sutra? It's a form of meditation."

"Oh," said the man with the turban. "So you think Billy might be enlightened."

"Well, I don't know about that, but he probably doesn't need to be slapped."

The burly man looked at Darrell, who nodded. He still hadn't said a word. The burly man let go of Billy who immediately started laughing again.

The man with the baseball cap started in with his questions.

Another man started rolling a joint.

One of the beautiful girls crawled over to me and gave me another flower, which I took.

The other girl crawled over and started peeling an orange at my feet.

Isabel was nowhere to be seen.

Emma was now sitting in lotus position, meditating.

And so it went for about twenty minutes. My mind sat with it. This is travel—ultimately there is no control. This is what can happen when you follow a girl you barely know across the world and directly into somebody's little wormhole of weirdness. This was drug-induced madness mixed with an obvious guru trip. A teacher who would allow a student to slap another student couldn't teach me anything I wanted to learn. I felt rising panic and an increasing clamminess from my own illness. How strange or violent would it get? I could see nothing from Darrell's face, hidden behind mirrored glasses. I began to dislike the man.

I recalled Gandhi's mantra: *Ram, ram, ram. God. God. God. It's all God, all consciousness. I am fine. I will be fine. No matter how long and strange a night unfolds, it ultimately will pass. I tried to relax.*

Rain spattered in large drops against the windows of the French doors. Thunder cracked off in the distance. Lightning pulsed a flickering light through the candlelit room. Perfect.

A beautiful golden Labrador came in the room, happy and whisking its tail back and forth. As it passed the drug-laden coffee table, the tail swept the cocaine onto the floor.

"Hey, watch zee drugs! Get zee dog out of zere!" shouted the man with the turban, in an accent that now sounded Belgian. A couple people galvanized themselves into action, clearing the dog out.

Darrell cleared his throat and the room fell silent. Even Billy stopped laughing.

"It's interesting how we all want to know what love is," Darrell said. "But when the dog, which is pure love, enters the room, we can only think of how to get the dog out of the room."

The room thought that one over. Not a bad teaching in the moment, I thought.

The man with the baseball cap renewed his staccato questioning.

"So is the dog love? The dog is love?" he said. "And *dog* spelled backward is . . . *God*! The dog is God, and God is love."

Darrell said nothing. People began murmuring among themselves. I bit my tongue to keep from laughing.

Then Darrell abruptly stood. He clapped his hands twice.

"Meet in the *chez* in twenty minutes." Everybody stumbled to their feet. Isabel appeared.

"What's the *chez*?" I asked her.

"I will show you. But you will want to get into some loose and comfortable clothing, as we will be getting physical."

Physical? I looked around me. *These people can barely stand.*

As I walked out of the grand salon Emma joined me. We said nothing as we climbed the stairs. When we got to our magnificent room, I shut the door. We said nothing as we got changed.

"Save me?" I finally asked. "Perhaps you have brought me here to save *you*."

"Darrell has his own methods. You can't judge this. We are coming into it in the middle of a retreat," Emma said. "Try not to judge this."

"I didn't sign up for a drug scene led by a guru. Been there, done that."

"You don't know what you signed up for," Emma told me. "Let's go—we don't want to be late."

"What's a *chez*?"

"The *chez* is what we call the stone building where they used to age the Armagnac."

We walked down through the château, which was lit by candles, and into the courtyard. It was pouring rain. We ran toward a large stone building and entered through a massive sliding wood door.

The room was dimly lit, and as my eyes adjusted, I recognized the people from the salon. They were dressed in sweats and T-shirts and looked normal. Isabel was there with a camera.

Then they broke into applause. I just stood there, unsure of what was happening. Then I got it. I began to laugh.

The whole performance in the salon was just that, a performance. The whole thing was a put-on.

My laughter grew from a deeper and deeper place within me. As I realized how completely my reality had been flipped, I felt an immense joy. It was the joy of being completely surprised. I couldn't remember the last time I had been completely surprised. Can you? Usually when your reality gets flipped it's negative, like during a car accident or a mugging or a heart attack. But to have it flipped into something positive and playful? To have my expectation of what was happening suddenly flip into what was actually happening? It had been a long time. In that moment I felt a kind of internal unraveling, the kind of joy one feels at the truly unexpected. This was of course coupled with the relief of not having to escape from a drug-soaked retreat with a Mansonesque cult leader!

Off to my side, a compact silver-haired man approached and shook my hand with a smile.

"Hi, Arthur. I'm Darrell," he said. "Welcome."

I looked around at the crowd, recognizing the "drugged groupie," the burly "bodyguard," and the guy with the baseball cap, which he still wore. Darrell later told me that he needed to integrate me in a sink-or-swim way with everybody who was already on the retreat, to put me in the experience.

"Nice to meet you all," I said, laughing somewhat sheepishly.

Later that night I thought about the day, with its unique challenges of fatigue, transportation, delays, illness, and expectations—all the uncontrollable elements inherent in any kind of travel. My experience of the play (in the truest sense of the word) in the salon was that every detail I observed reinforced a reality I had already "seen" and concluded was real. My mind was made up immediately upon entering the grand salon. The incense, the music, and the weird people could only add up to one interpretation: guru trip. Then I began looking for supporting evidence to my hypothesis and, not surprisingly, found it.

> The poverty of expectation—the failure of imagination—I found this just so interesting. We tend to hear what we expect to hear, whether it's good or bad. Human nature is that way. Unless something is jarring, you tend to stay on your track and get it reinforced rather than recalibrated.

This could have been said by a spiritual teacher, but it was actually said by the U.S. defense secretary Donald Rumsfeld, talking about the failure of converting intelligence "noise" into information that can be used for predictive capabilities.

This is particularly true when traveling using mass transportation. Because we don't have as much control over what is going to happen or the pace, we tell ourselves hypotheses, or stories about what we think is happening.

Behavioral scientists say that the eye doesn't really see reality fresh as it occurs because there is too much information—the brain is filling in most of the information from a storehouse of memory. That's why when you're a young child everything takes on a kind of hallucinogenic newness, a freshness that can make a tomato or a blade of glass the most interesting object in the world. This is what happens during certain drug experiences. When you are high on Ecstasy or mushrooms you slow down enough to become fascinated by the world. Every minute can last forever as your eyes see it all for the first time. You experience wakefulness as the small self falls away and you become one with and totally absorbed by the moment. You "see God," but unfortunately this taste only lasts as long as the drugs. This is one of the factors in addiction, this desire to experience oneness with all, to return to the source, free of the encumbrance of self. People literally trade their life for it, trying to get the original and strongest taste back, trying to retrieve the freshness of a childlike way of seeing.

During my experience in the grand salon my mind was reinforcing what I thought I was seeing, filling in the blanks.

"Aha" As I saw the track marks,

"MmmHmm" when I noticed the lines of cocaine.

Everything seemed to support my view of what was happening. But it wasn't true. And if I was open to the idea that something *else* was happening, I might have noticed other details, like the wig Darrell was wearing or the fact that the proffered "pill" was an M&M with the logo licked off. There was, in fact, a whole other reality going on, with plenty of clues to support it. What prevented me from seeing it, moment to moment, was the fact that my mind was already made up. I only saw the one reality that I expected. But in wakefulness this wouldn't be the case. In wakefulness I would be seeing each moment fresh, open to whatever new information arises.

Typically this is not an either/or proposition. We are never fully awake, nor are we fully asleep. When traveling we usually switch back and forth, filling in the blanks as we get in the cab or get on an airplane. It's useful to remember when feeling tired or sick or exposed, as one often is when using mass transportation, that wakefulness is more of a challenge.

EXPECT THE UNEXPECTED

Public transportation in all its forms offers us an unparalleled freedom to explore the world. Planes make the world a tiny place and give us the opportunity to be generous, curious, and surprised. Mass transit shakes up our routines, exposes us to different people, and broadens our horizons.

It also makes the world smaller in a way that isn't always reassuring, providing new challenges and fears, from SARS to terrorism. As mentioned in the chapter on violence, the mind can seize on these fears and narrow the scope of our lives. But in a time when, due to unfamiliar external stresses, there is an internal contraction happening in the hearts and minds of many, mass transportation forces us into the hurly-burly of life. It may force us to sit next to a person of a different race or sexual orientation or socioeconomic group. In doing so it stretches our tolerance for diversity and human contact. It makes us more adaptable and is an antidote to the mind's fears about the world.

Most of our journeys on public transportation are safe. And most of the strangers we travel with are harmless. Public transportation is a reminder of this. It teaches us the wisdom of insecurity (the title of an eloquent book by Alan Watts). When we are driving ourselves, on our own schedule, we become insulated to the vagaries of the world. We become preoccupied with comfort and safety, forgetting that life is made up of the *unexpected*.

As John Lennon said, "Life is what happens when you're making other plans."

The wisdom of accepting the essential insecurity of our *plans* for life is taught in a very real way on the planes and subways of the world. These lessons are an extremely valuable reminder that we are not in control of everything that happens and that sometimes bad things happen to good people. And bad things happen to bad people because this is the way life is. To expect it to be any different will turn us into people who need to have complete control of our environment—who are under the illusion that life can be controlled and made safe.

Life is not controllable. Life is not safe. No matter what lawyers or the government says, life is an essentially precarious endeavor. And that's fine. I had a spiritual teacher once who said that real power was not having the courage to stand on train tracks holding up a hand and commanding a train to stop, but rather knowing that a train is much more powerful than you are, being aware of when trains are coming, and crossing the tracks only when it is safe.

This is great—unless, of course, you don't see the train . . .

There is simply is no such thing as total safety, and we need to give up on the idea. So don't give your freedom to any individual or government promising safety. One of the beautiful things about travel in general, particularly while on public transportation, is that it reminds us of this fact. It places you squarely in the opportunity to live the unexpected.

You are also relieved of the necessity of actually driving or paying attention to the road. Every moment becomes a chance to watch the play of life that is happening in front of you, to meet it without expectation and to see it clearly. Thus the very thing that can be irritating about mass transportation, the lack of control or privacy, can become a source of pleasure. It can become an opportunity to intemally expand and accommodate different people and ways of life.

This can take place during the extreme day-to-day conditions of riding the subway or bus to work. The next time a rowdy youth with a boom box gets on, cursing the bus driver for telling him to turn it off, staring you in the eye, begging you to challenge him, relax. Enjoy the colorful display. See it clearly, and if you are truly bothered, move.

But in moving it is not necessary to create internal boundaries for yourself, or judgment of the other person. When the stranglehold of the small self is broken, our awareness merges with the greater self, which is all that is.

Out of this merging comes freedom and flexibility, even if we are on a subway in Japan and special "packers" are pushing and squeezing us in like sardines.

We are not separate. We are part of the one.

"SPARE SOME CHANGE?"

The "Smelly Bum" on the Corner

If I am not for myself, then who will be for me, and if I am only for myself, then what am I, and if not now, when?
—ETHICS OF THE FATHERS, 1:14

The questions come in the space of minutes while walking down the street: "Got any money for food?" "Spare some change?" or my favorite, "Can I have a buck for some beer? I really, really need a beer right now."

Every city has homelessness. I live in Santa Monica, a part of Los Angeles that has ironically dubbed by Harry Shearer as the "home of the homeless." Late at night on the Third Street Promenade, it can become like a scene from a Dickens novel. Every day I am confronted with an outstretched hand and pleading eyes. This is at the very least. One day a demented man set fire to some garbage and threw it on top of my car, which was parked in my open garage. Luckily a passing motorist stopped and put it out before the entire apartment building burned down.

In an environment where literally every five minutes you are confronted with a panhandler, sometimes an aggressive one, it's easy to shut down, to avoid the person by averting your eyes and quickening your step. But what is the cost of avoidance when confronted with a homeless person demanding money? I know when I turn the other way I feel a pang in my heart as I ignore this person in need. I always ask myself why it is so hard for me to pause and at least acknowledge their humanity.

And as I hurry away, I wonder what it does to my own humanity. What part of ourselves is amputated when we dine at a sidewalk café while somebody else goes hungry a few feet away? Is there a way to avoid numbness in spite of the overwhelming population? Is there a way to express compassion without going broke?

Perhaps no other aspect of city living is more difficult, draining, and painful than interacting with the homeless. Whether we are aware of it or not, they trigger fear, criticism, and even repulsion. On a deep level the fear is accompanied by the feeling "There but the grace of God go I." It is the shadow side of capitalism, where the weak are left by the side of the road to fend for themselves or die. Dealing with mental illness, the absence of family, and a lack of support, couldn't anyone end up in that position, given a combination of calamitous events?

There is a fear that homelessness could be also be contagious, so we don't want to get too close. We avert our eyes and hold the homeless at arm's length both mentally and physically. We try to avoid any suffering, in ourselves and others, not accepting it as a part of life. We judge: something must be wrong with them if they ended up on the street. They must be defective. This repulsion allows us to dehumanize them in our minds; they become the "other." If they're barely human—and granted, some of the ones suffering from schizophrenia who have been on the streets the longest can seem to be another species—then we can more easily ignore them. And so the homeless experience something worse than hunger, being shinned from the tribe, branded with a "Scarlet H."

Yet most spiritual traditions, including Judaism, Christianity, and Buddhism, say that he who learns from every person is wise. Ben Azzai is quoted in the Wisdom of the Fathers: "Do not be scornful of any person, and do not be disdainful of anything, for you have no person without his hour and no thing without its place."

What can we learn from the homeless? The question itself belies a prejudice, for the homeless are simply people who have a wide range of experience, education, and wisdom. But even if you never approach homeless people and learn what they have to offer individually, what about learning the lesson of gratitude? Gratitude for our circumstances, which, no matter how humble they may be, at least include a roof over our head.

Being confronted by homeless people can breed "compassion fatigue," a sense of being just tapped out. Following may be feelings of frustration, hostility, judgment, and anger, which lead to a deeper feeling of contraction and isolation as we question our ability to love.

Do we have only a finite amount of love or compassion to give? When we are connected to ourselves and to the sense of being indelibly a part of consciousness, which is infinite, can we run out of love and patience? No. This is an illusion of the mind, which is telling tales of limitation and lack. You can not run out of the love that you are.

Yet it feels like we do.

And the feelings of helplessness lead to strange moments.

IN THE SUFFERING MADNESS

If you cannot find the truth right where you are,
where do you expect to find it?
—DOGEN

One night in Boston I went to a 7-Eleven to buy milk. It was late, and the store was harshly lit with fluorescent lights that exposed the lines in people's face as if they were in an interrogation room. It was Saturday night, and the store was crowded with students prowling the aisles for snacks.

I grabbed the milk and settled into the line to people-watch.

At the rear of the store, three youths were raucously playing catch with a can of chili. An elderly lady drifted down the aisles, scrutinizing prices and extracting cheaper goods from the back of the shelves. The fat guard yawned and read *People* magazine. He occasionally looking up at the chili tossers but didn't bother to move.

A slim blonde worked the register with a bored expression. Pretty, she wore a red plaid shirt that suggested she was from New Hampshire and would rather be hiking.

The door opened and a man walked in, invading the sterile environment like a huge bacterium. His unrecognizable clothing was covered with a makeshift raincoat consisting of garbage bags. He smelled like urine, cheap wine, and vomit. I couldn't picture a personality under the blackened face.

All eyes watched him limp toward the chili tossers. The silent queue suddenly voiced a full scale of opinion, ranging from supercilious high tones to appalled low notes.

"Isn't that disgusting?"

"That is, like, *sooo* gross."

"The poor thing looks like he hasn't eaten in days."

"Something should be done about them."

I had no comment as the people tried to relieve their feelings of guilt, anxiety, anger, and disgust with various comments. I have seen it before in myself.

The line moved on.

Gradually the comments died due to a lack of any emotional concern. I inhaled the silence and pondered my own reaction to this human being. It was impossible to view him as somebody who had had a childhood, who had been a pink little bundle of gurgles and screams, and who had had a mother for at least a short while.

What had happened? Why? What really separated me from this person? What could I do right now? I felt helpless, like a beggar who has been luckily plucked from the gutter and seated comfortably at the banquet of life, with a brain that worked and people who cared for me. It all seemed so random.

The line moved on.

I was at the checkout counter and glanced at the blonde, who was looking at three security screens off to her side. I followed her gaze just in time to see the wretched man sneak something into a cavernous pocket. He shuffled out of range of the camera.

I caught the girl's eyes as she opened her mouth and swung around toward the security guard, who hadn't changed his position except to turn the page. The people in line shuffled their feet impatiently.

I lost myself in those green eyes, trying to fathom her thoughts and to express my own. Would she tell the guard or let the poor man go? I didn't think I was succeeding when, almost simultaneously, we both smiled slight, knowing smiles.

After a tentative peek at the security guard, she rang up my milk.

"A dollar thirty-nine, please." Her smile broadened.

The ragged old man stumbled out into the bitter wind with his loot.

Was it right? Was it wrong? On one hand, of course, it was unethical—I encouraged another person to ignore a crime. On the other hand, it was compassionate—the man obviously was in greater need. I know it was the only thing I could do in that moment, and I felt better for it because I wasn't passive.

Passivity in the face of the homeless is truly demoralizing and enervating. Passivity in general is at the heart of the banality of evil. The woman in New York who was attacked while twenty-three people watched from their apartment windows because they all thought somebody else would call the police was a victim of passivity. Passivity is what makes city living more dangerous and less pleasant, whether applied to a dangerous situation or to a person starving on the street in front of you.

The downside of doing nothing creates a calcification of the spirit. It creates layers of denial and hardness between your heart and the world. It smothers any sense of connection, because after the denial comes rationalization. And so you get a little further from the truth of who you are, which is pure love. I have experienced it myself, and every time I do I regret it.

Doing nothing just plain feels bad, even if you're not aware of it. And the first step toward feeling better is to come out of denial of what is happening and do something, no matter how small.

DO SOMETHING, *ANYTHING*

A life is either all spiritual or not spiritual at all.
THOMAS MERTON

Recently I was walking down the street with a friend and a man was fumbling for change at a pay phone. He had clear blue eyes, looked about sixty years old, and was fairly well dressed, but seemed confused. He approached us and asked for some change to make a phone call. We searched our pockets, and he searched his for the number.

"Got it here somewhere," he mumbled. He wouldn't make eye contact. He pulled out a small piece of paper. "Can you read this?"

We looked at a postage-sized want ad from a yellowing newspaper. It was advertising a small house.

"That's my son," he said. "Out in Palm Springs. My name is Robert. Can you dial that number for me?"

"Sure," I said, checking with my friend, who nodded. This was going to be a bit of a mission, but we had some time to kill before our movie. Thinking we could do a good deed, I dialed the number on my cell phone.

"Hello," a man's voice said.

"Yes, hi. I think I've got your dad here. He wants to talk to you."

"Nope," said the man. "My dad's sitting right here, watching the game."

"Really?" I said stupidly. "Are you sure?"

"Guess I should be." The man's voice took on a sarcastic edge. "Goodbye. Good luck finding your daddy."

With that he hung up. I looked at Robert, wondering if he wasn't suffering from some kind of mental illness. Perhaps he had wandered out of a hospital. Perhaps he was diabetic and his blood sugar was low.

"Robert, can I see your ID?" I asked.

"How about I pay you two hundred dollars to drive me to Palm Springs?" he said, handing over a license.

"Is your full name Robert Stone?" I scanned his license, mentally vetoing the idea of driving him to Palm Springs. The license was expired.

"Yup. Robert Stone," he answered.

I called the operator and tried to find a Robert Stone in Palm Springs. There were four. I called them all, getting answering machines for two. The other two people had never heard of a Robert Stone. On it went like that, with Robert producing more numbers and clips of newspapers. Scraps of yellowed paper with numbers of relatives, friends, neighbors . . . It was beginning to turn into a Kafkaesque burlesque, with every number that he produced leading to a dead end.

"Robert," I said, trying to look him in the eye," all these numbers are dead. What's the real story?"

Robert mumbled something and looked away.

"Do you need help?" I asked. "Do you want us to call social services?"

Robert shook his head. I looked at my watch. Half an hour had passed. I looked at my friend, who was using her cell phone to track down the numbers. She shrugged. What else was there to do?

"Robert, we're going to go now," I said carefully, uncertain what his response would be and feeling terrible that I wasn't able to help him. It was heartbreaking, really. He was probably homeless, dialing numbers to get a home that no longer existed.

Robert nodded. "Thank you for your help."

"Are you sure there's nothing we can do for you?" I asked again.

He just shook his head.

"Where will you stay tonight?"

"I got a place. It's okay."

"Well then." I shook his hand, feeling foolish. "Take care of yourself."

With that we turned away from Robert, who was stroking his gray beard. He reached out and clutched my sleeve. He didn't say anything, just nodded, his blue eyes clear but somehow unseeing. I nodded back, but he was already turning away. We debated if we should call the police or social services. We talked over the different possibilities, but none seemed to be right. In the end, we left Robert to his life and went to the movies.

Both of us were touched by his condition. Neither of us felt good that we weren't able to help him, but we weren't fatigued. We didn't feel drained. We had reached out and tried to do something for him; we didn't just walk by him and pretend he wasn't there. While there was some frustration that we couldn't resolve what was going on in that moment, I stumbled upon something that lessened my own sense of alienation: doing something, anything, creates human contact and connection, which lessens the sense of separation. And in any big city, it is easy to find opportunities to connect.

Later that afternoon I walked down to the beach by myself and sat, watching the sunset. The wind drifted a sheath of sand over the beach, like a woman pulling a veil over her face. Two beefy men threw a football, and beyond them surfers squeezed short runs from tiny surf.

A homeless woman, spitting Tourette's syndrome poetry, lurched across the sand, dragging a ratty blanket. In the corner of my eye, a child wearing pink swung from ring to ring, her body a candy-colored metronome, with her father anxiously hovering beneath her grin.

I watched the homeless woman and got as quiet as I could, relaxing my awareness. She screamed obscenities at the little girl, who swung away, ignoring her. She was beyond help in the moment, untouchable in her madness. I opened my heart to her.

I did nothing, and suddenly I was everything: the sand, the football floating lazily against the purple sky and the men throwing it, the surf and the surfers, the little girl and the steel she was riding, the homeless woman and the insane words coming out of her mouth.

In this awareness there was no separation. The world split open and I merged with it. I was being pulsed in the heartbeat of life, of

God, of consciousness. I was not separate from anything—it all originated from the same place. My heart grew until it swelled with love for everything. A smile grew on my face until it was a grin.

There was such a relief in it. It was so simple that it was laughable. No matter how strange or different or horrific you think the person is standing next to you, they are God.

The only thing preventing us from experiencing this is our fears, judgment, sense of superiority or inferiority, and subsequent disconnection. This product of mind is what separates us from what the mystics would call a connection with all, an experience of nonduality.

GIVE SOMETHING

The true meaning of life is to plant trees, under whose shade you are not planning to sit.

—NELSON HENDERSON

Okay, so you're not a "spiritual person" writing a spiritual book and having epiphanies on the beach. You're a busy professional on the way to work. You don't have time to talk to homeless people for half an hour. Or maybe you're so poor you don't have even a dollar to spare.

But what is the truth here?

A friend of mine told the story of being approached by a homeless man when she was dressed up for a job interview. She was the very picture of success and yet was poorer than she had ever been, living on a friend's couch. He asked her if she had a dime. She laughed, somewhat embarrassed, and said, "Honestly, I don't. I only look the part."

The man laughed with her, and for a moment they were just two human beings sharing a naked moment. He thanked her and said that she had given him something much more valuable than a dime; she had given him the first laugh he'd had in months. This is so often the case. Even if you don't have money to spare, you do have your presence, in the now. The response of looking homeless people in the eye and acknowledging their existence is often the most valuable gift you can give, to both them and yourself. What does eye contact and a nod cost in terms of time? In terms of money?

Many times we go out into the world with stories about a sense of not having enough—we are not wealthy enough, we need more money. If we are plagued by a scarcity mentality, we certainly don't have any money to give. But what is the richness of life? Isn't it being open to every possibility for love in our human exchanges? And isn't giving love what really makes us feel rich? To respond with compassion to a homeless person, even if you don't have money to spare, is a way to bridge the gulf between you and them and, equally as important, between you and your deeper self.

JUSTICE

After the verb "to Love," "to Help" is the most beautiful verb in the world.

—BERTHA VON SUTTNER

There is a word in the Bible *tzedaka*, that originally meant "justice" or "righteousness" but later came to signify "charity," in the sense of almsgiving. The emphasis is that the rich, in giving to the poor, are not doing them a favor but are discharging an obligation they owe as a matter of justice. Any assumption of superiority on the part of the givers is unwarranted. Even if they have made their money by the sweat of their own brow, they have perhaps been born into circumstances that allowed them to thrive, with a loving family, education, and financial support. And if they had none of those things, they were blessed with enough self-esteem to be able to work themselves up from poverty. And if they were actively abused, then their constitution was strong enough to withstand it and able to grow in spite of it.

At its root, this idea of justice points to a connectivity with our brethren that transcends the circumstances of our birth and into the realm of responsibility. For not only could they be us, in a very real sense *they are us*. Even dualistic religions like Christianity and Judaism point to the nondual ideal in Isaiah 58:6:

> Is it not to share your bread with the hungry, and bring the homeless poor into your house; when you see the naked, to cover him, and not to hide yourself from your own flesh?

The naked flesh of the beggar is our own naked flesh. To feel this fully is to know the connectivity of life. To feel it on a mystical level eliminates all sense of separation.

IT'S THEIR "KARMA"

As Catherine Ingram writes in her book *Passionate Presence,* some religions and New Age beliefs offer the happy excuse that the poor are poor because it's their "karma." Hinduism, with its rigid caste system, embodies this principle. Cows are sacred. Dogs, infinitely more intelligent, are less than dirt. Beggars starve because of their past life transgressions. This is all very convenient in terms of letting ourselves off the hook of caring or behaving responsibly.

In a sense this fatalism embodies the nondual idea that you are not the doer, as propounded by teachers such as Ramesh Balsekar. If everything is consciousness, including us, then is there such a thing as free will? If everything we are, everything we see, touch, and do, is consciousness, then who's in the driver's seat? And if this play of consciousness creates homeless people, who are we to feel that we should do anything? Isn't it all supposed to be as it is? Can't we walk away with a sense that all is perfect?

You are not the doer. Certain spiritual teachers stress this over and over again. As a manifestation of God, who is in control? Is it you, with all your wants, needs, and desires, all arising out of your ego? Or is it something infinitely more intelligent?

As Nisargadatta Maharaj said in *I Am That*: "When you demand nothing of the world, nor of God, when you want nothing, seek nothing, expect nothing, then the Supreme State will come to you uninvited and unexpected!"

Other nondual teachers such as Byron Katie say:

> I want reality to change? Hopeless. Let me change my thinking. Some of us mentally argue with "what is." Others of us attempt to control and change "what is," and then tell ourselves and others that we actually had something to do with any apparent change that took place. This leaves no connection or room for God in my life. In the peaceful experience of no opposition to God, I remain aware of my nature: clear, vibrant, a friend, a listener.

There is a great relaxation in accepting what is rather than endlessly striving for what we think should be. I've mentioned this many times in this book—that in giving up control, we are able to accept reality. If we are in the pulse of consciousness, then the heart that is beating everything, including us, doesn't need our help.

Another take on this idea is the concept of predestination. While we may make choices in the moment, it was already predestined that we make these choices, a kind of unfolding determinism over which we have no control.

This is all well and good, but ultimately who cares if we are not the doer? In daily life, there are still choices and decisions to be made.

And what about the other reality that every advancement of humankind comes from people who do not accept reality as it is, but rather work to change reality for the better? Aren't they doing?

So how does one deal with this apparent dichotomy? On one hand, if everything is consciousness or God, then what real choice does the "I" have? On the other hand, how do you avoid the New Age clichés, with their "you create your own reality" mantra offering an easy justification for not feeling compassion or responsibility to the less fortunate? (This pronouncement is usually tied to some technique for sale that will help you "realize your dreams" or "manifest your goals," or give you some other illusion of control.)

But a nondual experience of the world doesn't mean that no decisions and choices are made. They are made in each moment. In the now, one may stop and give a homeless person money. The initial impulse is a spontaneous decision that happens in the moment, arising almost unbidden from the heart.

You don't pause at all. It's like this: there's an impulse to help. It must be acted on immediately in that moment. If you wait, it may disappear, or when you eventually act on it, it might feel forced or stilted.

So don't wait for yourself to ripen in order to give love. You are already ripe. Just do it, say it, or follow the original impulse of the heart, before your mind builds a barrier between the impulse and the action. Because whether it's saying a kind word or rolling down your window to pass money to a person with a Will Work for Food sign at the light, it's only fresh in that instant. As soon as mind enters into the equation, with "She's just going to drink" or "He should get a job," then the action will stall and feel stilted, if it happens at all.

In the moment, the decision to act is yours.

What you don't do is expect anything to change. You are not thinking about the future. You don't expect the person to thank you. You don't expect the person will stop drinking or get a job or take their antipsychotic medicine. You are not in control of the outcome. In fact, my experience with Robert Stone is probably typical. You act out of a spontaneous compassion that arises from your recognition and connection with the person, but you then freely in the next moment let it go. Again, you have no control.

Moment by moment you are awake and doing, but you have no identification with the action. You don't feel you are a superior person. Sometimes we can't control these feelings—for who among us is perfect?—but we don't feel smug or sanctimonious.

The action arises out of your own heart, being beaten by the same force that drives the universe, and allows you to connect with what is happening around you. It allows you to act on that connection in a free way, no matter what other people's response is.

LEARN THEIR NAME

Things do not change, we do.
HENRY DAVID THOREAU

A friend of mine told me a story about driving down a steep access road to get onto the Pacific Coast Highway in Santa Monica. She was at the stoplight at the bottom. A woman, disheveled but clean, was walking by cars and holding a sign: Please Help. My friend was hunting in her purse for some change when she noticed the woman looking past her. She glanced in the rearview mirror and saw a brand-new black Mercedes convertible. In the car was a young, beautiful movie star putting on makeup. My friend rolled down the window and gave the begging woman some coins, exchanging a few words of kindness. The woman thanked her profusely and moved on to the black Mercedes.

The movie star glanced at the woman and didn't stop putting on her makeup.

I think I know this homeless woman. She is a regular in that spot. I've given her money before. But because of the nature of the traffic in that area, I'm never stopped there for long, and I haven't had time to learn her name. I do know the names of several homeless people in my neighborhood, though. There's James, a large and amiable man who hangs out near the Wild Oats market. There's Harold, a slender, gentle man with a radiant smile, who holds a tin can outside Barnes and Noble and with whom I have discussions almost every time I see him.

Now, I am a not a saint. I can get as irritated, self-absorbed, and selfish as the next person. But I noticed something interesting when I took the time to talk to the homeless people I encountered in my daily rounds. They became human to me. Not a lump of smelly, faceless humanity, but actually human, with concerns and individual life histories that I gradually got to know.

And more to the point, I became human to them. I was not just another mark, another person from whom they could get money. I was Arthur. Many times when I was broke I couldn't give them any money, or whatever I gave them was merely a token. But I no longer felt a tightening in my stomach when I saw their outstretched hand. I no longer ignored them. Unlike the movie star, I no longer had to shut down some part of my awareness that didn't include them as a part of my reality. For in doing that, I was the big loser, not the homeless person who was begging. In denying their humanity, I was denying mine. In closing off my awareness, I was missing out on everything that was surrounding them. I was actually denying a portion of reality.

In reaching out, in connecting to the homeless people even with a warm hello, I was including all the realities around me. When James got beaten up by two drunken men and showed up on his customary corner with a bandaged head, I could listen to his story. I could ask him if he needed anything in particular, in this case Tylenol because the aspirin he was taking was upsetting his stomach.

At the core of most religions, sometimes well buried, sometimes hiding in plain sight, is usually a nondual idea. Christ's main teaching of the Golden Rule, "Love your neighbor as yourself," is often interpreted as "Do unto others as you would have them do unto you." But this is quite different from "Love your neighbor as yourself." This positive command can be literally interpreted: love your neighbor as yourself because that person is a manifestation of consciousness, the same as you. To love them as yourself is simply to see this reality, ending the illusion of your isolated identity. This is almost exactly echoed by Buddha in the Dhammapada when he says, "Consider others as yourself."

As you slowly build relationships with those less fortunate than yourself, you will learn about their circumstances, their addictions, and their mental illness. I found that instead of being drained by the emergence of a homeless person, I was nourished because it allowed me to be in the flow of my own love. Not all the time, but sometimes. They wake me up, I wake them up. It's reciprocal.

After a while it becomes possible to look at the whole world and every interaction within it in this paradigm. It is all consciousness in the process of waking itself up: the good, the bad, and the ugly.

Oftentimes I will approach homeless people I know and they will be reciting "Spare some change" over and over again as people walk by them without even looking. They will see me and their whole demeanor will change. Suddenly they are not operating by rote. They are alive and in the moment, smiling at me, saying, "Hey, how ya doin?" Sometimes they remember my name, sometimes they don't. Usually they don't even ask me for change, preferring the human interaction.

Psalms 41:1 says: "Blessed is he who considers the poor." It doesn't say "Blessed is he who gives to the poor." When you learn a person's name, you don't automatically just give. You give in a way that is more specific. If I'm going into Wild Oats for the salad bar, I'll ask James if he would like something. It allows a specific response to specific needs. So much about what it means to be human is to have choice, and sometimes offering that choice to a person in need restores his or her sense of humanity. Several times I have bought James lunch.

In this mode of being, all of a sudden you are part of an organic whole. This breeds understanding, and understanding lessens judgment, separation, and frustration. The kindness also expands your heart and breeds more kindness. Gradually you become a larger person, able to engage and interact with the world and all its attendant beauty and heartbreak.

Again, it is impossible to do this with every homeless person you see. Sometimes just in walking to the movies I can be approached twenty times for money. One of the things that challenge people in dealing with the homeless is that the problem seems so huge, so unsolvable. What can one individual do?

Perhaps the solution here is to stop thinking that we need to fix everything at once. Or even fix anything at all. This brings us into the reality of the moment, and we can reach out in whatever human way we can, for ourselves and others.

So I try not to walk by without at least acknowledging their request, even if it is to say, "Sorry, not today." Sometimes their response is a negative "Fuck you." But just as often it is a "God bless you," accompanied by a smile.

Is this wakefulness sometimes tiring? Not if you don't resist what is happening. Ultimately it isn't nearly as debilitating, lonely, or draining as ignoring the very real needs of the humans around you.

There is no such thing as the wrong time to share yourself.

WHAT IS HAPPENING AND DOES IT MATTER?

One day I was walking down the street with Tammy, my girlfriend at the time. A woman approached us. She was cleanly dressed but looked somewhat disheveled. Her face was haggard and emotional.

"Excuse me, please. I'm . . . I need help." The woman was barely holding it together, as if by saying the words she was becoming internally unglued. Concerned, we stopped.

"What's wrong?" I asked, thinking she might have been recently attacked.

"I . . . this is hard to explain." she said haltingly. "I've lost my place to live . . . due to an abusive relationship . . . and I spent last night in a park. I don't have any family, and all my friends have taken his side."

The words now started coming out in a torrent. She began to cry.

"I don't know what to do. I just need some money to get a room and try to put my life back in order." She was now fully sobbing, almost hysterical.

"It'll be okay." I frantically searched my pockets for money as I searched my mind for words. "I know it seems impossible right now, but it'll be okay."

I pulled out my wallet. There was one bill in it, a twenty. I was pretty broke at the time and didn't really want to give her that much money.

"Do you have any money on you?" I asked Tammy, who shook her head. I looked at the woman sobbing and said to myself, *What the hell*. I gave her the twenty. Tammy looked at me like I'd lost my mind.

"You take care of yourself. I'd give you more if I could, but I'm a bit financially embarrassed myself," I said.

"Thank you, thank you," the woman said, grabbing my hand and trying to hug me. "Thank you so much."

I gave the woman a hug and watched her walk away.

"Wow, can you believe how hard it is to be alive sometimes?" I said to Tammy.

"I didn't believe a word she said," Tammy said flatly. "I think you just got conned."

I stared at Tammy with disbelief. She was a struggling artist but also had some money issues. When I met her I had more than enough money, so it didn't matter much. But I was living the screenwriter's life: large chunks followed by periods of scarcity until the next large chunk came in. And I was waiting for the next chunk.

"You've got to be kidding." I said. "If she's a con artist, then that was an Oscar-winning performance. She should be an actress."

"Maybe she is," Tammy said tartly. "We *are* living in LA."

We argued about that for a long time, about charity and generosity and whether or not people should even give to the homeless. Tammy wasn't sure, saying that the money could be used for drugs or alcohol. I agreed with that but felt there were ways to ascertain whether a person was drunk or on drugs, and that didn't mean one shouldn't buy them a sandwich or give them money for a room.

Tammy said it was demeaning to give them money, and I agreed, musing that the ideal way to give would be to preserve the other person's dignity by giving anonymously or by giving him or her a little job to do. In many third world countries, especially those with a large poor population, there is a whole contingent of people who will watch your car while you are in a restaurant or shopping. They are unarmed and if somebody wanted to steal your car, they certainly wouldn't do anything to stop it. But for a couple of pesos or rand, they will watch it. This amounts to little more than charity, but it allows the giver and the taker to engage in a miniature transaction that at least mimics productive work, perhaps getting the recipient ready for self-sufficiency.

Still, none of it felt appropriate to this situation, and I felt that perhaps Tammy's reaction had more to do with her lack of generosity than anything else. Is what is happening in the moment of being asked for help a nuisance or an opportunity to expand your heart, to ask yourself, "Is this person so different from me?" Is not their need and hunger an opportunity to experience consciousness in another form? I was annoyed with Tammy for not being more generous.

Six months later I was walking down the street by myself and I saw the same woman. She had the same haggard expression on her face and was imploring a young couple. I stopped and watched. She was saying the same exact thing: she had just lost her apartment due to an abusive relationship. The couple gave her some money and hurried on.

The woman turned to me and with pleading eyes began her spiel. It was as honed as the work of any actress I had seen in acting class or worked with on films. It was the same exact performance, and I marveled at the same exact nuances showing up in the same places. I interrupted her.

"Excuse me, but you told me the same exact story six months ago. I gave you twenty dollars." I said. "I'm just curious—are you really homeless?"

She looked at me for a moment and then wheeled away in complete silence. As I watched her bounce away, her short, frizzy blond hair forming a halo, I found myself deeply amazed, torn between amusement, outrage, and sympathy.

Tammy had been right after all.

Some would say that this is a disgrace and that this woman is a con artist preying upon the gullible. Perhaps. But what is really happening here? She had to be one in a million to come up with such an elaborate and emotionally convincing story. It wasn't an apathetic "Can you spare some change?" line. The whole experience had a feeling of theater. If life is a stage, then this performance was well worth the $20.

But on a less flippant note, here was somebody so desperate that she was debasing her emotional life for money. She was still begging on the streets; what a difficult life! Certainly the rejection, emotional exhaustion, and self-inflicted damage were harder than working for a living. Is she not worthy of our compassion even if the story she told to get the money was a complete lie?

Some would say I'm being too generous here, that she was a con artist and belonged in jail. Maybe.

But so what if it's con job? Do you curtail your generosity because you're afraid of being conned? Then you have allowed your spirit to be diminished. Perhaps reaching out when it feels right is the more important thing. Perhaps you prefer to give to a reputable homeless shelter than to give directly to the homeless. Perhaps you take food to go from restaurants and give it to homeless people on your way home yourself.

In any case you choose connection over rejection.

PUNISHMENT VERSUS REHABILITATION

> Hatreds do not ever cease in this world by hating, but by love; this is an eternal truth. . . . Overcome anger by love, overcome evil by good. Overcome the miser by giving, overcome the liar by truth.
>
> —THE DHAMMAPADA

America is very punitive in its mind-set. Currently we have the highest per capita rate of imprisonment in the world. The total prison population is 2,166,260, a new record, and is up 30 per cent since 1995. We keep building jails and locking up not only violent criminals but also 1.4 million nonviolent criminals, two-thirds of everyone who is incarcerated. We lock up those who are suffering from drug addiction. (Unless, of course, they're upper-middle-class white people; then they go to a eighty-day rehab instead of state prison.) We lock up juveniles and execute the mentally ill. We spend six times more money to house prisoners than we do for child care.

This punitive view is often applied to our view of the homeless. What comes up in our mind as we go by them? "Get a job"? "Get lost"? Or "How can I help?" "Are you okay?"

Things are not always the way they seem. For every ten people you help who need it, perhaps there is one person who doesn't need it and is taking advantage of your kindness. But who loses in that exchange? Certainly not you. You have expanded your heart to include that person, even in his or her duplicity.

It is said that a real thief walks around and instead of seeing a full and whole reality sees only the monetary value of something: your watch, your clothing, your car, your earrings. Such a person cruises through life seeing only dollar signs.

This is what this woman with the spiel about the abusive relationship did with her life. Every day. The whole world was whittled down to what she could get from people. What a way to live. What a price to pay.

Do you feel compassion or do you want to punish her?
What punishment would be more than what she is living?

CONTEXT

The trinity: mind self and spirit, when looked into, become unity . . .
"Nothing is me" is the first step. "Everything is me" is the next.
NISARGADATTA MAHARAJ

One day I was walking down the street and I passed a man leaning against a wall in a nice shopping district of Los Angeles. He was elderly and his hands were shaking. His skin was peeling from some strange disease. *Poor guy,* I said to myself. *Drinking, probably homeless.* I rushed on to my appointment.

A half an hour later I passed the same spot and the man was still there. I looked more closely. He was struggling with some sort of neck brace that extended down his back and wrapped around his waist. It was designed to support his head, which bobbed left and right. He was immobile, barely able to tolerate the exertion of standing. I couldn't walk by him.

"Can I help you with that?" I asked.

"Yes. Thank you so much." he answered in a crisp English accent. "I can't get the bloody thing on my head."

I helped him with the harness, which was incredibly elaborate. It rested on his hips and wrapped around his rib cage like a corset. The spine of it ran up his own spine and neck and had a shallow basket to hold his head. We struggled for a good ten minutes to get the strap wrapped around his head, holding everything in place. It was intimate; his skin smelled like baby lotion and was flaking off in small pieces the size and texture of bread crumbs. The whites of his eyes were red but offset by startlingly blue irises.

"Thank you," he kept saying, hands shaking. "It's this bloody Parkinson's."

"Yes, almost there . . . Okay. How's that?" I said, finally getting the contraption on him.

He straightened up, balancing a bit like the Tin Man from *The Wizard of Oz*. "Perfect," he said. "Thank you. My name is Jerry."

I introduced myself. It turned out that he was waiting for a friend to pick him up. When he found out I was a screenwriter, he said that he was a producer. We chatted a short while until his friend pulled up in a black Mercedes. It was hard to believe that when I first saw him I had thought he was homeless.

Jerry tried to walk to the car but was a tottering accident waiting to happen. I carried his canes and allowed him to lean on me, loading him into the car. His body was frail inside the metal and cloth brace, and he clung to me without pride.

"Chuck, I would like you to meet a delightful young man. He's a writer!" Jerry said to his friend with such enthusiasm that I couldn't help smiling.

"Nice to meet you. Sorry I'm late," said Chuck in a rush.

"Are you in the Writers Guild?" Jerry asked.

"Yes," I said, smiling, keeping it short. The moment was too perfect. We had shared such an intimate experience that I didn't want to sully it with the ubiquitous networking for which LA is famous. Jerry immediately sensed this and put out a trembling hand, which I took.

"I wish you the best of luck," he said. "Thank you for stopping and being so kind."

I suddenly found myself not wanting to let go of his hand. I had such a feeling of tenderness toward this man and the stoic vulnerability with which he let me help him. I had helped him, but he had given me the gift of allowing himself to be helped. I realized it felt wonderful to be needed in that way. In that moment, like a Good Samaritan, he had given me the opportunity to give.

In Malcom Gladwell's book *The Tipping Point*, he describes an experiment that was done at a seminary. A psychology professor wanted to find out what the different factors were that affected

Good Samaritans in their decision to stop and help people. He wanted to test if context had anything to do with the decision to stop. He decided to use seminarians because he thought, given their chosen profession, he would have a better chance of people stopping.

He broke them into two different groups. He told one group an important peer review was taking place across campus and that they had only ten minutes to get there. The other group was told they had an hour to make the ten-minute journey. The chief determining factor of whether or not the seminarians stopped to help wasn't disposition, temperament, or professed piety, but whether or not they thought they had the time.

This was something I experienced with Jerry. On the way to my meeting I glanced at him but kept on moving. On the way back I had time to look more closely and saw the actual reality of the situation. I also had the time (it turned out to be twenty minutes) to get involved.

But don't we all really have the time? What is more important in our lives? By what will our lives be measured on our deathbed?

It is useful to ask yourself during the day, *Am I rushing? What might I be missing if I am rushing? What might happen if I do rush?* Recently a woman who was driving an SUV too fast and talking on a cell phone turned a corner and killed a bicyclist. Her children were in the car with her. In that split moment, her entire life changed. She was charged with vehicular manslaughter and imprisoned. Her marriage crumbled under the strain.

Most situations aren't as dire as this. But context does affect wakefulness. How open are we to what is happening around us? Can we even see what is happening, or are we speedily skimming the surface of our lives?

Here's an experiment to try: leave early. Of course, this feels nearly impossible in today's world. Everything is a rush. We're all trying to get so much done that we rush through everything. But see what happens for a day if you give yourself less to do; and really take the time to experience it. You may find that you touch many more people and actually experience much more of the day.

Walk through your own neighborhood and notice your experience when you rush down the street. Then slow it down a notch. Really look into the faces of the people who are asking for your help. What do you see if you catch their eye? Relax your awareness and merge with them.

Are they not God and deserving of a moment of our time?

Every time we walk outside our front door, we have an opportunity to grow and experience more connectedness to the world. Instead of ignoring reality, you can embrace it. Instead of saying no to consciousness in it's multiplicity of forms, you can say: "Yes! Nothing human is alien to me."

"ME. ME. ME. WHAT ABOUT ME?"

Urban Rudeness and Narcissism

> Try not to achieve anything special, you already have everything.
>
> —SHUNRYU SUZUKI

In the supermarket a woman slams her cart into yours while trying to get ahead of you in line. What do you do?

The next day you are standing in line with a full cart in front of a person holding just one item. What do you do?

When a car has its turn signal on, do you slow and let it in? Or do you speed up and close the gap? And how do you feel being rude? How do you feel being generous? Rudeness has more to do with your relationship to the world than what people are actually doing.

After the terrorist attack on the World Trade Center, people related to each other differently. There was a sense of tenderness when encountering even total strangers, a sense of connectedness to our fellow humans. We all saw, in horrible detail, the fragility of life. There was a reprieve from the general decline in civility, which goes much deeper than mere rudeness. This decline is rooted in the belief of an isolated identity in competition with its fellow human beings. It includes a form of impatience that is born out of a fear of not gaining or, more frequently, of losing something. This is a harder and more active kind of rudeness, one that views other people as objects in the way. It promulgates a bottomless well of need because in the small self's quest for control and domination, nothing is ever enough. The dynamic of *me, my story, my plans,* and *my life* crowds out what is actually happening in the moment. What "I" want subsumes what is. Eventually the little "I" hardens into an entity that loses touch with anything but its own needs.

This can be found in any environment, any community. I'm often amused when I go to a crowded yoga class in Los Angeles and see people push and shove their way in so they can get the spot they wanted. It is ironic how much stress and anxiety get generated around going to an activity meant to reduce stress and anxiety. It proves that the dynamic of selfishness can be present in any circumstance, even in so-called spiritual circles.

Rudeness is not a huge event in our lives, but it is a quality-of-life issue. The steady drip of the small infraction often adds up to relentless stress with effects as problematic she as those of larger events like violence. For every rudeness says, in effect, "You're not as important as I am."

CONTENTION TO CONNECTION

But is there any comfort to be found?
Man is in love and loves what vanishes,
What more is there to say?
—W. B. YEATS

I am not immune to the temptation to be rude. At the yoga studio I teach at, parking is at a premium. It's so crowded that I often don't bother trying to find a place outside the studio, which is on the second story of a block of stores. On the same block, right across an alley, is a parking lot that is almost always empty. It services four stores and is an easy walk to the yoga studio. I discovered this secret parking spot and happily began to park there, despite the warning that it was only one hour parking and violators would be towed. After about a month, one day I pulled in while a slender man was hosing down the parking lot. He saw me with my yoga mat walking toward class and called out, "There's no parking here for the yoga studio." I looked at him and then looked around the empty parking lot. Thirty spaces, and three were taken. And I was late for class.

"Doesn't seem like there's any shortage of parking here. Do you mind if I catch this class and not park here again?"

The slender man nodded, and I thanked him and went off to my class. Two weeks later, as I was circling the busy shopping district for a parking spot, I gave up and returned to my secret spot. The lot was almost empty as I parked my car and walked toward the studio.

"Hey. Hey!" I heard from behind me. I was pretty sure it was directed at me, but instead of acknowledging it, I quickened my step and ducked into the yoga studio. I was late for class and in a hurry.

After my yoga class I came back for my car. It wasn't there. I looked around at the empty parking lot with a sinking feeling, hoping that I'd been mistaken, that maybe the car was here and I'd just missed it. But there was only a Mercedes.

This is unbelievable, I thought. *It's been stolen.* In the corner of the lot I saw the same slender man painting a railing. He was studiously avoiding me. And then it dawned on me. For the first time in my life, my car had been towed. After a moment of relief that it hadn't been stolen I became furious. Instead of feeling happy that I still had a car, even if it wasn't right there, I could only focus on how I had been wronged. I stalked up to the slender man.

"Did you have my car towed?" I demanded.

"I told you there was no yoga parking here."

"So you had to have my car towed?" I sputtered. "Congratulations. You've managed to ruin my morning. And probably cost me a hundred dollars."

The slender man shrugged, as if to say, "Whose fault is that?"

"You heard me call you. You just ignored me," he said. "I'm just doing my job."

"Now those are some famous words throughout history," I said. "And I didn't ignore you."

"Yes, you did," he said. And of course he was right. But that didn't stop me.

"What's your name?"

"Louis." He sighed and kept on painting the railing.

"Well, Louis, way to go. Feel really proud of yourself. You kept the world safe from illegal parking today."

"Don't park here again," he said simply, with no gloating or ego. I just stood there silently. What else could I say? He was totally right and I was completely wrong. In addition to that, I was huffy and lying and completely out of balance. And I just couldn't accept the fact that my car wasn't there.

"Congratulations for a job well done," was my lame parting shot. I walked away, leaving him to paint in the hot sun while I went off to lead my privileged life.

Does it get any ruder than that? I don't think so. I trudged across Santa Monica, hating my circumstances and hating myself. There was a familiar internal dialogue of: *How could this happen? This is unbelievable. This sucks. I can't believe my car is gone. What if it got scratched while they towed it? What is that guy's problem? Who cares if I parked there? The lot was empty. This is so unfair.*

I called the number I'd gotten from the sign that said Unauthorized Vehicles Will Be Towed. Yes, they had my car. It would cost $150 to get it out of hock.

This *me, me, me* dialogue passed fairly quickly. My ego was affronted. It couldn't accept the reality that I had acted badly and been completely busted for it. After a few minutes' walk, I came around to accepting it. I shouldn't have done it. I should have left myself more time to look for parking. But my mind's machinations were still more about how I should have avoided the results of my selfish actions. As I walked in the hot sunshine, this too eventually passed. My mind settled into the now, enjoying the walk, adjusting to the fact of losing the money and wasting my time. It accepted the powerlessness of being carless in a city where everybody was busily driving themselves crazy. It accepted that there was no taxi and that in the time it would take to call one I could actually walk to the tow yard. Eventually, the mind came right with it all.

Then came the self-recrimination. I began to feel terrible at how I had treated Louis. I had taken his initial generosity of letting me park there the first time and run with it. I had lied to his face when he said I ignored him. I had been careless, greedy, and condescending. I hated the way I had treated him. The walk disappeared. My mind became a battlefield of guilt and self-recrimination.

And I'm not saying I shouldn't have had this reaction. It shows a sign of conscience. But as my teacher Catherine says, along with much psychological literature, there is a difference between remorse and guilt.

REMORSE VERSUS GUILT

I was feeling remorseful for my treatment of Louis. It was a true feeling. It was deserved, given my actions. But when it moved into guilt, it became a knife that my mind began to use to stab me.

Remorse is a feeling, but guilt is the result of a thought.

The mind is always looking for primacy. It has no compunction about asserting its mastery at every moment, using anything as a cudgel, particularly our own failings. We are all coping with the pressures of big-city life, and we will all at one point or another act carelessly or with rudeness. This is inevitable because we are not yet anywhere near the enlightened state of Buddha or Christ.

But after you have acted badly and felt remorse, there is not much else to do except make amends. The event has passed—it is gone forever. If you are besieged by guilt, at this point you must recognize what is happening: the mind is running rampant.

Yes, I had acted carelessly, with rudeness and narcissism, but I wasn't generally a careless person. The only thing I could do about the litany of guilty thoughts could happen only in the present moment. I forgave myself for my failing and resolved to apologize to Louis the next time I saw him. I was wrong and would admit it to him. From that moment on, the guilt disappeared. I felt lighter and back in the moment, no longer bludgeoned by guilt.

It took a month before I saw Louis again (I certainly wasn't parking in that lot!). I parked at a meter one cloudy afternoon and there he was, hosing down the pavement. I called out to him.

"Hello, Louis." He looked up at me warily. I walked over to him, completely without any charge. "How are you?"

"I'm fine," he said. "I'm surprised that you remembered my name."

"How could I forget?" I joked. "You caused me much reflection and consternation."

He just looked at me, not sure what to expect. He was a young man, serious in demeanor and the way he did his job, and also with an inherent dignity.

"Listen, Louis." I stopped joking around. "I'm sorry for my behavior. I heard you call down to me that day and I ignored you. Then I was snotty to you after the car had been towed. There is no excuse for it. And I hope you'll accept my sincere apologies."

He turned off his hose and gravely offered his hand.

"I accept your apology," he said. "I'm sorry for the inconvenience it caused you."

We shook hands and smiled at each other.

"We are all still learning here on planet Earth," I said.

"Yes we are," he said. "Sometimes too slowly."

I nodded. He had that right. Now when I see Louis, we smile and wave.

A point of contention had been turned into connection. A feeling of anger had been replaced by warmth. Rudeness had been transformed.

GIVING VERSUS TAKING

Giving is the highest expression of potency.

—ERICH FROMM

So much urban rudeness has to do with a mind-set. Aside from adhering to an isolated identity, that mind-set is "What can I get?"

versus "How can I give?" This applies to time and space as well as objects. My time is more important than yours, so I'm going to shove ahead of you. My space should be inviolate, therefore I'm going to guard it assiduously and push you out of the way.

Ego is always grasping and trying to figure things out. It is always doing rather than being. It thinks it is in control and pushes and shoves its way through the day, looking out for number one. But this simply ends in exhaustion and resentment, no matter how much you come out on top. It is like being in a bad love relationship: if you are interested only in taking, no amount of love will fill you up. A feeling of love can be perpetuated only by expressing love, by giving love to your partner.

The same is true of your relationship with humankind in general. If you are only interested in taking, then you will never have enough. It's like a law of physics, some strange inverse correlation of the universe. The more you give, the more generous you feel toward your fellow human, the more you will feel like you have enough.

Don't take my word for this. Check it out with your direct experience. Instead of trying to get ahead, treat total strangers with generosity and see how you feel. On a toll road, try paying the toll for the car behind you—you won't believe the level of amazement of the other driver as he or she catches up to you and waves a thank-you. Try giving up your seat on the subway to somebody with a lot of bags. Not even an old or infirm person, but just somebody who's more burdened than you. Make room for somebody who enters a yoga class late and is looking for a space. Actively seek out ways to lighten a stranger's load.

How does it feel when you give versus when you take? Spend a day doing this and see what the results are. I guarantee you will end up feeling more relaxed, happy, energized, and content than if you stride through the day trying to get ahead of other people or ignoring them altogether.

But again, don't take my word for it. Spend a few hours being really rude. (Better make it just an hour.) Cut in front of people.

Grab the last item on sale at the store. Get in an argument with a total stranger over a parking spot.

How does that feel?

Part of our conditioning means competing for everything. Competition is actually seen as a virtue in our society. We want what we want, and we want it now.

Just notice it.

One night I went to a gathering for an organization trying to come up with a solution for peace in the Middle East. It was started by an Israeli and a Palestinian and involved a grassroots effort to create peace by circumventing intractable leaders on both sides. About two hundred people showed up, and it was a great success.

Afterward, everybody left at once. As I waited with my friend in the valet parking line, I noticed we weren't really moving ahead. We had started a conversation about the evening with another couple, and we all remarked that the line seemed to be moving very slowly. After paying attention for a few moments, I realized that people were ignoring the line and going right up to the valet station to pay the parking attendant. The line wasn't moving because the attendants were too busy handling the line crashers.

"Peace in the Middle East seems like a lofty goal right now, eh?" I said.

When we began to mention to people rushing past us that there was a line, a few looked at us as though we were being the rude ones for impinging on their right to move to the head of the line. But most apologized and took their place in the queue, saying they hadn't noticed it. They simply weren't paying attention.

GIVE PEOPLE THE OPPORTUNITY TO GIVE

Anywhere there are large groups of people it's useful to be awake to the behavior. Once in a while I go to Costco. I hate the store, which is just overwhelming, but like everybody, I love the prices. I needed to buy a box of writing paper, so I stopped in. As I got in the shortest line at the row of twenty cash registers with my one item, I was behind a woman with a full and enormous cart. I waited for her to notice me and let me go in front of her.

She didn't. It wasn't that she didn't see me; she did. She just ignored the situation.

I debated asking her if I could pass in front of her. But somehow I didn't want to ask this person for anything. Although attractive, her face was drawn tight in a perpetual mask against the world. The vibe was "Don't mess with me; I'll win." I could see her saying, "You'll have to wait your turn," and I didn't want to put myself in a position of being refused. So I waited, like a dolt.

Later, when I thought about it, I realized that I was operating out of a subtle form of protective egotism. I didn't want to ask for help in that moment because to do so would be to put myself in an apparent position of weakness to a possibly unpleasant person. No way was my ego going to do that! I was also living in a sense of worry about a future outcome—again a sign the ego-mind was strategizing about what was going to happen next. This is what the mind does—it ignores the present moment or only uses the present as a means to an end. Notice that most of our thinking is in this vein.

One of the aspects of being loving and awake is to allow other people the opportunity to give. It's putting yourself in the seemingly vulnerable position of receiving, whether with loved ones or with strangers. Now, it's possible they will refuse or resent you for forcing them to be polite. But how bad you feel will only be a measure of how much you identify with how people treat you. If your sense of self is dependent upon this, then inevitably you will suffer because inevitably somebody somewhere will treat you poorly.

If I had been feeling free in that moment in Costco, then what difference would the woman's response have made? I wouldn't even have been thinking about the response, as it's simply a form of the mind factorizing. And if I wasn't experiencing my own freedom, would any amount of generosity have made me feel it?

What all this mental activity in fact does is corrupt the moment of spontaneity. I could have asked her spontaneously and without the need for her to say yes (a preference, of course, but not a dire need) and she could have responded in whatever way she would respond. By not doing so I prevented her from having the opportunity to be giving, and for us to form a moment of connection. If I had interrupted the woman's tight stance against the world, giving her the opportunity to come out of herself, maybe I would have actually been of service in the moment.

This may sound convoluted, but it's not. It's in giving that we can experience connection in the moment, breaking up our isolation. It's in giving that we experience the greatest form of pleasure, even when it's in giving the other person a chance to give.

The Tao says: "All streams flow to the sea because it is lower than they are. Humility gives it its power."

When being humble in this way, every single situation becomes an opportunity to exercise the generosity of receptivity. Giving people a chance to give is a service.

IGNORING AS RUDENESS

The immature think that knowledge and action are different, but the wise see them as the same.

—BHAGAVAD GITA 5:4–5

There is another kind of rudeness that is less hardened but no less insidious. I call it the "you're not there" syndrome. It consists of things like talking on the cell phone while paying for something at a store's register. Haven't we all done this? You're fumbling for money, listening and talking on the phone, asking "How much is it?" while the clerk waits with arms folded. Meanwhile you're sharing your entire conversation with everybody else waiting in line, whether they want to hear about your previous night's activity or not.

Distracted, you're not there for either the conversation or the transaction at hand.

But it goes further than that. The "you're not there" syndrome doesn't just refer to your lack of presence; it refers to how you're treating the other people in your environment. They are simply not human, having been reduced down to the purest form of the transaction, namely, taking your money. They might as well be an ATM. When you don't acknowledge the other living, breathing human in front of you, it increases both people's sense of separation. Because they are at work they will not say anything; they have to be polite and put up with the rude behavior because their jobs depend upon it. But just because they don't say something doesn't mean they aren't thinking it.

The interplay of our actions with our feelings of either separation or connection to the world is profound. Talking on the cell phone makes people lose a sense of themselves in relation to their environment. They simply forget where they are. They are not present or aware of their surroundings and the people in it. When in this forgetfulness, they become stuck in their own narrow world, wrapped around itself in an endless spiral.

Talking on cell phones while driving results in an estimated 1.5 million auto accidents, resulting in 2,600 deaths, 330,000 serious injuries, and $43 billion in damages. If it distracts you to the point of causing a car accident, imagine how rude and unaware it comes across at the checkout counter.

Instead of wanting people to be less rude, be less rude yourself. And don't bother trying to change other people's rudeness, but rather simply adjust your own attitude.

As Anaïs Nin said: "We do not see the world as it is. We see it as we are."

Ultimately, rudeness arises, but how it affects you is up to you.

PLAY WITH THE RUDE WORLD

After getting my MFA from the University of Southern California's film school I worked as a waiter in a popular, hip restaurant in Venice, California. It was the perfect job, as it allowed me to write during the day and have a social outlet at night. I was optioning my scripts at the time but not yet making enough money to live off my writing, so I needed a mindless job to pay the bills.

In general the clientele were regulars who were well behaved. Occasionally there would be rude people who seemed to need more than good service and expected a certain level of groveling. It was another permutation of the bouncer syndrome—they had a small amount of power in a limited circumstance and enjoyed it a bit too much.

Some nights every table seemed to fall into this category. Rude. Demanding. Impatient. Nasty. After a while I began to ask myself what was going on during these FUBAR nights (FUBAR is a military acronym for "fucked up beyond all repair"). Why were they happening? Was there anything that I was doing to contribute to their rudeness?

What I began to notice was that these nights coincided with nights that I didn't want to be there. I was tired or cranky or just sick of asking people if they wanted soup or salad with their entree. Or maybe I was feeling above the job with my Ivy League undergraduate degree as well as a master's degree. Or perhaps a Hollywood professional with whom I had a meeting earlier in the week showed up and I felt that person no longer saw me as a writer but as a waiter. And maybe even the very worst had happened: a fellow graduate of USC came in and I had to wait on him or her. These were times when not only didn't I want to be there, but I wanted to crawl under a rock. Such was my egotism.

Though I always performed my job with competence, I began to notice that on the nights I didn't want to be there, the people would behave horribly—sending back food, complaining to me or to the manager, or being downright rude or dismissive.

After I noticed the connection I began to wonder what I could do? It was happening right as I was beginning to be exposed to these teachings, and I realized I had a choice as to how I could view my job. In every moment I was free to make a different choice from the one I was making. Was I a failure or in service to my dream? Were my customers jerks or needing attention? It all depended on the way you looked at it.

Eventually I tried to see bringing food to people's tables as literally bringing life to them. I tried to see it as an honor and a chance to be giving. Some days I would be in this zone, but many days I wouldn't. People weren't treating me well, and I didn't know what to do.

Then one Friday night when it was extremely busy, I had the table from hell. A middle-aged couple sat down. I saw them from across the restaurant but had four things stacked in front of me to do before I approached the table.

"JB on the rocks and a glass of chardonnay," the man barked after I greeted them. He didn't look up.

I returned with the drinks within minutes.

"Is this what we can expect? To be ignored all night?" The man still didn't bother looking up. "Because if it is, then you might as well get the manager right now."

It just went on like that. They sent back the soup: not hot enough. They sent back the salad: too much dressing. They were rude in manner and in speech, saying peremptorily, "Take it back."

By the time the entrees were ready to be served, I was ready for homicide. And in a kind of horrible unconscious chain reaction, my other tables were "going rude." It was like I was a whipping boy for the egocentric, the needy, the demanding, and the dismissive. A whole gallery of unpleasant people, pushing, pushing, pushing.

In the middle of the insanity, I paused and took a deep breath by the bread station in the corner of the kitchen, trying to find my balance. What was going on? What the hell did they want from me?

I had a small epiphany. They wanted attention, but more than that, they wanted love. And they were picking up on the fact that I wasn't about to give it to them. That I was actually withholding it from them. I wasn't rude. I wasn't hostile. In fact, I was friendly enough in a cool and professional way. I was serving, but without love or joy, and that's what they wanted. They wanted *connection*.

This is true of *any* kind of service, even service at a much higher level than waiting tables. Activists who were initially spurred by outrage or anger but haven't moved beyond that may, in their frustration, become bitter. Instead of being joyfully *for* their cause, like the environment, the activists become bitterly *against* those in opposition. They walk around in a state of perpetual contraction and rage. This actually doesn't help a cause or spread respect and understanding in the world. It just adds another layer to the acrimony and hostility pervading the front lines of debate.

We are talking about rudeness in this chapter, but I think the dynamic is the same in any conflict. As the Dalai Lama wrote, "If we ourselves remain angry and then sing world peace, it has little meaning. So, you see, first our individual self must learn peace. This we can practice. Then we can teach the rest of the world."

I decided in that moment by the bread station to conduct an experiment in peace. I would go back out on the floor and give my tables as much love as possible. I would shower them with affection and positive attention.

My ego immediately rebelled. Why should I go the extra mile? They were odious. Why should I grovel at their feet, obsequious, when they were so spiteful? Somebody as decent and talented as myself? The little "I" went into a paroxysm of fear and protection, rebelling against its apparent self-abnegation.

Still, against this litany, I stowed my attitude and went out to the floor. I walked up to the most difficult table and really looked at the couple for the first time. The first thing I noticed was that they were unhappy. They were unhappy separately, and the way they were hunched over their entrees, not looking at each other, told me they were unhappy together. There was no life between them, as if the pall of a horrible disagreement had hung over them for years. They were miserable and in such suffering that a splendid feast could have been laid on their table and they would have sent it back. I approached them on a wave of compassion.

"I just wanted to check in with you and see if everything was all right." They nodded without looking up. It was going to take an act of real generosity to crack these two.

"I'm pleased you're enjoying it," I said kindly. "Can I get you both another drink on the house?"

"What?"

They looked at me directly for the first time all night, and I swear that it was with suspicion. They had reaped what they sowed for so long in their personal exchanges, they were so used to being met with the tight formality one gives to an unpleasant person, that they couldn't understand what I was saying or the warm energy behind it.

"It would be my pleasure to buy you a drink," I said.

"Why, yes," said the man, his dour face suddenly cracking into a smile. "Would you like one, dear?"

"Yes, I would . . . thank you very much," said the woman.

"My pleasure," I said. I went and got them their drinks. When I returned, the two of them were talking to each other. They both smiled at me. I put their dessert menus on the table.

"Please take your time and enjoy your drinks," I said. Then I went around to every table. I didn't buy any more drinks, but I took a moment to slow down and really inquire how they were. I looked beyond their demands, rudeness, and egocentricity and saw the insecurity that was driving it. The kinder I was, the better I felt, and the more the night turned around. By the end of the night, even the most difficult people had warmed up. I was flying along, absorbed in my work, cracking jokes, connecting. I no longer felt above the job and I no longer resented the people, even those who were rude or snotty or demanding.

After that night, I saw in those shifts as a waiter (and there were only four a week) an opportunity to give love to total strangers in each moment.

And every time I was hit by a dose of really difficult people, I checked myself and my attitude. Was I feeling superior to the situation? Was I on automatic pilot? This self-inquiry became second nature whenever I found myself frustrated or annoyed by other people's attitudes. I began to be able to almost instantly change my heart and my mind and meet them in the moment with compassion. The worse they behaved, the more love I expressed. The restaurant became a living experiment.

Sometimes the universe seems to reveal the machinery of its inner workings. You get a whiff of how things are related and attracted to each other in a way that seems almost magical, but isn't. It is usually the result of deep insight into the natural connectivity of things. This happens only by fully being in the now, dropping any identification with the thoughts that are running in your head, judging, comparing, and separating. In my case it was letting go of *I like this person but not that person* and *This job sucks* and *I'm too good for it.* When I dropped those thoughts by coming into the present moment, I was able to see more clearly and deeply what was going on and what my job really was, which was to give love.

It's everyone's job. And our real reason for being on the planet.

One busy night I walked down the length of the restaurant and people at every table said hello. There were my regulars (people who used to request me as their waiter); there was a development exec from Hollywood who had almost optioned one of my scripts; there was a friend from USC who had just sold a spec script. Not one was rude. As I got to the end of the restaurant I turned around—I felt such a connection with whole place and everybody in it. There wasn't even a hint of shame or the idea that I shouldn't be there. I was there, really there. Fully in the moment. Awake.

I had a distinct thought that came to me like a bolt—not so much a thought, but a deep experience of knowing: *I am done with this place. I have integrated all parts of my life in this one walk of absolute liveliness down the length of the restaurant.*

The next week I got my first Hollywood job, and it enabled me to quit the restaurant for good.

POSITIVE PERSPECTIVE

We do not see things as they are. We see them as we are.

—THE TALMUD

Rudeness and narcissism are phenomena that arise like any other; we can seem to be at the mercy of our own and other people's attitudes all the time. As our own reactivity gets provoked, as our experience is obscured by a balloon of conditioning that completely obliterates the moment, we can instantly be reduced to a primal level, screaming our heads off at somebody for being rude. But all it takes is a pinprick of awareness to pop the balloon of reactivity. And when it happens, all the conditioning disappears, leaving only what always was and always will be: consciousness, love, being.

One day I was walking down the street approaching a corner. At the end of the block I heard screaming. As I looked I saw a big man running down the street toward me with two Chihuahuas on leashes. They were galloping along trying to keep up on their spindly legs, yapping away, looking up at their master like he was playing a game. But the guy was seriously angry.

"You motherfucker!" he shouted. "I'm going to kill you!"

He was charging right at me like an angry rhinoceros. I had never seen him before in my life. I braced myself for impact. But, breathing hard, he ran right by me, stopped at the corner, and gave the backside of a BMW the finger.

"I'll fucking kill you next time I see you!" he screamed, apoplectic, at the car. The dogs danced at his feet, yapping encouragement.

With that he turned around and walked back toward me. Everybody in earshot had stopped and was staring, including myself. The vision of the large man with the tiny dogs would have been funny except for the size of his anger.

Then a window slid open in the building we were standing at.

"Shut the fuck up!" a guy shouted out the window. "Who wants to listen to your bullshit?"

"Who you talking to?" screamed the big guy. "I'll kick your ass!"

"I'm talking to you! Keep your big mouth shut! I'm trying to sleep!"

With that the guy slammed shut the window and yanked the shades closed.

It was like watching a surreal comedy as people passed the hot potato of rudeness and anger from person to person. I found myself staring in momentary amazement at the reactive dance, one set of conditioning meeting another.

"What're you looking at?" the big man snarled at me, looking for an outlet for his anger.

"I'm not quite sure," I blurted out, still amazed by the man's behavior.

"That guy drove across the crosswalk while I was still in it," the big man fumed, pointing in the direction of the now absent BMW. "He's supposed to wait until the crosswalk is clear. He could have run over my dogs."

"That's rude," I said sympathetically, kneeling down to pet the little dogs, which started licking my hands.

"It *is* rude. Fucking rude." The man looked up at the window balefully. "This whole city is rude."

With that he walked away in a huff. He had no idea how rude he was being by subjecting the world to his cursing and anger. He was in pure reaction mode, responding to the rudeness he perceived he was experiencing.

But even though I felt a rising tide of reactivity in me, as I watched how careful he was with his dogs I suddenly saw it from a positive perspective. All his anger and rudeness was simply because he loved his dogs. He was afraid of losing them or them getting hurt; it was the cause of his reactivity. When I saw this, instead of provoking reactivity in me, it actually created compassion for the man. He was doing the best he had with the tools he had. And the man in the window was just somebody who had been woken in the middle of a nap.

We can be saved from our own reactivity and narcissism by seeing the positive or neutral intent of the other person.

Breathe half a breath of another person's life, and you will find it impossible to hate that individual. You will understand that person's pain, his conditioning, his suffering. You will also understand that while you get to go on in your life just by walking away, that person has to live with himself 24/7.

YOU'RE NEVER STUCK

One time I was on a yoga retreat and had carpooled with three women, all strangers to me but friends with each other. Let's call them Michelle, Jane, and Heather. On the way home, Michelle and Jane wanted to drive straight back to Los Angeles. Heather and I wanted to stop in Santa Barbara and see the sights, perhaps getting lunch. A huge battle erupted among the three women and it got quite heated, with some ugly words exchanged. Michelle finally drew the line.

"I'm driving. It's my car. I need to get home. That's it, it's final," she declared. "We're not stopping."

"That is so rude!" Heather sputtered. "Oh, so it's your car and you get to make the decisions? What about democracy? What if I was driving? Would it be fair that I make the decision?"

"This isn't a democracy."

Heather went ballistic. I, on the other hand, had voiced my opinion and desire and was largely silent. I didn't want to get in a huge fight with strangers, especially not after a yoga retreat, the energy from which was draining away with each rude exchange. But the three friends continued to go at it as only close friends can. As we passed Santa Barbara the tension in the car mounted. I finally spoke up.

"Michelle, could you pull over here, please?" I said.

"Pull over? Why?" Michelle was puzzled. "Are you sick?"

"No, I'm going to get out."

"Get out?" All three women turned to me.

"What do you mean, get out?" Heather asked.

"I'm going to get out of the car," I said. "It's a beautiful day and I feel like lunch in Santa Barbara. I can catch a bus or hitchhike back."

"Hitchhike?" Jane said. "Are you crazy?"

"Not at all," I replied. "I hitchhiked around North America for six months when I was twenty. You can hitchhike anywhere."

This touched off a firestorm of debate. It was as if I had suggested that we all strip and walk down the center of the highway stark naked.

"You can't hitchhike," said Michelle.

"You want to go home, and I respect that." I said. "Heather and I want to stay. It doesn't have to be an either/or proposition. I really don't mind. I'm sure there's a bus."

I looked at Heather, who was amused behind all the chaos.

"You're welcome to come with me if you want," I said to her.

Michelle pulled the car over. More debate. They could see I was sincere in my intention to stay. Finally it was decided we would stop for lunch in Santa Barbara. We drove in silence. They were truly nonplussed by my behavior—they couldn't figure it out. Eventually everybody relaxed over lunch and we had a fine time.

My request to stay in Santa Barbara wasn't a bluff or a power play. It's just been my experience that you can always get out of the car, both literally or metaphorically. When you are confronted by rude or narcissistic behavior, simply leave. You are rarely truly stuck anywhere, even in a car that's being driven by someone else. You just have to be willing to accept the consequences of your freedom.

One of the keys to freedom is to avoid trying to change people's position. Michelle didn't really need to go home. As was revealed by the argument, she didn't really have anything to do. She just liked to mentally get herself together for the upcoming week. Now, you could argue with that need, as the other women did, and have an encounter rife with bad feelings. But it's better to be generous and accept her need at face value.

Try to receive all people as beautiful exactly where they are, even if that place seems tight or controlling. Just as you are on your journey toward wakefulness, so are they. Don't expect them to skip an important step, which is wherever they happen to be in that moment. Not only is it useless—think how many times people have told you to snap out of whatever it is you were doing—but you would want them to accord you the same respect. Although wakefulness is available in an instant, my experience has been that everybody has to go through whatever process they have to go through.

When you encounter rudeness, it's like having somebody spit in your face. If you spit back, by either trying to change the other person or trying to win your point, you create anger, conflict, and separation—ironically, the same things that happen when you try to get ahead by being rude.

NARCISSISM IN LINE

The present, the here, the now,
That's all the life I get,
I live each moment in full,
In kindness, in peace, without regret.
—CHADE MENG

My friend Simone loves to crash movie lines. She just thinks the rules don't apply to her and revels in her lawlessness. Recently I went to the movies with her and another friend named Jack. We bought our tickets and then saw that the line stretched around the block.

"Okay," said Simone, eyeing the line. "Let's see where we can cut in."

Jack and I looked at each other. We wanted to get good seats for the movie and possibly even to sit together. The only way to do that was to crash the line, but Jack would have none of it. I reluctantly agreed with him, more out of a sense of duty on civility than because I wanted to. Simone, however, disagreed.

"You can be sheep if you want to be. Not me."

With that she split off, and Jack and I went to the back of the line. After a few minutes Simone reappeared.

"Come on, you guys, get with the program," she exclaimed, grabbing my arm. "You've got the tickets to get in. The lady at the front is holding our spot."

Jack and I were confused—didn't she have her ticket? We allowed ourselves to be dragged up to the front of the line, right up to the woman ripping tickets in half.

"Here are my friends," Simone announced. Other people around us gave us withering looks. Jack and I hesitated.

"Give her your tickets," Simone commanded. And we did. In that moment there was a bit of a thrill from beating the system. But it was a Pyrrhic victory. Even with all that stress and hustling, the theater was nearly full. We were going to have to split up and sit separately. Jack went to the back of the theater, where he liked to sit. Simone and I sat in seats separated by a row in the middle.

"Arthur!" I heard Simone call my name. She was motioning me to her row, where a seat had magically appeared. I got up and moved.

"Did you ask the whole row of people to move down?" I asked, noticing that a formerly empty seat was now occupied.

"No, I didn't ask," Simone said. "That woman just organized it so we could sit together. She saw we were separated and she moved the whole row so we could sit together." Simone pointed to a woman engaged in a conversation with a friend.

"Notice the difference in your behavior and hers," I said dryly to Simone. "You cut in line, alienating everybody along the way, and she actually is awake enough to see that we are sitting in separate rows. She then takes the initiative to move the whole row down so we can sit together. We should be sitting at her feet."

I raised an eyebrow at Simone. We often give each other a hard time, acting as each other's conscience, watching each other's back for slips into a lack of wakefulness. "Don't you feel terrible now?"

"Terrible," responded Simone, not feeling terrible at all. We laughed.

"Bad girl," I said, slapping her wrist lightly.

"You Americans are such good little rule followers." Simone is from Kosovo. "I like coming from an essentially lawless place, where people just do what they want."

"Spoken like a true spiritual adept," I said.

"Like that woman over there. The skinny, dyed blonde?" Simone pointed. "She said to me in line, 'That's really uncool.' I told her that I was more than capable of taking responsibility for my actions without her opinion."

"So you were rude and then rude about being rude."

"Yes. But I was consistent," Simone said. We laughed again, both recognizing that it is occasionally a relief to be spiritually incorrect.

Rudeness comes in many forms, but at its core is a kind of narcissism. Think about your friends who are always late. They always have an excuse for leaving you waiting, but what they are essentially saying is that their time is more valuable than yours, that they are more important than you. They are breaking their social contract with you out of a momentary lapse into narcissism. The best way to deal with the chronically late is to accept this as a flaw and not expect them to be on time. But no matter how you slice it, when somebody is always late, they are being rude.

And we have all done it. We all have our moments. Sometimes we will even be gleefully cognizant of our rudeness. It is not a way to live life, for all the reasons enumerated in this chapter. But as mentioned earlier, after the rudeness is done, what is there to do about it? It's gone. The behavior is dead.

Again, only this moment is livable. So the game of the moment can involve the conversation about the rudeness. Not as a way for self-flagellation, but as a way of play and learning and fun. While we all try our best, there is no point in adhering to a sanctimonious, squeaky clean vision of life and then beating ourselves up for every infraction. That can be as rigid, controlling, and unforgiving as any other past story or identification that makes us believe "I'm a bad person."

We are constantly given the opportunity to experience, examine, and then forgive our own rudeness and our reactivity to the rudeness we encounter, but why make it like drinking castor oil? Treat yourself and all situations lightly. Let it all be play, even when learning the lessons we are here to learn.

So it is best to see rudeness, like all other phenomena, as an opportunity instead of a problem. Eckhart Tolle writes: "There have been many people for whom limitation, failure, loss, illness, or pain in whatever form turned out to be their greatest teacher. It taught them to let go of false self-images and superficial ego-dictated goals and desires. It gave them depth, humility, and compassion."

There is a deep lesson hidden in every negative experience or moment of sufferings although it might be unseen by you at the time. Spiritual failures such as lapses into rudeness provides a chance to look more closely, understand more deeply, and view with compassion and humor the battle we have with our conditioned greediness.

In this way of learning and seeing, in every moment of every day, there is an opportunity to be helpful, generous, and alert to your fellow man's needs, from the small to the large. Every day we can take the opportunity to be kind, like the woman in the theater, rather than selfish. Every day gives us the chance to be engaged with the world, moment by moment, awake to our own rudeness, conditioning, and behavior. It is a beautiful and self-regenerating activity only available in the here and now, in which we learn to see what ultimately matters and what is dust in the wind.

In the end there is only one antidote to conditioned selfishness. It is only through giving that the fossilized small self cracks like a glaze of ice on a winter tree, leaving something behind that is warm and alive to the gifts of the moment.

It is only in this way that we encounter the unencumbered self.

SCARING OURSELVES TO DEATH

Transcending Media Negativity

The map is not the territory.
—ALFRED KORZYOSKI

Three years ago I went to Machu Picchu in Peru. It was a stunning journey to the ancient spiritual city floating in the clouds above the western edge of the Amazon jungle. A couple of days later I found myself walking down the crooked streets of a tiny and very poor village of Peruvian Indians. It was dark, and except for an occasional dog the dusty streets were devoid of life. Once in a while I would see a kerosene lamp in a window.

I thought happily, *I am truly in the middle of nowhere.*

Then I looked in the open doorway of a small hut. Inside were three people huddled around a tiny television, which was playing the movie *Robocop*. I stared at the scene: the dirt floor, the kerosene lamp, and *Robocop*. It was a moment that slammed home the far-reaching effect of American pop culture. I wondered what vision of America was being taken from that movie. In a moment of history when globalization is a foregone conclusion and our pop culture seeps into the oldest civilizations on the planet, watching them watch *Robocop* was positively surreal. As someone who sometimes wrote junky action movies, it made me deeply question my own role as a screenwriter.

THE BIG SLEEP

All in all, it's just another brick in the wall.
—PINK FLOYD

The creeping spread of American culture across the globe is a sad thing to watch. Inexorably, the mystery and danger of the world are being drained and replaced by a commodity, something easily digestible for the largest number of people.

The German philosopher Immanuel Kant wrote the following in 1784:

> After the guardians have first made their domestic cattle dumb and have made sure that these placid creatures will not dare take a single step without the harness of the cart to which they are tethered, the guardians then show them the danger which threatens if they try to go alone. Actually, however, this danger is not so great, for by falling a few times they would finally learn to walk alone. But an example of this failure makes them timid and ordinarily frightens them away from all further trials.

The same could be said today, with the word *media* substituted for *guardians.* In the West we are drowning in media and can't even see it; a source of nonstop information, stimulation, and hype, the media are as ubiquitous as the air that we breathe. They affect how we live, ensure the timidity of our lives, and control our vision of the world. They impact almost every subject in this book, from homelessness to status envy. Conformist values are relentlessly hammered into us at every turn, making living an alternative life not just like swimming upstream, but like swimming in a completely different stream altogether.

The media create a collective vision, often of fear or consumerism or mindless reproduction, that not many people question.

In fact, it's a vision that the rest of the world is busily absorbing and a lifestyle to which they now aspire. The third world looks to the fast pace and the materialism of the first world and wants in on the action.

In this way the media produce the opposite of a spiritual life, which has simplicity and silence as its by-products. The media, in all its forms, are about *adding* sensation—their natural by-product is stimulation, their message is more, more, more! This is not to say that the media can't be used for deeply spiritual forms of communication or can't be included as just another form of consciousness. My teacher's teacher, H. W. L. Poonja, used to love to watch cricket and bad Indian soap operas. It was just another phenomenon arising in his awareness. But very few of us are marinated deeply enough in nondual awareness to be unaffected by unending stimulation.

We are taught to devalue our direct experience because we're told it's not as valuable as what we see in the media. It's not real unless it's on television. It's not glamorous unless it's in the movies. We are told our lives are humdrum in comparison. In the end, we can become jangled, numb, and bored to the subtle revelations of the world.

We can also end up misinformed thanks to the tsunami of exaggerations, staged events, and spinning press releases we view on a daily basis. Sometimes these hoodwinks work: sometimes they backfire. But no one cares, because the media, in their breathless search to hold our attention, have already moved on. Whether we move on to war or the next celebrity murder trial, little attention is paid to any mistakes that might have accrued along the way. Once the carcass of one story is gnawed over, it's on to the next.

We all probably remember Eric Rudolph, the survivalist who at one point topped the FBI's most-wanted list and is accused of bombing the Olympics in Georgia. Does anybody remember Rick Jewell, the original suspect, whose life was destroyed by the original media frenzy around the story? It doesn't matter that he was the wrong man. The idea is to get the story or, if it's not there, to create it in as compelling a way as possible.

Even a venerable and respected newspaper such as the *New York Times* is not immune to manipulation, as evidenced by the Jayson Blair confabulations in dozens of stories. Another mini-mediathon in its own right, it touched off storms of debate about affirmative action, among other things. Blair will be long forgotten by the time you read this, but the fact that you can't always trust what you read in the newspaper, even the *New York Times,* shouldn't be.

The media hold our attention for a moment and then push everything out of our consciousness with the next story or entertainment event. It almost feels like there's a conspiracy to keep us jangled, overstimulated, and working too hard to pay attention to deeper and more important issues. Couple this with the cuts in budgets for basic education (a school in Oregon has resorted to a blood drive in order to buy books—could anything be more symbolic?), which are symbolic of the decline in the level of education in a country where 53 percent of the people think that Vietnam is in North America. This dumbing down then makes us more susceptible to lies about our reality coming from more and more media sources. With the rise in the ethos of news as entertainment, the already blurry lines between spin and news, fiction and nonfiction, and newsmakers and journalists have all but disappeared. George Orwell said to use language precisely so we can name things correctly, lest we fall prey to the phony and untrue. I believe we live in Orwellian times, where a program to log in wildlife areas is called a "healthy forest initiative" and a program allowing thousands of coal-burning power plants to spew greater quantities of poisonous gases into the air is dubbed the "clear skies initiative." In a self-fulfilling cycle we spend less money on education, creating a less literate populace incapable of deciphering lies from the truth, and more easily distracted by the media from what is truly important.

While there may not be a vast conspiracy that is orchestrating this, there is something about human nature that is very drawn to this way of being. We are drawn to the stimulation of more, more, faster, faster. The answer has to do with avoidance, mostly of our own death. In this way we use the media in all forms to circumvent questions of our own mortality that may arise in quieter moments. Better to distract ourselves with the hurly-burly of digital life.

This media glut doesn't bring us knowledge and it certainly doesn't bring us wisdom. Ironically, the very source we turn to in order to forget about the deeper issues like life and death makes us more afraid of death. The media plays on our neurotic fears and narrows our experience of life.

If we simply stopped chasing the next media high, we might be able to sit still and feel our mortality as a natural conclusion to life. We might be able to be quiet enough to hear our deeper selves. But first we have to wake up from our deep media sleep.

UNPLUG FROM FEAR

The news, with its "if it bleeds, it leads" philosophy, aggravates this feeling of impending doom and anxiety, especially in today's environment of terrorism, war, and economic hardship. But whether it is anthrax, police chases, shark attacks, child abductions, orange terror alerts, or any number of stories to stoke our gory imagination, these are usually not our direct experience, but rather are the global equivalent of urban ghost stories. Those who see the world only through the prism of the media are destined to have their reality created for them by other people. Can your bathroom kill you? Tune in at eleven for the full report.

We are taught what to fear, what to think, and what should concern us in the future. The media present an unrelentingly negative picture of the world, and so America lives in a culture of fear that has very little to do with fact or direct experience. Over the past ten years homicides are down 20 percent, but the coverage of them is up 600 percent. Child abductions are down from the years 2002 and 2001, but one of our last mediathons makes it seem as if we are undergoing an epidemic. The truth is that family members involved in a custody battle perpetrate most child abductions, but you would never know it from the news.

Forty people a day are getting murdered, giving us eleven thousand homicides a year (fifteen hundred of which were accidents). As a result of what we see on the news, we are all locking our doors and not talking to strangers. But in America, *70 percent* of murders are done by people who know each other: husbands and wives, boyfriends and girlfriends, fellow students and colleagues. Locking the door is useless against people we know and welcome into our homes.

The dark side of human nature is within each of us. We all have the capability for every kind of behavior, from the most altruistic to the most heinous. If we are honest, we see that we have within us both the murderer and the saint. But it is much easier to blame externals for our own fears and problems. And the media are only too happy to oblige us, finding the bogeyman du jour to blame our fear on. The news would have us believe that the danger is everywhere without, rather than mostly within ourselves and our inner circle. This is turn makes people more fearful, distrustful, and malleable. Sometimes it backfires and the media itself become the bogeyman, blamed for behavior beyond their control for events that could be more easily traced back to family dysfunction. But that doesn't stop them from beating their drums of negativity.

All this adds up to avoiding looking closely at ourselves and reality. Even with the terrorist threat, we are much more likely to be hit by lightning than be hurt in a terrorist attack. We are more likely to have a car accident than either of those two events, yet the media continue to keep us in a state of paralyzing fear. From this fear comes the lie from certain quarters of our government that if we give them our freedom, they'll make us safe. And in our lack of discernment, we buy the lie.

We all like this kind of fearful entertainment, a sort of global gossip over which we can shake our heads in amazement or judgment. But it is not entirely harmless; how can we question the very real economic and social injustice that is happening right under our nose as long as we are transfixed by the media, in a trance? While the crisis in the environment continues unchecked and a distinct species of plant or animal becomes extinct every twenty minutes, Dr. Donald Levin in *American Scientist Magazine* we dither about shark attacks, our fear of which primarily stems from *a movie*.

According to the United Nations, 50,000 children a day die from starvation (roughly two a minute, seventeen million a year). We, in our insularity, become more concerned about the latest celebrity who got arrested for a DUI.

It makes us seem as if we are frantically rearranging deck chairs on a the *Titanic*. We are afraid of this or that but aren't seeing the larger picture because we are willfully keeping ourselves blinded by the media glare.

Meanwhile the ship is sinking under our feet.

SEEING THROUGH ANOTHER'S EYES

The important thing is not to stop questioning.

—ALBERT EINSTEIN

The media can either connect us to the world or insulate us from the world.

But the absence of critical thinking engendered by the media, those "guardians" to whom we hand over much of our decision-making capability, has reached epidemic proportions. Either way, more and more people are getting their vision of life through the filters of the media. But understand that the filter has somebody else's agenda and subjective reality smeared all over it. It is not reality!

The case of Jessica Lynch in the war on Iraq is a perfect example. What was portrayed as a heroic rescue in hostile territory, was actually an assault on a hospital with no soldiers in it, just doctors and terrified patients. I have nothing negative to say against Jessica

Lynch; she has suffered mightily and been private and discreet about her ordeal. It's the media and their handlers that are difficult to swallow.

Was Jessica Lynch a hero, somebody who knowingly risked her life to protect others? Not when you think about it; she was part of a supply team that took a wrong turn in the desert. But in their search for a pretty, blond heroine, the media, in a truly *Wag the Dog* moment, tried to spin her story of a victim in harm's way into a golden story of heroism.

We believe these stories because we want to have a heroic vision of ourselves in the world. This in turn makes it easier for the military to recruit future "heroes" from the ranks of poor Americans. Fed a nonstop story of heroism, real and imagined, or forced by economic circumstances, these young people join an army expecting not just a job, but an adventure. They are then sent into pre-emptive war with a lot of flag-waving by the very elite who wouldn't dream of letting their sons and daughters go. But we should look askance at anything that manipulates the truth, which is like writing our myths in disappearing ink. In the long run it only makes people more cynical.

We can't discern the truth because we are not out in the world having a direct experience. Whether you were for or against our recent wars, the coverage must give us all some pause. The sanitized, bloodless representation of war, presented and framed with slick logos, pounding music and "patriotic" jingoism, doesn't begin to convey the reality of the dead and the maimed. It doesn't convey the terror of the soldiers and civilians on the ground.

And most importantly, it doesn't begin to convey the idea that everybody involved is human and the death of an Iraqi civilian is no less worth mourning than the death of an American soldier.

The media insulates and separates us from the rest of the world. We have the feeling that we've been to places because we've seen them on television. But because we don't travel, we don't have direct contact with other countries—they aren't real to us. So the countries are more easily demonized for legitimately disagreeing with us about something like the war in Iraq, even if they are our allies who have seen the devastation of war firsthand, such as France and Germany. (Did we ever think we'd see the day when we were saying to the Germans, "Hey, you're not militaristic enough"?)

In the rush of war coverage, the "enemy" isn't shown as having the same concerns and feelings as us. But an acquaintance of mine who was in Baghdad before the bombing started said that life continued as it does the world over; people were eating, going to cafés, and working. They were also extremely friendly to her as an American, despite the fact that war between the two countries was imminent. But if you relied on the stock footage of Iraqis in the streets waving guns, your vision of the country would be very different indeed. In any military conflict, the opposition is demonized into the animalistic "other," the monster that we should fear and destroy.

I'm not advocating we all go to war zones to see what is happening; obviously that's impractical. But we can at least search for different sources of news (overseas, Internet, alternative press, etc.) to balance the shifting agendas of the different media conglomerates.

We must also remain focused on the reality of the people behind the images, whether of war or of other news.

We must never let ourselves be manipulated out of the truth of their humanity.

NEWS AS ENTERTAINMENT

Enlightenment is not imagining figures of light
but making the darkness conscious.
—CARL JUNG

News is now coming at us as a form of entertainment.

The ultimate way this happens is in the phenomenon of the mediathon. Whether it's the killing of Nicole Simpson, Princess

Diana's death, or Kobe Bryant's trial, the mediathon is another way in which we are glued together around the television set, creating connectedness through external events.

I want to be clear that I am not above this. In fact, I watch most mediathons with the kind of drool reserved for crack addicts staring at a full pipe. But I also realize that it's an indirect way of connecting with people. And I never lose sight of the fact that I am being given a version of the world that is highly editorialized, even if only by what is included or omitted. It is a distortion of reality, a subjective view, owned by conglomerates with their own agenda. And even if you agree with the ideology being propounded, it is still the equivalent of junk food.

The nonstop drip of stimulation that seduces us away from the richness of direct experience makes us less vital, less skeptical, and more passive. It weakens our discernment and intelligence because it is an essentially shallow experience, offering up reality in a filtered, edited, and packaged view of what is essentially a very messy world.

There is a place for the mindless slurping of pop-culture junk food, but I usually try to do it in the company of friends who like to shout at the TV and turn watching it into an interactive sport rather than a passive swilling.

Still, too often I find myself in front of the television alone, killing time or tuning out. Again, there is nothing wrong with this, but *it is not a direct experience of anything but the media*. Ultimately the only way to have that is to unplug the TV and walk outside your house or apartment.

SNAP OUT OF THE TRANCE

I was getting my MFA at USC film school when the LA riots happened. Even before the hysteria of that day, South Central LA was depicted every night on the news as a dangerous place filled with predators, crack addicts, and gangs. After the riots, the mediathon depicted it as a war zone. Yet I drove through those neighborhoods daily on the way to USC, both before and after the riots. I ate in the restaurants, shopped in the stores, and listened to music in various local (noncollegiate) bars. I interacted with the residents in small and large ways, and at no time did I feel threatened. If my own experience of that community was confined to depictions on the nightly news, I would never even have ventured into South Central, missing out on the warmth and richness of its residents. I would have been held hostage to the terrorist within me, with all his stories and fears.

When you get up from the couch and go for a walk, you experience life in all of its glory and uncertainty. When you go into a new part of your city and walk around, you are seeing for yourself what it is like. What you see, what you experience, is unique to you, not somebody else's vision. Every time you go into an unknown part of your city you have the opportunity to deconstruct stereotypes, become present, and learn from direct experience.

When you experience the wall-to-wall coverage of a mediathon, you are not seeing the people involved as real. When Princess Diana died, she was deified to the point of unreality. She became Saint Diana. The media gave the people what they wanted, even though the stories were no more true to the reality of the people involved than the coverage of her wedding and marriage was. The truth of Diana the person was flattened into an image for our own consumption.

The real danger here is that we are given the message that all people are not the same, that some are more important than others. This is something the media are constantly reinforcing: certain people are unique and important and others aren't. Therefore we should listen to the unique and important people in our world and discount the invisible and unimportant, including ourselves. We should trust the people on television because obviously they are important enough to be on television.

I know this is a radical thing to say in our typically hierarchical way of looking at the world, but *every single life on the planet has the same value*. Every human being, if you scratch the surface presentation and conditioning, feels pain, has hopes and fears, and enjoys the capacity for love. Every human life. This is an inalienable spiritual truth that the media refutes daily in its separation of people into leaders and followers, enemies and friends, rich and poor, heroes and villains, watchers and participants.

Don't fall for it. No one person is more valuable than another. Not the president or a rock star or the pope.

You can stand in their company simply because *you are*.

THE MAP IS NOT THE TERRITORY

It's become appallingly clear that our technology has surpassed our humanity.

—ALBERT EINSTEIN

Mating butterflies will fly to a picture of another butterfly instead of a real butterfly right next to it—as long as the picture is bigger than the actual butterfly. In much the same way, we are addicted to the media buzz of more, faster, louder, bigger. We are after the bigger bang. When we get used to a certain level of stimulation, we gradually go numb and need more and more to get off. It becomes an addiction. But after the hit is over, there's always a bit of a hangover.

The human equivalent of this butterfly effect is our relationship to magazines, pornography, film, and the Internet. We can become so enamored with the representation of beauty that we lose our sensitivity to the real thing. It becomes very difficult to resist a twenty-foot head with a four-foot smile.

Recently I was sitting at a café, people-watching, when I saw a perfect little scene. An attractive man had his nose in *Maxim*, flipping through the pictures of beautiful woman. Right next to him were two attractive women who were checking him out. They were whispering and one of them was pointing him out to her friend. The man didn't look up.

The interested woman, egged on by her friend, grew bolder. She sidled up to him and did what women do when they are interested in a guy—she hovered. She tried to catch his eye. He turned a page of the magazine. Finally she looked at her friend and shrugged. As they walked away, the woman said to her friend, "He's in a trance."

I thought it was the perfect summation of what can happen when you are choosing the picture instead of the reality. When the map overtakes the territory, you are in a trance, inured to the riches of the flesh-and-blood world. When you become a media spectator rather than a participant in your precious life, you become more and more passive as time leaks away.

Carl Jung talked about the "collective unconscious" that we all participate in and which connects everything. The media—television, movies, music, the Internet—have created a digital version. We are all plugged in, dreaming it at the same time. It is a form of glue that adds cohesion to our daily experience. But watching a documentary about Machu Picchu is not the same as trudging up the mountain, experiencing the perils and the pleasure of third-world travel. Staring at pornography isn't the same as making love to a real person and can in fact numb you out to true human interaction.

Expectations of a woman's beauty and a man's power are inflated to impossible standards by the media. So the genders live in a shadow of unreality when dealing with each other. Women expect men to be powerful and don't look for that power within themselves. They concentrate instead on their external beauty, desperately trying to fit an impossible image. They then take their power by proxy from the men they marry, men who won't make the grade unless they can live up to media-induced visions of power promulgated by myths from *Cinderella* to *Pretty Woman*.

This results in men striving harder and harder to gain the external power that can be flashed as a draw to women, a power that trades on control and domination. Rather than building on *their* internal personal power, grounded in integrity and honesty and the realization of the value inherent in all people, they buy into the power game, striving constantly to accumulate more and more to meet women's unrealistic expectations.

Men, in turn, have become addicted to anorexic, Botox-injected, surgically altered "perfect" visions of femininity, as reflected in the media. When men look up from their hypnotic state and encounter a flesh-and-blood woman, she seems plain in comparison. So men use and discard women in the search for that unattainable "one" that has been programmed into them by millions of images over a lifetime. But they don't realize it doesn't exist. The image is a product of lighting, hair styling, and makeup; it is hardly more real than a Barbie doll one buys in a store.

Both genders end up feeling insecure and dissatisfied, staring at each other over the digital fence with a combination of expectation and suspicion. We are told what is beautiful and what is powerful, but when we adopt these values as our own, they don't feel right. The end result is more aloneness and alienation.

The best way out of this conditioning is to experience reality directly—and if that reality is a magazine, to recognize it for what it is: an object.

"The map is not the territory" applies to information as well. Most of our visions and opinions of the world are parroted. We watch TV, we read magazines, we scan newspapers, and we regurgitate op-ed pages. In a world where so much secondhand information is available, we become like fish swimming upstream as we struggle to stay abreast of the latest. When we focus on this information as knowledge, it is difficult to cull wisdom, which is mostly the product of firsthand direct experience.

If you feel you must expose yourself to this much useless information, try to digest it and keep whatever nutrients you can cull, and then, like the body, let the waste products be flushed away.

Ask yourself how you know something is true. Make no assumptions that what you hear is true. Take no opinion that is not carefully thought out as your own. Unplugging from the media means forming your own impressions of the world and the people in it.

DO LESS NOW!

> The world is sacred.
> It can't be improved.
> If you tamper with it, you'll ruin it.
> If you treat it like an object, you lose it.
> —THE TAO

In the media, the virtues of doing are extolled nonstop and the simple pleasures of being, with nothing added or subtracted, are completely ignored. Eventually life itself gets distorted, if not by the content of the media, but, as Marshall McLuhan intimated in his famous quote "The medium is the message," by the sheer volume and stimulation of its delivery system. This stimulation can lead to numbness, anxiety, and a restlessness that is never sated, no matter how much stimulus is absorbed.

It can also lead to the worship of false idols, from film stars to whoever is the latest fad. We watch enviously as other people lead a big life, and we are constantly told that we are free to do the same. We can buy anything we want to buy. Go anywhere we want to go. Be anything we want to be.

But how free are we when the average American watches three hours and forty-six minutes of TV each day (more than fifty-two days of nonstop TV-watching per year)? By age sixty-five the average American will have spent nearly *nine years* glued to the tube. Nine years of passive training as one's precious life drips by.

Almost all television programming exists only to sell you something. Nine years of your life spent learning to consume. Like it or not, this is a massive dose of conditioning being mainlined directly into your mind. To absorb it in a state of passivity breeds more passivity. And although it may seem to relieve loneliness, think of the last time you watched a lot of television. Did you feel more or less connected to life at the end of it? Did you feel more or less lonely and disconnected? And when you shut it off, were you recharged or drained? Did the silence replacing the television feel sweet, or did you want more television?

This is how elephants are trained. They start out with a chain staked to the ground and the baby elephants are tied to the chain. As they get older, the elephants are easily able to break free of the chain by simply walking away. Yet they don't. They have been conditioned to believe that they can't break the chains, and so they don't even try.

In much the same way the media conditions us, especially the tremendously potent medium of television. It's important to see through this conditioning that is telling us how to live, what our values are, what our politics should be. We need to identify the ways in which we are being conditioned. Most people aren't aware of the extent of media dominance in our culture, but the world is saturated with messages selling something. According the Center for Media Literacy, Americans are exposed to over three thousand lads a day through different forms of media, including sixty channels of TV, movies showing at the local theater or on video, airwaves full of radio talk and music, newspapers, magazines, and books. We are like robots programmed to consume from early childhood, told what we need to be happy. America, with 6 percent of the world's population, owns 59 percent of the world's wealth, and yet we still don't feel like we have enough.

The truth is, we need nothing beyond the simplicity of the moment. But commercials create an itch that can never be gotten rid of.

Even the Internet, touted as a source of connection and information, can be used as a way to hide out, a way in which people can interact with a simulation of reality rather than the reality itself. There has been a huge spike in the amount of time teens are spending on the Internet (an average of 9.3 hours a week), adding another form of communication that doesn't involve direct contact with the outside world—another way in which we can avoid talking to each other face-to-face.

At least at the beginning the elephants know that they are chained. We don't even know the chain exists. We think we are so free. Powerful. Rulers of the world.

But how free are we?

To understand how powerful the conditioning is, one need only know that 81 percent of ten-year-old girls are afraid of being fat. Seventy percent say they would rather lose a parent or suffer a nuclear war than be overweight! There is a cause-and-effect mechanism at work here. The average height and weight of women in the United States is 5' 4" and 140 pounds. The average media representation of women is 5' 11" and 110 pounds, thinner than 98 percent of all women.

This conditioning is as ubiquitous as the air we breathe, but there is a constant opportunity to see through the fear it perpetuates and to break free of its tyranny. But first, as in the case of the elephants, we must understand what is possible. And this takes a fluidity and responsiveness that release the conditioning before it gets locked in. This can only happen moment by moment.

It only becomes possible by waking up from the media dream!

At a barbecue a two-year-old girl fell into a swimming pool. Everybody stood horrified for a moment as the girl struggled, not knowing how to swim. The mother jumped in and grabbed the girl, rescuing her before disaster struck. She pulled the toddler out of the water as everybody rushed forward with great concern. But before her daughter even had a chance to start crying or any of the people could open their mouths, the mother laughed and jumped back in the pool, still holding her daughter.

She turned the moment into a game, and the daughter, instead of crying, squealed with delight. Instead of the child being conditioned to fear the pool and fear the water, the fear of the moment was dissolved into play. This was brilliant and intuitive and happened without thinking. It was a releasing of the conditioning at its inception.

In the same way, we must act moment to moment to observe what habituates us now. Releasing our conditioning to come into our unencumbered self can work only as long as we are aware of the entraining happening every day.

Because our conditioning by the media is as omnipresent as the air we breathe and nearly as invisible, we must be as vigilant as this mother was about not allowing any conditioning to be set. We must observe the possibility of conditioning and release it before it gets absorbed. This can be as simple as hooting at the television and making fun of the message. Humor is a fantastic way to pop the trance.

I nearly went mad in my first silent retreats, without books, music, radio, and television to distract me. The thundering constancy of my own story pulsed in my head like a dancer who still moves after the music has stopped. *What do you mean, just sit around and do nothing?* I felt like I was wasting my time.

This was such a clear example of the way I was using a steady drip of stimulation to distract me from myself. Once that stimulation was turned off, my head clanged with restless thoughts. But it exposed the fact that diversion, like drugs, only works temporarily. Once my nervous system was slowed down, the ordinary miracles of everyday life were fully revealed, as resplendent and simple as a bird flying across an open sky.

By the end of the retreat I was lying so still in the driveway that a lizard crawled up on my arm and basked with me in the sun. But the first step was to unplug.

CONTROL

The media give us a false sense of control.

We can watch humanity from the safety of our armchairs rather than the uncontrollable reality of the world. We are in control of the intensity and the duration; we can change the channel, adjust the volume, look away, put it down, or turn it off. In a video game we direct digital actors on our behalf to kill, maim, and hunt. When we die, it isn't permanent. This is one of the comforting things about a media experience versus a direct experience: there is always a second chance or a possibility of a happy ending.

This false sense of control extends to life, death, sex, and violence.

We get to have momentary feelings of power, living vicariously through the adventures of our heroes on the big and small screens. By reducing the wild world into an image on a square box and spending a huge chunk of our waking hours in front of that box, we reduce the world to something manageable.

But control is an illusion, pure and simple.

Real life is uncontrollable. Most of us don't have the power to say who lives and who dies, and barring suicide, none of us can control when we die. This is one of the first spiritual principles worth mastering. There is so much freedom in letting go of control: of other people, of one's experience, of thoughts about the way the world should be and what should be happening.

There's a great scene in the satirical movie *Being There*, based on the Nabokov novel and starring Peter Sellers as a simple-minded gardener named Chance. Although Chance has only gardened and watched television his whole life, his homilies about gardening get mistaken for political genius by an easily misled elite. When his boss dies, he is told to vacate the only home he has known. Upon doing so he is accosted by hostile thugs, and he pulls out his remote control, pointing it at them and pushing its buttons as if to change the channel. They, of course, just laugh at him.

But real life isn't controllable. Nor is death. Nor are other people. And the more we are subsumed by the media, the less we master this reality.

As I write this the most popular video game on sale in the United States is Grand Theft Auto: Vice City. Every time a player steals a car, beats up a woman, sells drugs, robs people, hangs out with a prostitute, or kills someone, he collects points. In one sequence a woman is kicked to death. The game is flying off the shelves. In violent video games we get to enact our darker fantasies without any lasting repercussions. Although the level of harm we do to our psyches by kicking a woman to death for entertainment in a video game remains to be seen, our country's fascination with guns and violence, both locally and globally, is already self-evident. On television, guns are the normal way to solve conflicts.

Now, I don't want to get into a long debate of about whether violence in the media creates violence in real life; studies have proven a correlation between the two hundred thousand murders a child will see on television by the age of eighteen and increased aggression. Although there is ample evidence of the connection, I still don't think adult programming should be tamed to accommodate the lowest common denominator of mental health. Real violent mental illness is created by genetic or behavioral conditioning stronger than the latest action movie.

But this isn't my point. The real issue is that all forms of media reinforce the idea that the wild and woolly world can be tamed and controlled. The more we live life through the media, whether it be video games, television, or computers, the more we feel like masters of our domain. We are lulled into a false sense of control over our environment. We take it for granted and forget that reality is uncontrollable.

So two things are happening when we interact with the world through the media: we are frightened by the representations of the real world and therefore avoid that reality, and we are given powerful feelings of control within the medium, reinforcing how nice it is to stay there. Neither is true, but both are debilitating if you don't see through the conditioning.

I'm not saying to become a media Luddite. Why would you want to? It's impractical, if not impossible. As you are exposed to it, moment by moment, go for the ride. But never forget that it is just a ride and that, like a roller coaster, its thrills are perfectly controlled and timed and manipulated.

Unlike the real world.

FRAMING THE DISCUSSION

Like the beating of our own hearts, the media (and the technology that drives them) are omnipresent and invisible at the same time. We don't see their effects on the world, how they intentionally and unintentionally shape how the world is seen, perceived, and absorbed. The hand of power is hidden but iron-fisted.

Beyond simple story selection and editorializing, the media can't help but communicate the bias of its purveyors. In a fascinating study done by Brian Mullen of Syracuse University and outlined in Malcom Gladwell's *The Tipping Point*, the reporting of the three network news anchors during the 1984 presidential campaign was analyzed for the emotional content of their delivery when talking about Ronald Reagan and Walter Mondale. Dan Rather and Tom Brokaw were fairly neutral, but over at ABC Brian Jennings' facial expression lit up when he spoke about Ronald Reagan. When ABC viewers were polled, they voted for Reagan in far greater numbers than those watching NBC or CBS, even though ABC was shown to be the network most hostile to Reagan overall! When all the other factors were considered, it was proven the subtle pro-Reagan bias in Jennings' face affected the way people voted.

So the media are framing the debate unintentionally, no matter what their conscious intent, like the theory of quantum mechanics that posits that by observing particles you change their behavior. And so the media affect us, just by their existence.

At first I thought this was a phenomenon that existed only in the United States. But when you visit other countries you see they all have their version of the nightly news, with its blow-dried anchor exuding a kind of plastic attractiveness, bantering with other anchors in a banal attempt at folksiness. They are framing the news in a certain way. I realized the phenomenon was universal; it's almost as if the news had to come from the most antiseptic source possible because most news is bad news. It had to be sanitized like war coverage, protecting us from harsh realities.

Indeed, now in the United States there are media consultants who advise networks on what aspect to show of a story. During the war with Iraq, they told the networks that people didn't want to see blood and dead bodies. And so we didn't. But this, in turn, has a profound effect on our own proclivity for war, because we don't see its consequences.

We are only seeing a small slice of reality, and it feeds and informs our direct experience. As William Faulkner once wrote, "Facts and truth don't really have that much to do with each other."

What is missing is the deeper truth beyond the symptoms. The fact that most crime is directly correlated to poverty and a lack of job opportunity is missing from the television news programs' shallow summation of the symptoms. What is left out is the underlying cause of the poverty. And by showing just the symptoms—the murders, rapes, and robberies in all their gory details—we get more hardened in our positions on opposite sides of the digital fence. When interacting only through the distorting prism of the media, we get separated from the other, whether that other is a country, a person, or an idea.

You need only turn off the television and step out the front door to come out of the hallucination of media in all its forms. Dive into direct experience and swim in the deep waters. Become fluid between direct experience and the absorption of belief systems taken from different media sources. Don't protect yourself from the wild and raw world. Escape the distorting effects of hype and advertising and the attendant feelings of "not enough."

Meet real people who are three-dimensional and not flattened out into cartoons.

As Henry Miller said: "The aim of life is to live, and to live means to be aware, joyously, drunkenly, serenely, divinely aware."

This can't be done secondhand.

ANOTHER DAY, ANOTHER DOLLAR

Avoid Working Stiffness

Chop wood, haul water.
—ZEN PROVERB

"Some days I wake up and I can barely get out of bed."

This was said to me during a long talk with Roger, a male nurse who has been working in the emergency room for twenty-five years. He said he was always worried about what each of the doctors, whom he knew well, was going to say or do. What were they going to complain about? Which one was going to snap at him for some perceived flaw? Roger was so tired of the ER, he had become a certified massage therapist, which he enjoyed a great deal. But when he pictured himself going to the local spa and doing it a couple of days a week, he thought, what would that be like? Pretty soon, even though he used to be excited, he became completely depressed about the idea—which in reality was just a thought about the future.

Often no other area is more difficult for people than work. It can combine stressors in all aspect of city life, from the commute to competition. Layoffs, downsizing, bad bosses, and scapegoating for poor performance beyond one's control are just a few of the challenges. The need to put in useless "face time" contributes to the sense of exhaustion and burnout that 61 percent of Americans feel.

Yet what is work at its most fundamental level? Is it not an opportunity to be with people in a creative way? A chance to be compassionate, supportive, and patient with oneself and other people? Much of people's stress around work has to do with expectations about what is going to happen in the future. Will the project they're working on turn out well? Will their boss like them? Will they get the promotion they're up for? Roger admitted that most of his anxiety around work came from anticipating problems that never occurred.

Work is an area that occupies almost as much of our minds in the future as in the present.

"PERHAPS"

Monica, a friend of mine, is the owner of an art gallery. She is endlessly creative, teaming up with different sponsors such as Absolut vodka to promote her exhibits. The gallery is a growing success. One year she landed a huge client, which began buying art and ordering more and more. My friend had a friendly relationship with the CEO, who had just presented her with a list of paintings for her to acquire. She was so excited that the gallery was going to be taken to another level that she designed her business plan for the following year around the company. When she shared the name of her new client with her colleagues at other galleries, they were green with envy.

Then the bottom fell out. The huge corporate client? Enron. She ended up getting subpoenaed by the FBI to be a witness. The basis of her business plan for the year evaporated.

The end of the story regarding work or success is often not the end of the story. It's like that tale of the son of an Indian chief who went riding one day and came back with a string of wild horses. Everybody gathered around and admired the horses.

"Isn't your son so lucky to have found these beautiful horses!" people exclaimed to the chief.

"Perhaps," he replied.

The next day the son was riding one of the wild horses and it bucked him off, breaking his leg. Everybody gathered aroun the chief.

"Isn't this terrible—your son has broken his leg," the people sympathized.

"Perhaps," said the chief.

A week later a neighboring tribe went on the warpath. All the able-bodied men went out to battle and half were mortally wounded. Because the son of the chief couldn't fight, he was spared, and when he grew older he became chief himself.

The purpose of Monica's story and that of the chief's son is that you are *always* at a point in life where the future is unknown. And, as I have mentioned, the future never arrives except in the form of the present moment. Comparing yourself to others in their work life is actually not to see the situation clearly. You don't know where anything is truly going with the people with whom you are comparing yourself. You don't see what's really happening, how they feel about it, what's going on in the rest of their lives behind the apparent "success."

You also don't know where you are in the unfolding of your destiny. So you are also missing the point of the game, which is to be the best *you* can be in each moment along the way. There is always going to be somebody who is more successful than you are. But don't look to other people to find out who you are; look to see if you are fulfilling your own potential in the best way you know how. If you are envying other colleagues, then you can't be doing that.

Instead of comparing, you want to work in the moment with joy and wholeheartedness, without expectation of any results. In fact, work and let go of results completely.

EXPECTATIONS

Just as fog is dispelled by the strength of the sun
And is dispelled no other way,
Preconception is cleared by the strength of realization.
There's no other way of clearing preconceptions.
Experience them as baseless dreams.

—Milarepa

Expectations around work can result in the unexpected. When I had just graduated from USC film school, my thesis script was called "Kiss God Goodbye," a gritty story about AIDS. It was a character-based drama and one of the few screenplays in Hollywood at that time that dealt with the disease. I had dozens of meetings around town in which everybody expressed their admiration for the script, using words like *brilliant* and *moving* and *funny*. A well-known director got attached, and then a huge producer. I began to believe my own press.

One studio meeting in particular stands out. I was ushered into the corner office of a small man with glasses, whom I'll call Mr. Bismark. He sat down and looked at me.

"This script is genius," he said. "I actually cried."

"Really?" I was modest, but by that time I was feeling like: *Of course it was genius.* "Thank you."

"Your work with character development was brilliant," he continued. "It's so rare to see that in scripts these days."

"Thank you again," I said, soaking it up.

"Very funny, too." Mr. Bismark smiled, as if remembering the script. "I laughed."

It went on like that for a few more minutes, and then he got down to business.

"So let me tell you what we're looking for," he said.

"Yes, please do," I said, full of confidence, eager to hear how much money they were going to be offering me to write their next Oscar-winning script.

"We're looking for a story about a pig."

"A pig?" I just sat there, waiting for him to crack a smile. He didn't.

"Yes, a pig—for children. A pig with a bunch of barnyard pals."

I laughed, but my stomach sank.

"What makes you think . . . ? what makes you think I can write a story about a pig?"

"Your natural ability with character development."

It was at this moment that, after six months of meetings, I got it. He was just throwing writers at the wall and seeing who stuck. There was nothing special about me; the studio was just pitching the idea to anybody who had any buzz, regardless of what his or her skills were or whether that person was a good fit for the project. At the time I was fresh out of film school and didn't know that flattery was just the warm-up—it was the way these guys talked for a living. *It didn't mean anything*, but to me it had meant everything.

It's laughable now, but when I left the meeting I was very off-balance. What was real? What was bullshit? Would I ever be able to tell the difference? I realize now it was a valuable lesson on the nature of expectation. I had been expecting a certain result, and when I didn't get it, I was cast on the stormy sea of mind.

Expectation actually works against you in the work environment, because you are seeing what you want to see, rather than what is. So you might miss another opportunity that exists right in front of you. But even more important and ironic, if you have expectations about the future, you are not giving the work you are doing your full attention, which is the only way to bring about the expectations you have for the future!

The old Zen proverb "Chop wood, haul water" means to do one thing at a time, with your full attention. When you're chopping wood, you're just chopping wood. When you're hauling water, just haul water.

In any kind of job this is important; in some jobs it is a matter of physical well-being, even life or death. An acquaintance of mine from yoga just chopped off a half inch of his finger while working at his job as a chef. The doctors sewed it back on, and amazingly it looks like it's going to take, but as he said, it was a painful price to pay for a moment of inattention.

At any point on the drive home from that fateful studio meeting, which was like a wake-up call about my career, I could have abandoned the stormy seas of mind. I could have returned home to myself in the moment, driving, parking the car, and so on.

The same thing is true for the work itself: by being absorbed in the vibrant now, it is possible to work fully and then relax, letting go of the results. Think about it: the past falls away and the future never comes. It is just a never-ending string of now, now, now.

In this awareness, there is no room for expectation about the future to take root.

There is also no room for endless regret about the past, the sense that *I should have done better* or *I could have said this* or *I should have been able to turn the situation around*. We will always make mistakes in our work world. We will screw up. It's inevitable. But once it's done, it's done. It is immutable, and there is no sense ruminating over spilt milk. You clean up the mess, working in the moment, and then you move on. Any mental replay or self-flagellation about the mistake is a waste of energy and time.

Simply allow the present moment to crowd the past and future out of your awareness.

JOB VERSUS PATH

Work and play are words used to describe the same thing under differing conditions.

—MARK TWAIN

The distinction between job and path, which Twain points out as often false, is the cause of much angst. One of the most difficult and fraught journeys in our life is the search for meaningful work. We are taught from an early age to try to find our meaning in life through what we do. This conditioning, some of it very well-meaning, is the cause of much misery. We should find our path and do what we love and be successful. As we look around at figures in the media, we see people leading fabulous lives and doing interesting and meaningful work. It's sometimes impossible while leading a simple and humble life not to feel completely invisible and unimportant.

But it is not what you *do* but rather how you *are* while you do it that creates happiness and meaning. Unlike many books on spirituality, *City Dharma* is not a how-to book about "getting the life you deserve" or "manifesting success" or any other kind of quid pro quo around your spirituality. To do so would be to buy into the trance that you need success to be happy. What kind of freedom and happiness can be based on externals like success? The world is full of successful people who are miserable and modest achievers who are happy. No degree of accomplishment makes a difference to your happiness, because happiness is an inside job.

DON'T SEE YOURSELF

The first steps in self-acceptance are not at all pleasant, for what one sees is not a happy sight. One needs all the courage to go further. What helps is silence. Look at yourself in total silence, do not describe yourself.

NISARGADATTA MAHARAJ

"I just started a small company but I don't like doing all the boring day-to-day stuff," an intense young man said to me during a dharma conversation. "I just don't see myself that way. It's depressing."

"How do you see yourself?" I asked.

"As a visionary—I'm a big-wave surfer, a mountain climber, an entrepreneur. I want to own many different businesses."

"But right now you are a small-business owner, yes?"

"Yes. But I believe that you create your own reality. And I want to hold a larger vision for myself as the head of lots of different businesses."

"You know," I said, "let's look at that belief that you create your own reality. Schizophrenics create their own reality. For the rest of us, there are certain realities that exist, especially in business. There are realities of the marketplace, supply and demand, timelines, market saturation, or education. Lots of different factors."

"But in business, you have to have the vision first, and from the vision you create the reality. Six months ago I ended a partnership because he just didn't share that vision. It turned out he wasn't really into the business to start with."

"Then you were right to end the partnership. From a financial point of view, what was the vision for the business that you saw?"

"Two hundred repeat customers within six months. Five hundred by the end of the first year."

"And how many customers do you have now?"

"Thirty." The young many looked at me. "It's been much harder than I thought. I just keep working away and we're breaking even, but I'm not making any money."

"So this idea of creating your reality? Can you say it's worked out?"

There was a long pause as the young man struggled with his emotions. "No. It's been depressing. It's not the way I see myself."

"Then don't see yourself."

The young man looked at me as though I had asked him not to breathe for the next hour.

"I don't think I want to live that way. Not to have a vision of myself, of who I am and where I want to go . . ." He trailed off.

"But it's your vision of yourself that is causing your suffering. It is the disparity between what is and what you want it to be that is causing depression, fueled by this idea that you create your own reality."

We spoke for quite a while, but I'm not sure he was convinced. He felt that if he wasn't creating his own reality, then it was somehow his fault. He wasn't clear enough in his vision, or he had doubts, that he then tried to expunge. This tightly controlled vision actually got him further from having a realistic picture of his business and work.

There is a whole cottage industry of New Age thinking that subscribes to this idea of completely creating your own reality. It has been around for a while, beginning in the cancer wards in the 1970s. People who were dying were often asked what they were doing or not doing in their lives to "create" this disease. This was, in a real sense, blaming the victims. Now, sometimes this is absolutely true. Different lifestyles and eating habits create different stressors; if you smoke and are overweight, you are much more susceptible to many illnesses. Thus behavior has an effect on one's health. In this sense the cancer was "created."

But just as often disease, especially cancer, is simply a genetic time bomb waiting to go off. No amount of meditation, diet, or exercise is going to prevent it. It reminds me of the *New Yorker* cartoon that has two ducks sitting in a pond. One duck says to the other, slightly depressed duck: "Maybe you should ask yourself why you're inviting all this duck hunting into your life right now."

The whole idea that you have control over every aspect of your life is something that many forms of pseudospiritual practices promise. Self-help books are a billion-dollar-a-year industry that has made many of the purveyors of this "truth" rich. Channelers will help you create your own reality and be more financially successful; healers will do extractions to clear your chakras and optimize your potential; shamans will go back to the past and re-create your future (I kid you not) to help you find your bliss; psychics will perform psychic surgery or any number of other bogus therapies designed to manifest your dreams. Other healers will pass an egg over you and then crack it, revealing tar in the egg as evidence of an evil spell, after which they will charge a pretty penny to remove the spell. There are even hucksters who will sell you a way to live forever.

There are all manner of gurus available to tell you how to transform yourself and get what you deserve. This hocus-pocus of magician's tricks doesn't stand up to the slightest scientific or statistical examination—they have been proven to be frauds over and over again. Yet we want to believe because to do so is our way (the ego's way) of trying to exert control in an uncontrollable world.

But what these frauds are really delivering is this: "If you pay me, I will sell you a nice story to give you the illusion of control, and then you will *get* what you want in life." And since most people reside full time in the land of desire, they go for it.

Aside from being fraudulent, this kind of quid pro quo approach to spirituality rarely has lasting results because it is transactional and ego-driven. Its main premise is that you don't have everything you need to be happy, that you need to do something, *anything*, to create your own reality and become a successful human being.

This is, quite simply, a lie.

No matter how hard we strive at our work, we can't control all the factors, economic or otherwise. There are ups and downs that are often inexplicable, and sometimes they have nothing to do with talent or hard work, never mind creating your own reality.

I have a friend who produced an Emmy-winning movie. She found the writer and nursed the script through countless rewrites, and yet when it came time to hand out a producer's credit, she was overlooked by the studio. Is this fair? No. Are qualified people passed over every day in the work environment? Yes. Yet people's lives are fraught with identification about their work—they tie their whole happiness to how it's going. In fact, people become so identified with their work that a large percentage actually die within a year of retirement. They no longer have a reason and purpose to exist.

SUCCESS

The "you are what you do" conditioning is so ingrained in our culture that nobody even questions it. We live to work, as opposed to having the work-to-live philosophy of so many European countries, with their six weeks of vacation a year. Capitalism, the Protestant work ethic, remnants of Calvinism, and an external definition of success in this country keep our noses to the grindstone. Workaholism, as a way to avoid looking at one's life or at difficult feelings, is a syndrome that's just beginning to be understood. It's the one syndrome, unlike other addictions, that is actually rewarded with approbation in America. And yet the majority of people in this country wish they had more time: to think, to read, to relax, and to be with their families. They feel stressed out and on an endless treadmill, trying to get their head above water financially or trying to reach some external benchmark of "success." Meanwhile, they have no time or energy to stay informed about politics or the environment.

But *any* identification is going to create a lack of freedom. Any identification is going to put you on that roller coaster, riding the highs and lows, depending upon how the work is going. The result is often the kind of paralysis that Roger the nurse experienced, living in the nightmare of his own mind, identifying with every thought about work as if it were real. And I don't exclude myself; we've all been there.

But what is free about this?

A woman I know who is a successful writer spoke about the time she was on the *New York Times* best-seller list. It was something she had dreamed about for years, and she was on it for one week. Because of the two-week lead time the *Times* has to determine the list, she already knew her book was not going to be on the following week. So as people called her and congratulated her, she knew the bittersweet truth of the passing nature of this success. Instead of reveling in this lifelong dream, she found herself wishing the dream would last for two weeks. Then she realized the irony of this, and it taught her a powerful lesson on the fleeting nature of success.

Success is like a shark, which never stops moving, Each level of achievement spawns a hunger for another goal. This is as natural as breathing for some people, spurred on by the mind and by their conditioning that a person is more valuable for what he or she does than for who he or she is. But in the same way a shark needs to keep moving or it will die, people who are overly identified with their work experience anxiety and fear with any perceived threat to their identity or success. The extreme form of this was when stockbrokers jumped out of windows after losing everything in the crash preceding the Great Depression.

The mind, with its great habit of comparison, often ties its self-worth to external levels of accomplishment: *I have accomplished this goal, therefore I am valuable.* Or *I have failed at that, therefore my self-worth is negated.* This is purely a structure of mind. It is illusion.

Some of the most interesting people I know haven't accomplished very much in the world. They haven't striven to make money, they aren't overly identified with what they do, and they don't care much about their level of external success. The riches they have to offer the world are their presence and the wisdom gleaned not from chasing a narrow margin of existence but rather through wide-ranging direct experience of the world. They have taken the time to learn about the world in a raw and direct way, and so their take on the world is outside the box.

Even if you are successful in our "you're only as good as your last success" culture, it's never enough. There is constant anxiety about losing that success. So you can be successful externally, while internally you can be compulsively rushing, grasping, and feeling like it all may disappear.

And if you're overly identified with what you do, if *it* disappears, then *you* disappear.

But to a person who has internal balance, it doesn't matter what is happening with work. Conversely, if work is going well, if you're extremely busy and successful but your internal balance is off, then your enjoyment of that success will be limited.

In a way this can be intimidating to contemplate. Are we not supposed to be affected by anything? Are we supposed to be robots, dispassionate and detached? Work goes well, great. Work goes badly, great. Nothing that happens to us makes a difference?

Well, yes and no. We are not supposed to be robots and ignore the ups and downs of life, but neither is it pleasant to be at the mercy of what we can't control.

So, where is the balance?

PERCEIVED VALUE

When internal examination discovers nothing wrong, what is there to be anxious about, what is there to fear?

—CONFUCIUS

One day after dinner a friend was lamenting that everybody else at the table had a book deal, had just published a book, or had a movie deal to write a script. She had published a book of short stories eight years earlier and had been writing a novel for fifteen years, the last five of which had been filled with rejection from dozens of publishers.

"Everybody here is a success except me," she said with self-deprecating humor, but she was feeling down about it.

"Then you're not worthy to sit at this table," I joked. It was her house.

We talked about the vagaries of the publishing world and how hard it was to be a writer. You put all this effort into a creative work and then nothing comes of it. You are rejected. Your work dies on the shelf in some publisher's house. It's true that rejection is the lot of any creative person—it goes with the territory. Whenever I go to the offices of my agent or my publisher, and especially the people developing Hollywood movies, I see stacks and stacks of manuscripts, each representing six months, a year, or more of somebody's life, buried on the shelves like so many little corpses.

The very next day, we were all sitting around the lunch table, which was filled with delicacies and flowers and wine, when my friend walked in.

"I've had the most extraordinary news," she announced. "I just got off the phone with a publisher and they want to publish my novel. They called it a 'narrative gem.' "

Everybody burst out with congratulations. It was very good news after so many years.

"I guess you may now pull up a chair," somebody joked, provoking laughter.

But what was the difference between the two days? Was her book any better or worse? Was she less or more valuable as a writer? As a person?

I had a similar experience with a script I wrote. I was trying to get an agent and was sending the script everywhere. Nobody would bite. I was getting depressed and wondering about my ability as a writer. Then I approached a well-known independent director who had come to USC to preview his latest film. He loved the script and attached himself to it. The next week I came home and there were twenty-three messages on my machine. Agents I had contacted before were suddenly interested, and producers I'd never heard of wanted to meet with me. My perceived value had suddenly gone up.

But nothing had actually changed. Nothing was different except the way the external world validated or saw me.

William Goldman wrote in one of his books on Hollywood, "Nobody knows anything." He meant that nobody knows what will make a good movie, as every film is a creative experiment; each film is a form of research and development, and nobody can predict the outcome. I think this is true of most aspects of life and a very good outlook to have when it comes to creative work. People can't really judge what is good or bad by themselves, so they wait for somebody else to like it. This is how the perceived value increases.

After years of meetings and near misses, the script I wrote never got made into a movie. What conclusion was I to draw from that? What conclusion should my friend draw from her experience with publishers? What should we think about all the artists and writers through the years who were not honored for their work in their lifetime, from Van Gogh to Keats to Emily Brontë?

It is incredibly difficult to live life without being attached to how one's work is received, no matter what that work is. But it has very little to do with the actual value of one's work.

And it has absolutely nothing to do with the value of oneself.

WORRY

Striving to better, off we mar what's well.

SHAKESPEARE, *King Lear*

A friend of mine manages a small business, very adeptly handling all their bookkeeping. One terrible day she got a notice from the IRS that they wanted to look at the business's books. It wasn't an audit per se; it was a spot audit to determine if a full audit was necessary.

My friend sweated and prepared for this non-audit audit. She talked about it day and night. If the books didn't pass this inspection, a full-blown audit would cost the company thousands of dollars and hundreds of work hours in preparation. She wound herself into such a state of general anxiety, she had trouble sleeping. When the day finally arrived, the auditor stayed for an hour and then left, saying casually that everything looked like it was in order.

During one of my dharma conversations a man spoke about feeling a vague kind of worry during his work. He repaired high-tech computers that were worth a lot of money. When they went down, it was usually an urgent problem, and he felt anxious about it until he could see his way clear to a solution. When I asked him if he could usually figure it out, he said yes.

I bring up these two illustrations to talk about worry, anxiety, and the niggling little fears that can come up during work situations. How will a project turn out? Will the boss like it? Will the company succeed? Will I do well enough to get the promotion? All sorts of thoughts can arise beyond the moment of simply doing one's work.

But these thoughts actually are not just neutral. They are meaningless in the big picture, of course, but on the level of work, they will prevent the outcome you desire because they are distracting you from the moment where the work is being done. You are in imagination.

I can actually talk about this kind of distraction personally. As I write these words, I've been wondering about this book. How good is it at communicating these teachings? How will it be received? Will it get reviewed? Will it be well reviewed?

None of this is actually pertinent to the writing of this book except that it can be used as an example of a kind of leakage of attention from the moment when the work is actually being written. Luckily, when you're writing a dharma book, this leakage is just grist for the mill.

In the book *I Am That,* by Nisargadatta Maharaj, he writes:

> If you just try to keep quiet, all will come—the work, the strength for work, the right motive. Must you know everything beforehand? Don't be anxious about your future—be quiet now and all will fall into place.

Another way of saying this is: do the work and let go of the results. When you can get in this state of mind, the work, whether it is fixing a computer or fixing the books, takes over the moment and you can lose yourself in your work. In fact, the statement "lose yourself in your work" actually inadvertently points to a form of waking up. Becoming absorbed in what is happening right now, without future or past, is why people like to work. It gives them a taste of freedom—they get to lose their small self and, in their absorption, experience right now.

The future will take care of itself.

FINDING YOUR "PATH"

Follow your heart. If you can't find it, just jump and your heart will start beating so fast you'll wake up.

—ANONYMOUS

Much angst is spent on whether we will find our path in life. What are we supposed to do with our life to give it meaning? How can we make a contribution? How can we be used to the best of our abilities? We ask ourselves this with heart-wrenching sincerity (unless, of course, we just want to make money). Sometimes we spend months or even years debating this issue.

Everybody would say it's very important to find one's path, to have meaningful work. But I say give up the search and concentrate on that which is larger than any job. And what is the difference between holding a job and having a path? Some people find meaning in their work, and others find meaning in their family and friends and life outside of work, which they treat as a means to an end. Is one intrinsically worth more than the other? Everybody would automatically say it's better to be engaged in work that is meaningful, that is part of one's path. But let's dissect this idea of "path" for a moment. In relation to the present moment, what is path but a future concept?

And who is to know what will lead to what? No job is more important than any other in terms of the present moment. The pop star getting mass adulation is not any better off than the carpenter doing his job. What is important is the dynamic one has with one's job in the moment. If the pop star is cynical, dissociated, egotistical, or narcissistic, then is what he is doing really fulfilling? Or is it just a search for pleasure (a high) that has inherent within it the opposite, pain (the low)? If the carpenter is fully engaged with his work, feeling peaceful and joyful while doing it, who is having the more fulfilling experience?

We are trained to believe that certain jobs are important and other jobs (our own), are of lesser importance. Musicians, writers, artists, teachers, and entrepreneurs are all looked at with envy because what they are doing is seen as meaningful. If they have reached fame and fortune doing what they love, then they are doubly important.

But how did they start? How does anybody start?

Understand that no matter what you are doing, you are already on your path; you just can't see the end of it yet. You can only realistically see right now, so let go of the idea of the path altogether. The caterpillar cannot know it has the butterfly within it. The seed cannot know it will be a flower. Not knowing where we are going is a difficult aspect of the journey of life, never mind work, but it is often the reality.

So you simply meet each moment of your present job with enthusiasm, realizing it is an opportunity. You say yes to whatever arrives in the moment. You keep following your own excitement moment by moment, without agenda. You will automatically grow in response to the opportunity that is presented each and every day, in the same way the flower grows through the dark soil and toward the light.

Let go of striving and winning, of being higher or proving you're special. There is freedom in that. Simply be wholehearted in your work right now.

EVOLUTION

Slow down and everything you are chasing will come around and catch you.

—JOHN DE PAOLA

Think about where you are right now regarding your work. It has been an evolution. One thing has led to another. Your work transforms you, and you transform it, moment by moment. You are on the journey.

It makes no sense to pine for the future because everything you do is intrinsically important in this livable moment. It is also important because what you are doing is preparation for a path not yet revealed. The struggle, the pain, and the process are all necessary and okay. Don't try to eliminate or control these. They are the anvil that will forge you into what you are becoming, so welcome the challenge. As the world says no, use it as an opportunity to increase your commitment to yes Picture any no like the raising of a bar, a way to purify your intent to be more awake.

I'm thinking of Lexi, a friend who decided to move to India with her small child eight years ago. She had so many expectations of India—how it was going to change her relationship to her spirituality, how she was going to work there, and so on. Within three months she was back home, completely broke, with her dream of India in tatters. She couldn't find work there, she couldn't keep up payments on her apartment here, and her marriage was failing. The only thing Lexi brought back from India was a trunk of beautiful clothes, jewelry, and collectibles. Within three weeks she had sold it all. This led to an import-export business, which led to a shop.

She had found her path! Perhaps . . .

But after a while the shop began to fail. When she got very quiet, she realized she didn't belong there. It wasn't in her heart. She no longer wanted to own the shop. Lexi had no idea what to do with her life, which seemed to just wander from thing to thing.

A day later a former student of Lexi's father showed up at the shop with a letter from her father, who was a renowned Shakespeare scholar and had died four years earlier. The student was in a class that had presented her father with a beautiful gold clock that had engraved on it, from *Macbeth:* "Let every man be master of his time." The letter he bore, which he felt the family should have, was her father's response to the class's gift and the statement from *Macbeth*.

Lexi read the letter with a lump in her throat.

Her father had written several years earlier to the class words that seemed so appropriate to her now:

> To answer the question, am I a master of my time. If you take the question to mean am I Napoleon or Churchill or any other great figure of history? No, I'm not a master of the universe. In the sense do I have control of my actual day? No, I do not. I live by the school bell. But if you mean, do I love what I do? Then yes, I absolutely love what I do and feel myself to be master of my time.

Lexi closed up the shop the next day. Somebody asked her to teach her how to cook Indian food. Lexi then began teaching Indian cooking classes in her home, and they became extremely popular. This led to leading groups on tours of India, exposing groups to little-known restaurants, five-star hotels and stunning camel rides through the deserts of India. She now works giving people trips of a lifetime, which she absolutely loves and is uniquely qualified to do. And who knows where it will lead in the future?

At what point was she not on her path? Even the boring, frustrating days in the shop—the "meaningless" parts of her history—were important, as they are for all of us. As the teacher Satyam Nadeen said, perhaps like an apple hanging on a tree, the fruit ripens and then drops from the tree. One minute it is hanging on the tree, the next it falls, not because it has forced itself or jumped, but because it was time. It recognized its ripeness and simply let go.

But the fruit could not have gotten to that point without its time on the tree. Should it resent this time or look at it as part of a natural and inevitable process of growth?

Frustration, being denied, bumping into internal blocks within oneself, stagnation, fallowness—these are all necessary steps on the journey. They are part of a ripening that *never* ends. So be in that moment of ripening and feel the ripeness *that you already are*.

Imagine if we could create ourselves anew every moment and step into every new instant free of the burdens of the past and unconcerned about the imagination of the future. Be like this. When it rains on your parade, know that you are ripening and enjoy that moment of difficulty. Although it will make you deeper and more qualified to occupy what you are becoming, the truth is that you already are. And you are fine just the way you are, even as you are being forged into a deeper, stronger you.

I have had many different jobs, including camp counselor, Good Humor salesperson, construction worker, waiter, short-order cook, roofer, night snow maker, ranch hand, teacher, salesperson, technical writer, management consultant, advertising executive, yoga instructor, screenwriter, and author.

Were any of them the true me? No. Were they important points in the moments when I did them? Absolutely. But only in those moments.

Think of your job history. Were any of those jobs *you*? The simple truth is when you say yes to what is presenting itself in the moment, you are on *the only path that exists*. Thus any environment, no matter how mundane or boring, is quite likely already transforming you, preparing you for another environment, with the irony being it won't happen unless you engage fully in the moment you're not enjoying.

Thinking about if you are on your path is like wondering if you are human. You are.

"Let every man be master of his time," Macbeth said.

It is possible, but only in the eternal now, where time doesn't exist.

GETTING FIRED

Nothing seems worse than getting fired, and it can be a terrifying experience. When people lose their job, their entire identity can collapse, and it feels like a form of death. There are also real repercussions. In Canada, people who lose their jobs don't worry about ending up on the street, because the government provides health care and social services. There's a sense that the rest of the country is looking out for them and that Canadians feel responsible for each other. In America, if you lose your job, you can actually fall through the cracks.

Mostly unemployment is a time when the ego-mind and the emotions feed on each other. The first thing triggering them is the idea that you were rejected. This in turn may trigger all sorts of stories, including some painful ones from the past. But what is the truth? Even if you were wrongfully fired, losing your job is an opportunity for deep reflection. It is an external alarm bell saying, literally, "You don't belong here. We don't want you." It is also usually a way in which life gives you a push in a direction you need to go, away from an unfulfilling job or a bad boss.

Who wants to be in a place where they are not wanted? This can be true of an entire profession. I have been a screenwriter for ten years. Nothing I've written has been made into a movie, which is quite typical of the screenwriting profession where only a tiny fraction of the movies developed actually make it to the screen. But I've worked on and off, been able to support myself, and been involved in some interesting projects, enjoying a very free lifestyle.

However, after a while Hollywood, which trades on the dream of seeing your work on the big screen, began to feel like a mirage. The ups and downs of the money, one year a big chunk, the next year nothing, began to feel difficult to manage. The main problem was a sense that my creativity was being poured into a black hole. Now don't get me wrong, I learned many things as a screenwriter. One of them was to enjoy the process and let go of the results.

Still, after ten years I began to let go of the idea, the dream, that I was a screenwriter. But just the contemplation of leaving it sent me into an unexpected depression. I had changed my entire life to pursue this dream. I had quit a good job, gotten into a great graduate school, worked hard for a long time. What was I if I wasn't a screenwriter? The whole industry began to feel like a great big candy store with my nose pressed against the window. Why wasn't I being rewarded on the same level as a few (very few) of my compatriots?

Then my agent called me and said I was up for a writing job. A producer wanted to take the old *Ironside* series from the sixties and make a movie about it. This seemed to be the trend in Hollywood at the time, from *Mission: Impossible* to the *Brady Bunch*. I liked the idea of a tough wheelchair-bound detective making his way around criminals, so I went in for the meeting. Sitting high above Hollywood in a conference room with three executives, I listened to their vision.

"We want this to be a cool movie," said one.

"Ironside was a reactionary figure representing the old guard's response to the cultural revolution of the sixties," I responded, having visited the Museum of Television and Film in Beverly Hills as part of my research. "He was cynical, tough, and funny, and the show poked fun at hippies and everything they represented. He's a great character we could update to be caustic about present day culture."

"Yes, exactly," said another exec. "But we want this to be an action movie."

I just stared at them. An action movie?

"But Ironside was in a wheelchair." I blurted out, trying to keep from laughing. "That's what made him Ironside. If you get rid of the wheelchair, then he won't be Ironside."

"Oh, we want to keep the wheelchair."

"I see. . . . Well, we could keep the wheelchair and come up with all sorts of stunts." I began improvising. "He could be a wheelchair marathoner, very agile and strong. The wheelchair could extremely high-tech, with all sorts of cool gadgets."

"Sounds like we're on the same page," said the third executive. He actually said that: *on the same page*. I bit my tongue to keep from laughing.

And so it went. I went home and spent a week working out an elaborate pitch. Nothing came of it. Nothing came of the project, which never even got developed. Hollywood, true to form, was all come-on and no payoff.

In the middle of it all I remembered my film school essay about cinema being an element for change, movies being important because they were the only stories some people heard, their only way of connecting to their own humanity through the stories of others.

I decided I had hit the bottom of the barrel. I was exhausted by the dance.

Hollywood was firing me from my dream of being a screenwriter, which I had poured everything into for over ten years. I had to move on.

But the further I got from my dream, the more depressed I got until I was essentially incapacitated. What would I do next? How would I live? I found myself stuck. I was not just being fired from a job, but from a dream, a whole identification with myself. I floundered around for months wondering: what to do?

Then I asked myself what it would look like if I let it all go? As my mind was going over and over it, I decided to just let my mind think of the worst. This is what it came up with:

I wouldn't be able to support myself.

I would lose my apartment and have to stay with friends.

I would lose my car, my freedom, and my creativity.

I would have to get a job I hated just for the money.

And so it went. *I., I., I. Me, me, me.* The mind went on and on. I just witnessed it. Then I felt something release. So what? What did I really need? I wouldn't end up on the street. I wouldn't starve. Something would happen. Or nothing would happen. I could be happy no matter what I did.

But the real truth was even though I had no job, what was happening right now? I had food in the fridge and a roof over my head. The irony is that my obsession with the imaginary horrors of the future simply prevented me from the doing in the moment what was necessary to forestall the dire events my mind was predicting! It was an endless cycle.

Inasmuch that I was identified with myself as a screenwriter, I was suffering. When I stopped, so did the suffering.

BAD NEWS CAN BE GOOD

There are two ways to go into any challenging job situation where the ego feels like it is under attack, from getting a negative work review to getting fired. You can either move forward with the intent to learn or hide with intent to protect. As long as you are guarding your job and your performance, as long as you are overly identified with it, you can't possibly grow and learn. You're too busy defending yourself. Staying with the intent to learn, even when getting fired from a job or a dream, helps keep you in the now. It can turn bad news into a growth experience.

While losing a job triggers all sorts of stories and dormant conditioning relating to rejection, freedom is as close at hand as the nearest moment. There is really nothing to do except relax the identification. It's like you are hanging from a bar and gripping it tightly, afraid to let go because the drop is thousands of feet to the earth. You (your ego) will surely die if you let go, so you grip the bar tighter and tighter. You face is contorted, your body rigid, your mind racing between fear and depression.

And then you let go. You simply relax and drop. And to drop into this awareness isn't a plummet of a thousand feet into a screaming void, as your mind (in self-preservation mode) would have you believe. It's a drop into a simple recognition of your true nature, which is peaceful, joyful, and filled with love.

It is remembering what you already know.

This is true no matter what identification is being shattered: whether it is work, a marriage, or even a dream. With just the slightest change in perspective, it can become something completely different.

You are not what you do.

JOB HUNTING

There comes a time when an individual becomes irresistible and his action becomes all-pervasive in its effects. This comes when he reduces himself to zero.

—GANDHI

After getting fired comes the equally stressful process of looking for a new job. This is another trial that brings up all sorts of identification, fear, and story. It can trigger intense feelings of hopelessness, of being judged, of inadequacy. A sense of not being enough can trickle in, feeding the idea that you have to prove your worthiness. There is plenty of advice out there on job-hunting interviews, including picturing the interviewer in their underpants. I will address none of that.

From a dharmic perspective, of course, you know that the person on the other side of the desk, the person you are trying to impress, the person your ego says holds so much power over you, is another manifestation of consciousness. The same intelligence that flows through them flows through you. They are not judging you any more than you are judging them. You are simply meeting another chip of consciousness and checking out if you will play well together.

The Gandhi quote talks about becoming irresistible by reducing oneself to zero. What does this mean in the context of a job interview? It means not paying any attention to the mind chatter that is going on about the need to convince, succeed, or shine in the interview. It is about reducing the *ego* to zero and simply being with what is happening between the two people in the room. By reducing the ego to zero, you are not there to self-aggrandize, but to serve. This in turn, becomes irresistible.

I remember a job interview I had many years ago at a magazine to sell advertising. The woman was shockingly antagonistic and combative. Her energy was extremely negative, and she challenged me on every aspect of my resumé, often being openly hostile and dismissive. By the end of the interview, I had developed a sincere antipathy toward her, the company, her desk, her bleached hair, the job . . . everything. I mean, I *hated* her by the end.

When it was finally over she said she was conducting a "hostile interview" to see how I would handle the stress. The whole thing was an act.

Whether it was an act or she chose the interview technique because she was feeling hostile and could take it out on somebody with impunity doesn't matter. I felt like I had been mugged. This was years before I was exposed to these teachings, and I ranted about the woman to anybody who would listen. There was no way I could ever work for a boss like that. I was offended and appalled. I was far from reducing myself to zero, as I'm sure my language and defensiveness communicated during the interview. I never got called back for a second interview.

Today, although I wouldn't want to work for a boss who starts out by playing mind games, I'm sure a lot more of her vitriol would have breezed by me. When you have reduced your self down to zero, there's nothing for any hostile energy to stick to. Any that blows by can become amusing rather than antagonizing. You own reactivity is diminished.

My point is that you have no idea what the agenda of the interviewer is. And while you mainly want to communicate your skills at helping their company achieve its goals, the deeper issue is one of accepting the culture of a company as it is and seeing if there's a fit. Like any other relationship, if there is a good match, not a lot of energy needs to be spent to maintain it. It flows easily without the constant rapids of drama. If you are awake to it, it is usually evident right from the beginning. So pay attention to all the signs that are there for the reading.

As a management consultant, I used to travel around the country to different companies, large and small. It got so I could tell the management style from the moment I entered the lobby and spoke to the receptionist. Were they friendly or frazzled? Welcoming or negative? Competent or bungling? Bored or overworked? As I sat in the lobby and waited for my appointment, the internal workings of the entire company were laid bare, like seeing an X ray of a person that shows the health of their structure and internal organs.

The same is true of a job interview. All you need to do is simply be awake. It will all be revealed to you. Watch your own desire arise, or your own fear of your own inadequacy. Stay in the position of the watcher, allowing it to all flow in front of you and meet the moment fresh.

You will then, without trying, shine in the interview.

You will also be able to see the reality of whether or not the relationship is a good fit for you, as well as for them.

ON THE JOB WITH DIFFICULT PEOPLE

One of the most challenging aspects of a job, any job, is you are sometimes trapped with people with whom you wouldn't otherwise choose to spend five minutes. You are stuck with the tyrannical rageaholic boss or the incompetent pot smoker or the suggestive sexual harasser or the dishonest supervisor pressing you to lie, cheat, or steal. Sometimes it is a matter of being with people who just aren't a member of your "tribe." You're in with a bunch of left-wing radicals and you're a conservative, or vice versa. And finally, but most frequently, you are in an environment in which dysfunctional family dynamics are being replicated in an endless drama.

This can be a source of tremendous stress because the freedom to move away from difficult people is curtailed in the workplace. Of course the obvious option is to quit and get another job, but it may not be feasible due to financial issues or a down economy.

I have a friend who has an addictive, negative, crazy-making boss who is constantly undermining the work that is being done by charging off in a new direction at the slightest whim. This boss is a total drama queen, takes credit where it isn't due, and blames failure on my friend and the other employees.

But my friend needs the job and doesn't feel she can quit. If it isn't practical to move, what can you do?

One thing is to stick to the code of professionalism inherent in every job, from janitor to president. Every occupation has a code of behavior and ethics, whether it is putting in a fair day's work or accurately reporting profits to the shareholders. This code is a guideline in any circumstance and actually might run separate from whatever corporate culture you may be in. So learn the principles of your profession and stick to them; don't be dragged down off your own integrity. Are you an accountant who is asked to fudge some numbers? What is the professional code you can use in defense of your refusal to do so?

In terms of interpersonal work relationships, understand that you can also keep to a level of professionalism no matter how difficult the people involved. Just don't expect work necessarily to be fun all the time.

If a person is wandering through the office backstabbing, gossiping, and pushing buttons, simply don't engage them negatively. Be consistently neutral and positive and eventually they will move on to more reactive targets who will give them the drama they are looking for. This requires that you be awake and aware when you enter the work environment, so you're not emotionally mugged. It requires a kind of mindfulness that, while still relaxed, is very alert.

The trick is not to take any of it personally; stay cool and professional. Understand that whatever is being thrown your way is their problem and not yours. Don't get sucked into any personal dramas. If you say nothing, without fear, standing in your own center, knowing who you are without defending it, the other person will be exposed. Don't try to win any arguments or try to convince anybody else. Don't gossip. Don't try to "fix" them within a work environment or you might end up replicating the original family dynamic that's causing the problem. It might ultimately lead to a power struggle and produce resentment, especially if you're not the boss.

Simply do nothing. Don't engage. Let the aggressor's fire rage until it burns out.

I hear the question. "What if it doesn't subside? Am I supposed to be a doormat?" No. Understand this: some people are bullies. They can't help themselves. They will take nonaction as a form of weakness. They respect nothing but direct and firm response and they will not be stopped until you stop them. So if it continues, try to have a conversation with the person during a quiet moment, perhaps out of the office. Tell the person his or her behavior is unacceptable. Most bullies are cowards and will back down. They may initially react badly to this confrontation, but underneath it some part of their higher nature is yearning to be stopped. For then, with your help, they can come out of their own misery.

Each situation is different, so whether you decide to confront or not, understand that water always rises or falls to the level of its own mark. In the end know that if you do your work in a wholehearted way and leave it at the door as you depart, the truth will out. It may take some time, but the person creating all the problems will eventually be clearly seen by all involved. I have experienced this time and again. People will notice how productive and well-meaning you are.

You will have maintained your dignity and harmed no one.

BOREDOM—FROM PRISON TO PORTAL

Nobody is bored when he is trying to make something that is beautiful or todiscover something that is true.

—WILLIAM INGE

Who hasn't felt bored in their work at some point or another?

I still have the scar from stitches in my head from one night of boredom. When I was twenty I worked a job where I was a night snow maker at a New England ski resort. I would work from 6 p.m. to 6 a.m., sleep for a couple of hours, and then ski all afternoon.

While it had its moments of crystalline beauty in the mountains at night, the job was often brutal, boring, and dangerous. It consisted in being taken up to the top of the mountain and then hiking down to adjust the water and air pressure coming out of separate hoses and merging in the snow guns. We had to wear rubber raingear over goose-down suits to cut the wind and keep us dry. We worked in pairs for safety, and often, to break up the monotony, we'd slide from gun to gun on our rubber raingear. It was a blast. But if an air hose got clogged, water would flow out of the water gun in a gush, creating a dangerous ice patch. I hit one such patch, slid twenty feet down into a tree, and ended up in the emergency room.

Boredom can lead to inattention, which in some jobs can lead to the emergency room. In most cases boredom is not even punctuated by bursts of excitement. And not everybody is doing work that engages them completely. Sometimes the work seems meaningless or repetitive, with no sign of William Inge's truth of beauty. Was his implication correct in that if you're not trying to create beauty or discover truth, then you're susceptible to boredom?

Let's take the toughest scenario. What about the person doing the same thing over and over? Like operating a machine in a factory, doing data entry on the computer, or reroofing an entire air force base—all jobs I've had for varying lengths of time when I was traveling the country. The same task over and over, every day. Surely I had a right to be bored. But what about people who can't leave for whatever reason or have to stay for an extended period of time? What about migrant farm workers who endure a treacherous journey to sneak into America so they can pick four thousand pounds of oranges a day in order to make $40 or $50 in backbreaking twelve-hour stretches? (Think about the luck of that draw when we complain about boredom at work.)

What are the options during the times of boredom inherent in any job?

There is only one: meditate.

No, I don't mean take a break and sit cross-legged muttering a mantra under your breath. I mean turn the task into a form of meditation. How does one do that? Well, start out by doing nothing.

Relax.

Concentrate your awareness fully on the task at hand.

Really focus on the movement of the arm, the stroke of the keyboard, the hammering of the nail.

Don't take any movement or moment for granted.

Use it as an opportunity to cease thought.

Fall into the most profound internal stillness.

Sink into a pool of infinity as each moment drips by.

Until only the task remains.

Over and over, in the moment.

Until "you" disappear.

Who, then, is left to get bored? You are free of everything except the task at hand. Free from thought. Free from judgment. Free from desire. Melting with the moment. Instead of stopping what you are doing to take a break and meditate, your whole day is meditation.

Instead of the job turning into a prison, it turns into a portal.

SEX AND THE CITY DHARMA

Seeking Love vs. Expressing Love

To see everything as the beloved, that is freedom.
—RUMI

"I love to be in love," Sally said at one of my dharma conversations. "I feel so connected, so at one with the universe. Perfectly happy."

She's not alone. One of the oldest societal trances people are caught in involves our belief systems around love and romance. How many times have we said, "If only I could find the right person, my soul mate, then I would be happy"? This idea, that love resides in one specific person, is one of the deepest myths of humankind, nurtured in the thirteenth century by poetry and plays and now, in modern times, by movies. It is so ingrained that to even question it seems heretical.

But how often does a love relationship end in dashed hopes and ruined expectations? How many times have we all gone through the pain of a relationship's end, a loss that feels like you can't breathe and your heart has been hollowed out from the inside? A loss that feels worse than a death, because the other person is still out walking around but no longer in your life.

As the old joke goes: "The least a former lover can do after they break up with you is die."

So often we live in the illusion of romantic love, which is frequently merely about infatuation, lust, projection, what we think or want the other person to be, or how we want them to perceive us. When the illusion falls away in one very painful shedding, our world is often rocked down to the core, ripping the scabs off old childhood wounds such as abandonment and rejection. And if we lose the *idea* of romantic love along with the lover, well that is a whole other level of loss. It can absolutely send you to the basement of your heart, dealing with your own psychic pain.

But try telling this to anybody in the throes of a full-on love affair. Even if it is only the plate tectonics of interlocking dysfunction, your words will go unheard.

And haven't we all been there? Could we have heard any words about the "impermanence of all things"? Or the need to develop "mature love?" Or find the love within us instead of looking outside?

Ha! Not likely! We were high on the ride of romantic love!

This chapter could easily be titled "Teaching What You Most Need to Learn" or "Do as I Say and Not as I Do," such are the legions of mistakes I've made in the arena of love. I am no expert. I am fumbling around just like the rest, and when confronted with the full-on flame of falling in love, I have been burned by my own romantic illusions as much as anybody. And in different relationships, I have been the one setting the fire to other people's romantic dreams.

There is a dharmic approach to love that I have begun to discover the hard way, after traveling through the trenches of confusion, depression, jealousy, anxiety, rage, and obsession. It has been a long and rocky road, but I have managed to come to a point of compassion, for myself and others. It is possible to move beyond expectation that the other person is going to fulfill every last need or desire.

For instance, at the time of the dharma conversation with Sally a couple years ago, I knew how she felt. I had just fallen deeply in love with Carla. We had met in a yoga studio and had the classic "melt into each other's eyes" moment. We were both deeply involved in the dharma and whenever we saw each other we talked endlessly about different philosophies and teachers. Despite our obvious connection, we didn't pursue it because she was in a relationship with this very wealthy man who, she later claimed, she was never attracted to and with whom she had never "been in love."

When her relationship ended, she called me. We had a picnic and then cranked the car stereo, laughing and dancing giddily as if we were drunk. And that was all it took. Carla was beautiful and intelligent, could quote the Upanishads, and danced up a storm. Although we knew each other not at all, we were soon madly in love. After she went out east for a couple of months in order to spend some time alone, she decided to move back to Los Angeles so we could be together. I helped her make the drive back.

Although we hadn't actually spent that much time together, we had talked every night on the phone, declaring our undying love. The feelings were certainly strong and sweet; I relaxed into knowing that I had finally found somebody for whom love was its own reward. But our personalities and responses to different situations were unexplored. Our ability to communicate with each other was untested, as was the depth of the partnership that gets explored when life gets challenging.

As we left Flagstaff, Arizona, she suggested we fill the tank. I said we should just get on the road and get gas where all the truckers gassed up. We drove for about three hours, involved in our conversation and completely forgetting about the gas situation until she looked at the gauge.

"We're out of gas!" Carla exclaimed, her voice slightly panicked. We were in the middle of the desert, with absolutely nothing in sight. I looked at the gauge; it was on reserve, but I figured we had at least thirty miles or more, given the gas mileage of a diesel car.

"We'll be fine." I assured her.

"I told you we should have gotten gas in Flagstaff," she said, accusation creeping into her voice.

"You're right. I'm sorry about that. I should have listened to you."

"Yes, you should have. Now we're going to be stuck out here."

"We're still moving. We have enough gas to go another half an hour, and we'll probably run into a truck stop in time." I tried to be reassuring.

"I doubt it." She was really annoyed.

"What's happening right now?" I said. "Anything bad?"

"Yes! We're running out of gas!"

"But we haven't *run out* yet. Nothing bad is happening except in our imagination."

"I can't believe we're going to run out of gas! This is pushing all my security issues."

I just stared at her. Security issues? Where had my dharma buddy gone? It was like somebody completely different had inhabited her.

"Okay," I said. "Let's say we run out of gas. We don't know if we will, but let's say we will. What's the worst that could happen? There's plenty of traffic. We're not going to die and leave skeletons in the desert. We'll be delayed for a couple of hours. It isn't the end of the world."

It went on from there, each of us unable to communicate with the other. She started going global with it, and there was no talking her down. In spite of our spiritual connections and yearnings, we were having our first full-on fight. Finally I saw a truck pulled over by the side of a road on a long uphill incline, still in the middle of nowhere.

"Let's pull over and ask those truckers if they have any diesel they can spare." There was no answer from her, so I pulled over.

When I got out of the car and approached the truckers, they turned out to be very hip young Italians who barely spoke English.

"Do you have any diesel you can spare?" I asked one, who was wearing a bandana around his neck.

"Diesel?" he repeated in a thick accent. "No."

"No extra gasoline?" I said, wanting to be sure I was understood.

"No."

"Okay," I said, glancing at the car with my stewing girlfriend.

"Thanks." I started to walk away. The other Italian ran after me.

"There is gasoline . . . eh, how say . . . station." He pointed up the long hill.

"Nearby?" I asked. "How far?"

"One mile, over hill."

I just stared at him, thinking we were having a language difficulty.

"One mile?"

"Yes. One mile." He broke into as grin, looking at my girlfriend. "That's good, eh?"

I grinned back at him, sharing a moment. "You have no idea."

I thanked him, we shook hands, and I walked back to the car. We drove over the hill and at the bottom of it, in the middle of nowhere, was a huge truck stop.

"Did you mention gasoline?" I asked. We looked at each other and cracked up laughing.

Carla wasn't wrong to be concerned. I wasn't wrong to be unconcerned. We just had different fears, styles, and reactions. I've been all over the world and spent a year hitchhiking around the country and Mexico and felt fine dropped anywhere. Carla liked to have everything planned out. We were learning about each other. And being spiritual doesn't mean you aren't going to have fights with your spouse, just that the deeper awareness is still there during the fights.

But whatever either of us thought was going to happen, either running out of gas or making it to the next gas station, was merely imagination about a future that never came. In the end, we were simply riding in the car. Nothing "bad" or "good" was happening. We could have simply put our attention on the direct experience of that moment.

Regrettably, it was just a hint of issues to come. Two months later she abruptly left the relationship to go back to the wealthy man. Five months after that, she was back on my doorstep, proclaiming her love—how she had never stopped loving me and that she had just "gotten scared" by the intensity of her feelings for me. She realized that the $5 million house she was living in meant nothing and that she was just "running her conditioning." She was finally going to leave the aforementioned wealthy man. We tearfully fell into each other's arms, my heart overflowing with love and forgiveness.

A week later she left a message that she still needed to explore her relationship with this man and would I please not call. This happened a couple more times, with her saying she was finally ready to end that chapter of her life. But it was always the same. No matter what she was saying, he continued to give her money, pay for travel, finance housing, and pursue her relentlessly. She always went back to him and, as far as I know, is with him now.

Carla, in spite of her spiritual yearnings, her knowledge of the all the relevant texts, and her ability to talk about it endlessly, was constantly seduced by the apparent safety of the material world. She wanted to live in the $5 million house. She wanted an unlimited credit card. She wanted to be taken care of in that way and never to be challenged by "running out of gas." It was deeply ingrained in her conditioning, which included not having a father. I just didn't want to believe it.

The point of this story is not to make a case against Carla; I sincerely hope she has found her happiness. I tell this story to point out how natural and human it is to always be talking about the other person: what they did to us, who they are, how they should change. It's understandable to create a big story about ourselves as a victim.

See how easy it is to fall into? See how easy it is to make the other person wrong? We want to blame them for our unhappiness, for our lack of love. It is a trap we can all fall into, especially if we think our partner's behavior is selfish or duplicitous or lacking compassion.

This dynamic of blame is the point of my story.

It is not about the other person. Blaming him or her has nothing to do with the love in your life. What goes on with the other person is ultimately unimportant to your own experience of love. The other person has to live with his or her own behavior and the love he or she does or doesn't create by choosing one way or another. You have to live with yours.

The deeper truth is that I chose Carla as a manifestation of *my* own conditioning. She reflected my own internal landscape at the time. It's almost uncanny; don't we always choose the person who is going to give us the *exact* lesson we need to learn? And don't we choose them again and again in the form of other people if we don't learn it? This is not to excuse duplicitous or harmful behavior; those perpetrators have to live with that themselves. But if I am scrupulous about my own dharma, who is responsible for all the pain I went through after the dissolution of the relationship?

Me.

The little me with all its desires and attachments. I was attached to Carla's beauty. I was attached to her intelligence. I was attached to the intoxicated way I felt when I was with her. It didn't matter that her insides weren't lining up with her outsides and that she wasn't who she said she was or wanted to be. I was attached to the idea that I had found the perfect person with whom to spend my life.

I was very much identified with the whole grand love story that I was living, so much so that I didn't see the real person underneath it all.

WHO IS IN THE MIRROR?

Love takes no pleasure in other people's sins but delights in truth. It is always ready to excuse, to trust, to hope, and to endure whatever comes.

—CORINTHIANS 13:4–8

I know a woman who constantly finds herself in entanglements, romantic and otherwise, with alcoholics. Her father was an alcoholic, and a relationship with a dysfunctional addict feels normal to her. Her caretaking role in the family is a deep part of her that becomes mirrored in the people she chooses to be with. She is ever hopeful that the addicts will change their ways—stop drinking and being emotionally abusive—but they never do. She spends all her energy focused on trying to change their behavior, rather than changing herself so that she will no longer attract and be attracted to that type of person.

The question isn't whether you can get the other person to change; it's whether you can accept them as they are, with all of their human foibles. Or not, and move on to find real love for yourself. Either choice can be truly loving to yourself and to them.

One time during dharma conversations a woman whom I'll call Marcy talked about how her boyfriend went off and had an affair. She was furious at him. We spoke for a long time about his infidelity, and I asked her if she had ever been unfaithful. No, absolutely not. Then I asked whether she had ever helped somebody else be unfaithful?

Marcy paused. "Well, not really," she finally said.

"Not really?" I pressed her.

"Well, I got a massage recently and the massage therapist is engaged to be married. It was very intense, and I ended up having a . . . a kind of emotional response." She hesitated. "We ended up heavily making out."

Marcy had done, to a lesser degree, exactly what she was accusing her ex-boyfriend of doing.

On the level of personality, your partner is a mirror of your interior landscape. He or she is your conditioning or your unfinished healing of an old wound, revisiting you and giving you the opportunity to figure it out. Again, for this reason it is senseless to complain about the behavior of your partner. You chose that person. Deep down and in the most important way, your partner mirrors exactly where you are.

It's like that joke about a man who thinks he's a dog. When a psychiatrist asks him how long he's felt like a dog, he pauses and then says: "Since I was a puppy." All of our conditioning is like that, so ingrained, so ancient, and so invisible to ourselves that we don't even know it's there. Yet we can get glimpses of it by looking deeply at the person we've chosen to be our partner in life.

So why did Marcy choose a boyfriend who cheated on her? Who is he to her? As Marcy and I spoke, we got deeper into her background. Her father had been unfaithful to her mother, and it had caused the marriage to end. This was the example that was set for

Marcy: her father was her first partner in life, and she was conditioned from an early age to replicate her mother's role while internalizing, to a lesser degree, her father's own behavior. She was conditioned to give her heart to a similar dynamic of unfaithful behavior as well as being unfaithful herself. When she encountered her boyfriend, he was mirroring her father's behavior, and they were off and running, ripping the scabs off the original unhealed wounds.

This is all on the level of personality and psychology. But it has spiritual implications as well. While the awareness that precedes thinking never disappears, it can, as I've discussed, be obscured by perceiving life from the idea of "I" or "me," specifically of "me, myself, and my story." This is particularly true in relationships. What matters is *remembering* the awareness that observes the thoughts, sensations, and feelings as they arise, and then dropping the baggage of the past in order to be fresh and present in your relationship.

We all have an expectation that what has happened in the past is going to happen again. This brings us into a place of fear. If you were constantly stood up by a previous lover and your present lover is late, you may have a very big reaction indeed, based on your expectations. The irony is you can't have a future with a new person if the past is present because you will be in reactive hell. The way to combat this is by stepping into the moment with what is and really paying attention. A good acronym to remember when in love and reacting to the past is NTR—not this relationship.

Still, telling a person like Marcy (and we are all like Marcy) to just drop the story isn't helpful if they she doesn't know what the story is. It is in witnessing the story endlessly repeating itself, mirrored in our lover, that we learn its origins. When we learn its root cause, we are able to identify what is happening more quickly and then drop that original story as well. You drop the surface story, and then you see and observe the deeper story and conditioning and drop that.

In this way we are not merely in a form of denial. We finally see it as it comes up over and over so that eventually we can simply shrug and grin when it arises. *Ha! There's the past again.* It can actually become a bit funny after a while. *There it is again! Look at me going for that same kind of person over and over and over and over.*

And we might be aware of it and *still* make *the* same choice, signing up for yet another round. This kind of willful blindness can be quite painful. While it is important to know from the roots of our being that this conditioning is not who we are, how do we avoid repeating a choice of the same type of person over and over? Or avoid staying in a relationship that endlessly repeats the same drama?

By being as mindful as possible and seeing as clearly as possible from the first moment you meet somebody.

Again, this has nothing to do with the other person. Awareness is an "inside job."

THE END IS IN THE BEGINNING

A heart can no more be forced to love than a stomach can be forced to digest food by persuasion.

—ALFRED NOBEL

My experience with Carla was beautiful, intense, sad, and painful. It was also all there from the beginning, as the story about running out of gas shows.

The bliss of falling in love provides the sense of communion and oneness that people want more than anything. To fall into a steady, blissful state of beingness in which the small self disappears creates a feeling of grace and non—duality—it's the ultimate high, and one that many people only experience from romantic love.

But it also puts us all in a dangerous place of not seeing reality clearly. We are so thrilled at falling in love, we are so happy to be tasting some relief from our ego-centered identity that we can fall asleep at the wheel and miss all sorts of clues about our lover.

The first step to realize is that the end of a relationship is always present in the beginning. A person's true nature cannot be fully concealed, and the thing that prevents us from seeing it clearly is our own desire. We *want* the person to be what he or she is representing. We want, out of our own need for romantic love or loneliness, to believe in that part of the person with whom we fell in love. This is fine, but it can become a problem when our awareness is so telescoped that this is all that we see. And if we want the other person to make us whole, we will have unrealistic expectations that will doom any relationship from lasting beyond infatuation.

This all falls under the rubric of simple projection. When we meet somebody for the first time, what do we know about him or her? Nothing. The person may have a winning personality, but what about character and values? That's impossible to know for sure, so we tend to fill this lack of knowledge with our own projections of who we think the other person is. We see only the part of the person we *want* to see, usually out of some kind of desire. This goes on for anywhere from six months to years. Then, after enough behaviour is displayed, we start taking back our projections, one by one, like little lost children.

Oh . . . he isn't kind.

Oh . . . her spirituality really isn't the most important thing.

After a while our lover is left standing there, naked, without our projections to serve as clothing. Then we see the other person clearly, and that's when the true relationship starts or ends.

If you are awake and not seeing everything out of your own desire, you can tell everything you need to know about a person shortly after meeting him or her. Most people aren't hiding it. In fact, everybody usually screams out who they are with each small gesture.

A woman told me recently that she is going through a massive breakup; it is incredibly painful for her. When she first met him, he described himself as a former smoker. However, the moment after they made love for the first time, when they began to feel like something was developing beyond the casual, he got out of bed, went on the porch, and lit a cigarette. When she went out and asked him why he had started smoking again, he said because he was afraid of the feelings that were developing.

It doesn't get much clearer than that. When I used to direct actors in film school, I would caution them to be very precise about when they smoked. Were they nervous, covering a facial expression, hiding emotion, or self-medicating with the nicotine? What was motivating them to smoke at that particular moment? In this case, at a moment of intimacy, why was her lover *walking out of the room* in order to go back to smoking cigarettes? You could say that because the feelings of intimacy were too painful for him to bear, he'd quite literally rather die than feel them. But even if she wasn't this observant, *he told her directly*. And when the time came for him to arrange his life to spend more time with her, he ended the relationship by refusing to follow through on the plans they had made. He permanently walked out of the room.

The end was in the beginning in full color, but she didn't want to see it.

So how can we see the truth faster about a person?

Again, essentially it is not about the other person. It is about seeing beyond our own projections and desires and fantasies in order to see the real living and breathing person in front of us. It is simply about mindfulness and paying attention to reality.

Because the end is in the beginning in the form of tiny bits of behavior, we can, if we are open and awake enough, see the truth pretty quickly. It's all there. The way a person treats underlings—how the person talks to a waiter (does he or she lord it over the server?), deals with the cashier at the grocery store (is he or she dismissive?) or treats people he or she will never see again—is a good indication of how that person will be in a relationship. How is your partner with people in need? How does he or she respond to a homeless person? Is he or she patient with children or impatient? How does your partner treat friends? How is this person with past lovers?

Often these bits of behavior are quite telling, come in many different forms, and will tell you exactly what is going on.

ENDLESS REFLECTION

Immature love says: I love you because I need you. Mature love says: I need you because I love you.

—ERICH FROMM

I have a friend who was dating a woman who later turned out to be a narcissist. Joanne was blond and the life of the party, and Dave fell madly in love with her. One day early on in the relationship Dave took Joanne to a dance/meditation class we both go to on Sunday mornings.

I noticed Joanne wasn't able to surrender to the dance, to really be with the people she danced with. She looked around a lot, checking out the scene. It was her first time, and the scene is pretty interesting (men with dresses), so anybody could be forgiven for being distracted. I also theorized that maybe because she was with Dave she didn't want to get too intense with other people, which I actually admired her for.

But when I watched her dance with Dave, she was just as disconnected—bouncy and a good dancer, but not really with him. I didn't think much of it at the time until I noticed that she was returning to the same place in the room, always facing the same direction, toward a wall. I was curious. Dave came up to me, and I asked him how Joanne liked the dance.

"She seems to like it, not a deep practice, but that takes time," he said.

"She certainly likes that part of the room."

"You noticed too, eh?" he said. "Let's go check it out."

We cruised over to where Joanne was dancing. She was facing a window into an office. The office was dark and the window was black, making a perfect mirror.

Joanne was dancing with her own image like, Narcissus with his pool.

Later in the relationship, Dave began to think Joanne was concerned only with herself. She was especially concerned with how she looked and what other people thought of her. She had a need for excessive admiration. A grandiose sense of self-importance and feelings of entitlement emerged. She seemed more comfortable with maintaining her presentation rather than revealing who she really was. Dave also felt she was interpersonally exploitative, using him for his connections to Hollywood. He was beginning to have serious doubts about the relationship.

"Well, the narcissism was there from the beginning," I said. "At the dance."

"You're right," he said. "How weird."

Dave and I stared at each other. It had been there, so clearly for him to see, right at the beginning of the relationship.

"Were there any other signs?" I asked.

Dave slowly nodded. It turns out there were many that he willfully ignored.

TELL THE TRUTH FASTER

The first and last thing required of genius is the love of truth.

—GOETHE

Dave told me a story of a time, perhaps the fifth time he had gone out with Joanne. They were coming out of a gas station on a fairly busy road, near a highway. As they pulled out Dave noticed that two cars were off to the side of the road. It was obvious that a pretty big accident had just occurred. A white Toyota, with steam coming out of the radiator, had both airbags flopped open. A young couple with two small children, both crying, was standing next to the car as other cars whizzed by. The other vehicle was a beat-up pickup truck, and the owner, who was wearing a security guard's uniform, was out in front of it, trying to direct traffic around the accident.

Dave and Joanne hadn't seen each other for a while and had plans to go for a hike and a picnic. But Dave, seeing the accident, slowed the car down.

"They look like they need some help," Dave said.

Joanne looked at the scene. "They look okay," she told him. "That guy is helping them."

"I think that's his car," Dave said, pulling over behind the smashed-up Toyota.

Dave got out of the car and approached the couple, who were obviously in shock. He ascertained they weren't seriously hurt, although the woman was complaining about her neck. He figured out how to turn off the alarm that was blaring and helped the couple remove valuables from the car in case it caught fire. Dave sent Joanne across the street to get some drinks for the children. In a very real way, they calmed the couple down so they could deal with their frightened children. They stayed there almost an hour until police and towing vehicles arrived. In short, he was in the moment, seeing the whole picture, both large and subtle. The couple was profoundly grateful.

Dave said that he had had the thought right then and there that Joanne was missing something important. That something was withered inside. But he ignored the observation. When I pressed him for the exact thought, he said, "I thought, *Oh . . . it's a shame. She doesn't quite get it that these people are more important right now than our plans*."

"Why didn't you pay attention to that thought?" I asked. "Be honest."

"Because she was so beautiful and smart and . . . we had such intense sexual chemistry."

Even though he saw the truth, his own desire prevented him from acting on it, and he caused himself two years of misery.

This kind of not-seeing can also be profoundly uncomfortable for the other person. You are putting him or her in an idealized box—a kind of unreality sets in, trapping your lover into a role-playing persona. Everybody wants to be loved for who they are: the good and the bad, the beautiful and the ugly. If you only see the part of the other person that you want, then ultimately what part of the other person do you love?

Why am I going on about mindfulness in this chapter on love? Because there is no other arena in which clear seeing is obscured as much as in romantic love. Wakefulness means being *awake* and telling the truth faster about who the other person really is. It also means telling the truth about who we are in terms of our needs and conditioning. It doesn't mean denial. It doesn't mean being a Pollyanna. It means clearly seeing the whole picture, including the early signs, the small actions that serve as a metaphor for the large ones.

The extent to which we aren't awake to the truth is the extent to which we are operating out of our own conditioning and unready for mature love.

Ovid says that the first and most important principle in finding a mate is: choose wisely whom you give your heart to. And the most important part of choosing wisely is clear seeing, beyond the necessities of loneliness, sexual desire, or familial conditioning. Otherwise the best we can hope for is the kind of magnetism born of dysfunction.

SEE THE BARBED WIRE

For one human being to love another: that is perhaps the most difficult of all our tasks, the ultimate, the last test and proof, the work, for which all other work is but preparation.

—RAINER MARIA RILKE

Dave chose not to see Joanne clearly because he was in the trance of desire. He had fallen in love with a part of her and was willfully ignoring the other aspects of her that were a huge part of her personality. They went round and round for two years, but the relationship ended when Joanne abruptly left him for another man. Dave was telling himself the story that if only she would surrender to him, then he would enjoy the part of her that he loved. If he could just get past the barbed wire fence she had put up around her, then they would be happy.

But the barbed wire fence is part of the person, not a separate entity.

Dave's misperception is a common one. Haven't we all done it? Underneath all the conditioning, everybody is a beautiful heart filled with wildflowers and teeming with love. When we fall in love, we usually get to experience this heart of a person. Then, after things get real, after intimacy and truth are exchanged and expected, the walls can either come down or go up.

Because we have had the experience of the beautiful heart of the other person, we assume that the barbed wire is there to be bulldozed, tunneled under, or climbed over. We don't assume that this is a part of the person, that it is intrinsic.

The barbed wire is the conditioning the person got as a child. So if he or she learned that love equals pain, you can bet that as soon as that person experiences true love, which is uncontrollable, which is just about the wild heart, he or she will be running for the door as fast as possible, before the other shoe can drop. *I'm feeling love? I'm feeling loved? Aaaaaahhhh! Pain is coming! Run for the hills!*

This barbed wire is not just the fence; it's a part of the person. And we all have it.

So what's the alternative? No romantic love? No more incredible rides? Are we to be alert to what other people are doing all the time, waiting, watching for a chink in the armor?

Nah. What fun would that be?

We handle love much the same way we handle violence—we are awake, observant, but not projecting. Present and open, we see and accept what is.

Also know that in a relationship sometimes people are like two parallel lines, seemingly never destined to truly intersect. This can happen at any point in a union, in the beginning or after thirty years. But it only takes one-half of the couple, one person to move a quarter of a degree off their way of doing something, in order for the two lines to eventually intersect.

Or for you to go off and intersect with a different type of person.

BALANCE THE HEART WITH THE MIND

I believe that every single event in life happens in an opportunity to choose love over fear.

—OPRAH WINFREY

The heart must be followed, for to not follow it would mean to shut down on some important level. It would be a betrayal of ourselves to fear and would affect us on a physical level.

When I am in a relationship that is emotionally unhealthy or not following my heart, the first thing to collapse is my health. I usually get sick in my lungs and end up with bronchitis. Or get a stomach flu that takes forever to recover from.

Does this ever happen to you when you talk yourself into something rather than follow your true heart?

If our mind betrays our heart, our body will be in continual revolt until we are back living in harmony with our true feelings. Our very search for safety, staying in an unfulfilling job or relationship, will ironically put us in an unsafe place. Our bodies are too sensitive to be shoved against the sharp edges of our mind's lie, which ultimately is telling some story that the body just doesn't buy. So any person who has made a decision against his or her feelings, either out of desire or out of fear, will pay a somatic price. The body will go to war with itself, in mute and silent repudiation of the mind. It will simply stop working, break down, or directly say, in ways that can be quite miserable, "Listen to me."

You can see it in people's faces, a certain strain or heaviness of the flesh. And in their bodies, a chronic illness and dis-ease. This is not a bad thing; in fact, it is quite moving when you think about it.

There is no picture of Dorian Gray in some attic, growing older for our life's dishonesty; it's imprinting right now on our tender flesh. If we ignore the heart in favor of the false reality of mind, the body's internal honesty will create the suffering necessary to either bring us down or bring us into alignment. This may take a while, but it is as inevitable as water wearing through rock.

On the other hand, if the body is saying, "Ooh, that person's body is fantastic, I want that body right now," and the mind is making observations, it too should be honored. If the mind is saying a person is neither nice nor kind, ignore it at your own risk.

The apparent dualities of mind, body, and spirit are just that: apparent. Our mind, body, and emotions should be honored because they are connected; they're not separate from each other any more than we are separate from the universe. This is simply the way, and it is beautiful and balanced and perfect.

So if you meet somebody and fall in love, it's the most amazing narcotic on the planet. It should be treated as a rare gift that doesn't happen to everybody in their lifetime. You must honor it, though; as Kahlil Gibran says in *The Prophet*, "its ways may be hard." This will take courage because true romantic love will bring up all your conditioning. Every story from your childhood when you were incompletely loved, or when love was abuse or when love was abandonment, will surface in a relationship in which true love, the feeling, is involved.

LOVE IS AN ACTION

If it's not meant to be, there's nothing you can do to make it happen. If it's meant to be, there's nothing you can do to keep it from happening.

—RAMANA MAHARSHI

But we don't need to give up love the feeling and go back to the time when marriages were arranged between families as a purely practical transaction. We simply need to add love as an action. And this starts by not trying to possess, hold, distort, or manipulate the object of our love. If the bluebird of love lands in our hand, then the most important thing (after buckling your seatelt for the wild ride) is to keep our palm open. The tendency is to close the palm in order to keep from losing that love, that person who is making you feel so incredible.

This is true in all relationships and particularly true about love.

The love you are experiencing is your own true nature. Look at the other person as an oil wildcatter who has drilled through the crusts of conditioning on your surface into the inexhaustible reservoir of your heart. The love that's there is yours and can't be removed, even if the wildcatter goes away. Know that it's possible to share this level of love all the time, with everybody you meet.

Even if the "one true love" doesn't ever appear, even if you are now without a relationship and have been so for a long time, you can still be loving in every encounter and therefore have a life filled with love. You can express love all the time. And if you are lucky enough to find that person and have the full-blown experience of infatuation leading to love and compassion, don't get lost in the perceived differences. As Catherine Ingram says, the nature of love is that it gives itself away.

When love lands, notice the tendency to engage in protracted power struggles as the ego resists surrender. This can take a form of religious, familial, and societal conditioning, but is all about ego.

I am reminded of a story about a couple who met and fell deeply in love. She was Jewish, he was Catholic, both strong in their faith. When they started to think about getting married, the question of conversion came up. They fought bitterly about it. They sought counseling, they consulted friends—nothing seemed to be working. They decided they were going to end the relationship over this issue and were on their way to a counseling session to deal with the end of the relationship. On the way to their appointment, they were both killed together in a car accident.

Our time on this planet is incredibly short. Know what is and is not important.

When you keep your attention on the love itself, you are not expecting anything from your partner in order for you to stay loving.

A mature love is all about action and expression, not beliefs or mere feelings. So you watch the feet and not the lips. Many people can be "in love," but their actions are anything but loving. I'm sure O.J. Simpson "loved" Nicole, even though he had battered her for years, pushed her from a moving car, and broken down her door after they had separated.

If people have grown up with a definition of love that equals pain, then that's what they will dole out when they say "I love you." If you are in the confusion of battered wife syndrome, you may be hearing "I love you" in between the beatings, so that you can't even tell which end is up.

When in a bad relationship, keep in mind the story of the frog in the boiling water. If you put a frog in boiling water it will, of course, immediately jump out. If you put a frog in cool water and slowly heat the water to boiling, the frog won't move. It will stay put and boil alive. This rather gruesome example is also true of somebody in a bad relationship. They don't even feel the heat of it anymore, because they've gotten used to the rising temperature of the abuse, neglect, or lack of intimacy. They don't hear it or see it until it's too late.

The simple way to see clearly in a bad relationship is this: when a person's actions don't match up with his or her words, trust the actions. This is where the person is at, even if he or she would sincerely rather be somewhere else.

Seeing somebody clearly and letting that person be who he or she is—that is the essence of any loving relationship, even if it ends.

The other side of the coin, of course, is seeing yourself clearly and what it is that you want, and making sure your actions are in alignment with this vision. If you are uncertain how you feel, take a look at your own actions. Are they loving? Are they tender and gentle? Are you treating the other person the way you would want to be treated? Are you giving him or her space, knowing that intimacy requires room to breathe, room to digest one's experience of another person? These are all ways in which we can examine ourselves and the people in our lives for loving actions, which are the signs of mature love, love beyond a mere feeling.

Real love is healing. It affects and changes people in a positive way. It makes them feel special. Its gifts are spontaneous and unintentional.

One of the most powerful effects of real love is that it makes people feel connected, which is a powerful gateway into the divine.

DIVINE LOVE

Look at you, you madman,
Screaming you are thirsty
And are dying in a desert
When all around you there is nothing but water!
—KABIR

The thing that Carla and I had most strongly was a presence that shone between us when we looked in each other's eyes. We *melted* in each other's eyes. When I say "we" I mean that all personality, conditioning, everything that was piled on top of our essential consciousness, just fell away. What was left was a radiance that was palpable and powerful, if ultimately unsustainable.

This is the very thing that gives people their first taste of nonduality: the forgetfulness of the small self that happens when we stare into the eyes of our beloved. There was no me. There was no her. There just was a sense of *being*, which manifested itself as love.

What many people mistake as desire or lust or love or connectedness is actually a moment of pure forgetting in which the small self completely disappears, providing for an immaculate instant a sense of profound connection and freedom in which love, the true nature of things, is revealed. Instead of keeping your eye on your partner and what he or she is doing or not doing, you keep your eye on love itself.

Up to now I've been discussing the intersection of psychology and spirituality, or what the experts would call transpersonal psychology. But you can take it a step further. Your lover is not just an external manifestation of you, reflecting you (where you are at). But in a spiritual sense, that person *is* you. If everything we see, feel, and hear is one blast of consciousness, how is your partner, as a manifestation of this consciousness, different from you? It is not a stretch to say that the people in our lives are actually parts of our selves. Like a dream in which we are playing all the roles, our partners and friends are doing that in our waking life.

It's all simply consciousness having a conversation with itself, whether it is in the form of you and your lover or trees blowing in a breeze.

Look deeply at your partner and see yourself.

Change your perspective and become free of self entirely.

When free of the small self, then mind, the one entity creating apparent separation from the larger Self, God, or consciousness, loses its grip. In this way all fear and separation is released and a sense of merging occurs.

There's nothing to be afraid of, because *we are not separate from anything*.

This connectedness and the added connectedness of sex is what Osho calls a vertical experience. A vertical experience is one in which horizontal time disappears. During the absolute now of laughter, orgasm, or meditation, there is no future and no past. When Carta and I melted in each other's eyes, all the conditioning disappeared, leaving just a taste of infinity, with no worry about what might happen. That was the ultimate strength of our attraction, and if we had been able to keep our eye on that beautiful flame, we would have been fine.

But this experience is not limited to one person or even a person. It is available all the time. A lover is unnecessary to experience this taste of oneness, this love, same way a partner is unnecessary for dancing. The whole universe becomes your lover.

To quote Kahlil Gibran, when you look at everything as the beloved, you become the lover and the loved, the gaze and the object being gazed upon. This is ultimately what we are all searching for. But we already have access to it, this infinite love, as close as our own breath. We only have to realize it.

So even when the conditioning is intense, even when you have identified it and know it inside and out, even when you have chosen the exact person with whom to play it out, know there is no "looking for love in all the wrong places." It's all God.

What is discovered in this awareness is the difference between being alone and loneliness. Loneliness is the absence of somebody, a negative state. Aloneness can include the full and vibrant presence of oneself. In loneliness we are *seeking love*; in aloneness we are *expressing love*. Real love comes not from trying to solve our neediness by depending on another, but by developing ourselves and our inner capacity for love. We are already full and need no expectations of others to fulfill us.

And as an irreplaceable manifestation of consciousness, *you can never be alone*. You are merged with all. Feel that and never be lonely.

So romantic love, even with all of its priceless tastes of freedom, even with its laughter and forgetting (to use Milan Kundera's words), becomes just another phenomenon. It is a beautiful phenomenon, but it is not necessary to experience freedom, happiness, and love.

And it can become a form of bondage, just like any other attachment

As Gabriel García Marquez intimates in this passage from *Love in the Time of Cholera*, losing one's illusions, while it can be a loss, can actually be a way into a deeper form of love:

> They no longer felt like newlyweds, and even less like belated lovers. It was as if they had leapt over the arduous cavalry of conjugal life and gone straight to the heart of love. They were together in silence like an old married couple wary of life, beyond the pitfalls of passion, beyond the brutal mockery of hope and the phantoms of disillusion: beyond love. For they had lived together long enough to know that love was always love, anytime and anyplace, but it was more solid the closer it came to death.

Romantic love, with all its attendant highs and lows, is the burning ground. But even within its flames can be the realization that you are the fire and the object being burned.

All is fine.

THE TRANCE OF OBJECTIFICATION

Love is the answer—but while you're waiting for the answer, sex raises some pretty good questions.

—WOODY ALLEN

When you objectify another person, treating him or her as a means to an end, this realization is harder to attain, for objectification is the opposite of connection.

Cities often have the largest groups of vibrant, attractive, and single young people. This presents all sorts of challenges and opportunities in places like Chicago, New York, Boston and Los Angeles, where the sheer availability of members of the opposite sex can create desire and competition. This puts increasing pressure on fidelity within relationships as one deals with one's libido. Sex is everywhere. Coupled with an obsession with youth and the use of sex to sell everything from tires to toothpaste, it is difficult to avoid the trance of objectification.

Mixed in with love and sex is a fear of old age and death that is reflected in social mores. People are increasingly reluctant to let themselves age naturally and opt instead for plastic surgery, becoming complicit in objectifying themselves.

This pursuit of love and sex also activates our competitive natures, in men for power and in women for beauty. Massive identification with external power or beauty simply adds fuel to the "me, myself, and I" story, and eventually causes suffering.

And so an endless circle gets perpetuated, based, in part, on the biological imperative. Men objectify women, valuing beauty and youth. Women internalize these values and treat themselves to a lifetime of beauty products, makeup, plastic surgery, Botox injections, furious exercise, and finally, at the end of it all, the depression that arises when the beauty fades and their identification as "desirable" gets stripped off them like yesterday's fashions.

In turn, women objectify men for their earning capacity, valuing in ways great and small their ability to make money and provide material comfort. Men internalize these values and begin to feel that money and power are all they need to be successful, treating themselves to competition, workaholism, an endless striving for more, and, in the end, a shorter life.

I'm not saying any of this as a form of judgment or castigation. It is just a paradigm that exists and may always exist. But what is beyond this cultural and biological trance of objectification? Is there freedom within this paradigm, even as it continues unabated? Is there a way to access our own tenderness and love while still in the madness of our world and our conditioning?

And what about sex, that easy provider of a vertical experience?

COMPASSION VERSUS FEAR

We will finally blossom when the pain of staying closed outweighs the pain of opening.

—ANAÏS NIN

We can't really talk about sex, casual or otherwise, until we talk about compassion versus fear. Compassion, the highest form of love, helps one overcome the fear of deeper commitment.

It is important to have compassion for our fear of being loved, of loving, of loss, of death, of pain. The one thing we yearn for with all of our hearts is that one true love who will understand us perfectly. Yet when he or she arrives we are struck with a shocking fear. There is all of a sudden something profound to lose. It's like playing poker for quarters versus playing poker with no limits. If you're playing for small stakes—for example, serial dating or being involved with somebody you don't love—then anybody can play well. They can bluff, bet large, be free. But when you play no-limit poker and the bets can be in the thousands of dollars, well, that's a completely different story. People crack under the pressure; they sweat, play stupidly, are run out of the hand, etc.

Love is the same way. It's easy to keep your equanimity if the game is tiddlywinks and no emotions are involved. But when we are tossed in the deep end of the pool and confronted with the tempestuous waters of love and emotions and infatuation and all the traps within them, well, that's when you find out exactly where you are in your spiritual evolution.

If you are going to ride the highs and lows of romantic love, know that it is about surrender into the unknown and the unknowable essence of another human being. It is surrender into the uncontrollable, and this takes a lot of courage and compassion for yourself because it means letting go of the grip of ego. Love teaches patience, forgiveness, tenderness, and service.

One of the ways we avoid all this risk is to have casual sex.

Now, don't misunderstand me. I've had the kind of relationship that is primarily about an exchange of affection and bodily fluids with a person with whom I have sexual chemistry. Between long periods of celibacy (believe me, they seemed to last lifetimes) and long committed relationships, I've been experimenting.

But the one thing I have learned over the years is this: there is no casual sex, either for men or women. (Although this is probably not as big a shock to women as it is to men.) It is impossible to share the most intimate act possible with somebody without feelings being exchanged. Ultimately, we are all sensitive creatures. Even those of us who seem the most armored and protected are sensitive. We are so sensitive from our previous pain that we can't bear to feel any more, so we hold tight to any kind of activity that might protect us from perceived pain, not realizing this armor makes us feel even worse.

But no matter how armored a person is, eventually feelings will develop during sex. Maybe not right away, because the first couple of times one's perception of the experience hasn't caught up to the reality. But after three or four times, no matter what is being said, emotions are activated, attachments developed, and expectations formed. Even in situations that seem to be *only* about sex.

A few years ago I decided I was done messing around—I had enough sexual experience and was going to "hold the space" for my next love to arrive. But after a year of celibacy I just got tired of being alone and tired of not being touched sexually.

That's when I met Alice, a yoga teacher. Our connection was immediate and purely physical—we didn't really have much in common except a love of yoga. She had blond hair down to her waist and was immediately up for anything. I was honest with her about how this was not going to be a relationship (I just knew right away) and she said she was fine with that. She was just out of a big relationship and not into anything heavy. After a year of celibacy, I dove in like a man who had found an oasis after being lost in the desert.

This is what men are told in our society, to go for it when it arrives in a beautiful package that requires no commitment. In fact, go for it with as many people as possible. The more powerful or attractive we are, the more opportunities we have to go from person to person. We think we are getting something out of it, pulling a fast one, getting over. We think we are living it up if we sleep with a lot of partners.

But what actually happens is that we reduce our capacity for intimacy. By going wide and shallow, we become inured to the pleasures of diving deep with one person. Eventually we are burned out, overstimulated, shallow, and in need of a psychic rehabilitation just to learn how to feel something again. The very intensity and stimulation we sought has produced a kind of numbness, which can be transcended only by further sensation.

Our society in general keeps raising the volume in order to feel something, *anything*, and it's an easy pattern to fall into, whether it's sex, drugs, activity, or consumption. But ultimately it is in the lack of stimulation that greater feeling and sensitivity arise. Less really is more.

Obviously orgasm has a lot going for it, namely, it feels incredible. But one of the unmentioned aspects of orgasm is the point where the "I" disappears into the "we," providing access to a powerful non-dual state. As the French call it, *la petite morte*—"the little death," the moment of orgasm—is a powerful way in which the small self dies for a moment. It is for many people their only taste of total wakefulness, the only time they are not self-referencing, their only release from the bondage of "me." Haven't you felt it? I'm convinced that aside from all the physical delights and the expression of love, one of the main pleasures of sex is this taste of freedom. This is an underlying reason that we go for it the way we do, all the way up to addiction and beyond.

All this is part of the dance of life and is neither more nor less consciousness than anything else. But when you try to disengage sex from love, it usually ends in disaster. With Alice it was no different.

I wish I could say our hedonistic bliss lasted for a long time, at which point we parted ways, but it didn't. One night at a party I glanced over at Alice as I was talking to another woman and I caught a momentary look of pain, anger, and jealousy. When I quizzed her on it later that night, she denied feeling anything. But that was just the harbingers of deeper feelings of which she wasn't yet aware. Because we weren't right for each other beyond our sexual compatibility, it completely blew up with hard feelings. She was hoping for more.

Ultimately, we don't need judgment or morality to guide us. We know that making love is just that: making love. We know that because it is human to know it. We know it because without it, immediately after orgasm there is emptiness and a desire to make the other person disappear. Without love you wish there was a button you could push that would make them vanish without a trace!

Without love it is just a matter of biological mechanics. And the more sensitive you become, the sooner it hits you, until you get to the point where you can't make love unless it's about love. You may be able to start out that way, but if it's not happening in the heart, then the act becomes an act of self-violence, not love. It is an act of self-violence because some part of you has to numb out in order to do it.

If you're having casual sex that seems to be going fine, just watch it and be prepared for the fallout. Feelings will out. Or you might end up in a relationship with somebody with whom you have nothing in common or whom you might not even like as a person. Or you might fall in love with a person who is unable or unwilling to move beyond the original agreement that it was casual and so you end up with a broken heart.

I'm not saying don't have casual sex out of any sense of external morality; it's just that there is no such thing. After a while you don't want to live life like a hit-and-run driver leaving a series of bleeding victims by the side of the road. I have done it. We have all done it at some point or another. And we have all been the victim of it and know it doesn't feel good.

The further down the path of wakefulness you travel, the less you will be able to enter these arenas without knowing the potency of the elements with which you play. You know the pain it's going to cause before you even take the first step and so you don't act on it. Because you know that being loving means taking your long-term spiritual growth and the other person's as the most important thing in a relationship.

This is not always easy, but in the process you can discover the thrill of flinging open the doors of your heart with another human being and saying, "I'm committed, you're it!" Free-fall into the depths of your own heart and discover the axiom that sex is much more intense, rewarding, and fulfilling when you take the risk of emotional involvement.

You become willing to risk getting your heart broken, for in the end, it's a heartbreaking world. But it's not so heartbreaking that the human heart can't encompass its tragedy and beauty. Whether in the arena of love, sex, family, or the horror of brutality between warring countries, you feel it all and know that your heart will grow and expand and survive.

This is how the courage to love is cultivated. We are on the planet to give and receive love, even as our challenges grow and we deepen and ripen. The only alternative is to contract, shut down, and protect. For in all love there is the reality of loss: loss of the ideal, loss of romance, loss of physical attraction, and eventually the actual loss of the person.

But expressing love is the way in which we approach divine love, a love that isn't outside of us, isn't dependent on other people or even an external deity. Divine love is a simple acknowledgment of this reality: it is all love. Even so-called evil is a form of love, just one that is deeply obscured or perverted by pain. As Marianne Williamson said, "It's all love or a cry for help."

So we don't have to be dead people walking. We don't have to anticipate the loss by killing off a part of our heart in order not to feel pain. Instead, we expand our capacity for dealing with loss by loving more. Instead of fearing any loss outside ourselves, we expand our internal world.

LOVE BEGETS LOVE

Every moment is made glorious by the light of love.

—RUMI

Ultimately love is our truest nature. Anything keeping us from experiencing that reality is pure obscuration.

Love obviously takes many different forms: romantic, familial, interspecies (think about how much love you give your pet). But the truism I would like to discuss here is how *expressing* love *creates* love. If you are unable to actually express love (the action), as opposed to merely feeling love (the emotion), then the love you have will whither on the vine.

In romantic relationships, we have all been in both situations—where we have been the one loving more or the one loving less. Although it may not always seem so, it is better to love more. The love that *you are* is then allowed to flow through you, renewed by an infinite source. The person expressing this love is getting closer and closer to expressing who he or she really is, acknowledging the true nature of things. This person is more closely plugged into the divine.

It is like a hose that expands or contracts with use. The wider the spigot, the more water flows. In this case the spigot is your heart and the water is the love. A love that flows connects with others, expanding one's capacity to love more—the hose gets bigger. A love that doesn't flow slows down to a trickle, and one's capacity to love gets smaller and smaller until it dries up.

Or as Mother Teresa said: "If we want a love message to be heard, it has got to be sent out."

Many people think that loving less is better because it gives them more control. When we are receiving, the other person does all the "work" of love. We bask in this, relaxing. And while it is important to be able to receive love as well as give, if we don't meet the other person's need for love, our capacity for giving gradually atrophies. There must be a balance of giving and receiving in order to avoid this internal withering.

In romantic love, this goes back to making sure you choose carefully whom you give your heart to, with the main criterion being somebody with a similar capacity to give and receive love. Ultimately you can't pour a gallon of anything into a cup. Even love. It will overflow and overwhelm the person who is receiving it, and to do so is not compassionate. It will, quite frankly, make the person feel bad or inadequate, and he or she will skittle out of the relationship as soon as possible.

To use another metaphor, you can't expect a sparrow to be happy soaring with an eagle. You can't expect an eagle to be happy flitting around with a sparrow. If you have chosen somebody and are expecting this person to be something he or she is not, understand that this is painful for that person. Being compassionate means seeing others clearly and then letting them be who they truly are, without going on a crusade to make them the right person.

All this straining is like holding water in your cupped hands. No matter how much effort you put into it, no matter how tightly you press your fingers together and how perfectly you make the cup, the water will eventually leak out and find its own level. This is true even if the water *wants* to stay in the cupped hands. So have compassion for yourself and for them. Keep your hands open and let things naturally flow into what they are.

Ideally we all would choose somebody able to give and receive love as close to our own level as possible. But if we don't do this (and how many of us really do?), what then? What to do when two people are surrendering to love at a different pace? What if you are the one loving more in a relationship?

Again, this is a matter of patience and acceptance. Don't put your attention on your partner. Put your attention on the love itself. How can you be more loving and understanding and patient? Don't get caught up in what is missing in your partner, for something will always be missing—we are all imperfect. If the relationship is not dysfunctional, not based on neediness, codependency, or abuse, if there is a real feeling of love and you are able to be yourself and blossom in it, then simply stay focused on the love.

And if you are at different depths of loving, instead of berating your lover to catch up, take the surfeit of love and spread it around. Give it away freely to anybody you meet. Express your love! Don't expect one person to fulfill every last fantasy for romantic love that you have been conditioned to have. Just to be clear, I'm not talking about adultery here. I'm talking about realizing that you might find more resonance with another person's humor or quick-wittedness or love of the outdoors, so you go there to fulfill that aspect of your personality instead of carping on your partner.

Understand that the love that you are is not bounded by one person. You don't need to find one particular person to love. Why be limited to just lovers and family? Every exchange with every person is an opportunity to express love.

And to take it one step further, you don't even need a person. Be in love with the world and everything in it.

When this is happening, where is the lack?

CALL IT LIKE IT IS

Of all forms of caution, caution in love is perhaps the most fatal to true happiness.

—BERTRAND RUSSELL

There is no other area in which more different stories are told about our experiences than those told in the throes of love or its aftermath.

When we don't name things appropriately, when we tell ourselves the story of "I love him" or "I can't live without her" or "Once I have that love, that person, that relationship, then I can be happy," we are not naming the situation accurately. We can succumb to a lifetime of caution around love, or it can easily become yet another way to look externally for what is already ours.

So being careful how you frame your experiences, how you talk about love, is important. For instance, when you say you love somebody, is it the whole truth? Sure, you love their intelligence, beauty, or humor, but do you love their narcissism or fear? No? Okay, so you love *parts* of them. Which is fine—the only unconditional love is between a parent and a child. If you are being treated badly by your husband or wife, your love will gradually disappear, so it has conditions.

This may seem like semantics, but it is useful to name things correctly. For it is in naming things correctly that we begin to dissolve the story we might be telling ourselves. For instance, when a relationship ends and you feel like you're dying, beware of what stories you are telling yourself to reinforce your feelings. A typical story might be that your former partner is the only person on the planet for you, your "soul mate," your one true love who is now lost forever.

Sound familiar?

It is simply untrue. Just think about it statistically: with five billion people on the planet, there are probably thousands of potential "soul mates" out there with whom you could live a happy and fulfilling life. Arranged marriages in which the families or a matchmaker is involved in choosing appropriate matches often result in very successful marriages.

It is not a matter of finding the magical right person, but a matter of accessing our own internal readiness for commitment and love.

A relationship with another person is explored through sex, love, and compassion, with the latter being the highest form of love. This begins with having compassion for oneself. The old cliché that you're not ready to love until you have learned to love yourself is absolutely true. How can you grow to have compassion for other people's inevitable weakness and foibles unless you can have it for that part of yourself? This is another aspect of mirroring; we treat the people in our life in accordance with the way the conditioned voice in our head treats us. Are we harsh or loving, stingy or generous, punitive or forgiving? Notice how what is happening externally usually reflects that internal voice.

At no time does this voice get louder and more difficult than when a relationship ends.

WHEN IT'S OVER

If it doesn't end well, it doesn't end.
—ANONYMOUS

An English hunter once shot a dik-dik antelope. Its partner, small and graceful, stopped running and stood over its fallen mate.

"Why isn't the other one running?" asked the hunter of his guide.

"She will die anyway," said the guide. "You have to shoot it. It is their way."

With great regret, the hunter shot the other antelope. It changed the way he saw the animal world, and shortly afterward he gave up hunting for good.

All relationships end. And unless you have the good fortune to die simultaneously in each other's arms, they all end with pain and loss. We all know this, and it is part of the fear that accompanies intimacy and commitment. So when your spouse is annoying you by being quintessentially himself or herself, know that someday you might yearn for the dirty socks on the floor or the sound of snoring.

The loss of a love, whether through death or through the dissolution of a relationship, can be one of the most painful experiences we go through. It will bring up denial, anger, bargaining, depression, and finally acceptance. The loss of a love is like a death, but without the benefit of finality. It can be a long road to acceptance, even if you're the one ending the relationship. Loss of a love can also trigger one of the most difficult and persistent thought forms: obsession.

One of the many ways to keep from feeling pain is to go into obsession. Whether it is about an ex-girlfriend, a lost job, or a promotion that was awarded to someone else (and people can obsess about anything), obsession is one of the most painful aspects of mind. It creates all of the suffering after the natural course of grief.

I am choosing to talk about obsession in the chapter on love because I think this is the most universal form. We have all been there. I've been on both sides of the equation, both the obsession and obsessed. Both are equally painful.

Typically when somebody is obsessing about you, he or she is not seeing all of you. The level of projection that happens has nothing to do with who you really are. It is a way of being crowded into a box with no breathing room, no space to digest. There is little to do about the person who is obsessing about you except to have compassion for him or her and not feed the obsession with contact.

The same is true when you are the one obsessed. Your entire life can be overtaken, as every thought leads back to your obsession. It can steal your life and, as I mention in the chapter "Hell Is Other People," it can turn your life into purgatory.

I have a friend who I'll call Mike who went through a breakup with his girlfriend Pamela a few years ago. Mike was unhappy with Pamela for a lot of different reasons: she was overly emotional, not intellectual enough, and overly flirtatious, and in general kind of annoyed Mike. He was critical of her, trying to get her to change. They had a tempestuous time until Pamela finally broke it off. She started seeing somebody within a month and is still living with this other man. Mike went through hell. He realized how much he had loved Pamela, how great she was, and how much he missed her. She became, in retrospect, what she never was in the relationship: the love of his life, the perfect woman.

Haven't we all been there? Do people ever look any better than through the rosy glasses of nostalgia and retrospect? Can anything create more obsession than the idea that we somehow blew it? That if we had one more chance, then it would all be fantastic, even if it never was fantastic in the first place?

So what is the solution? First know that the obsessive thoughts are still just thoughts. You don't have to define yourself as an "obsessive freak" because they are arising. The thought *I wonder what he's doing with his new girlfriend right now* or *She just used me and moved on* arise and fall away, only to be replaced by another one and then followed by a cascade of them, seeming to drown the stillness that is your true nature.

Try not to get caught up in attempting to make the thoughts stop. This is just another form of engagement.

Rather, just witness how easy it is to slip into focusing on the other person. As soon as you try to figure out the other person—why that person left, betrayed you, lied to you, or slept with your best friend—you are going to slide down the rabbit hole of obsession. You may never figure it out. And it's not necessary to. That behavior may be simply inexplicable. Any way you look at it, it is a fixed and unchangeable part of the past.

Your freedom isn't dependent upon getting rid of these thoughts. It isn't dependent upon a lack of suffering.

As my teacher Catherine Ingram rhetorically asks: "What kind of freedom would it be if it did not include suffering?"

I want to clarify that there is a difference between pain and grief, on one hand, and suffering, on the other. Suffering is usually increased by the mind's tricks, one of which is obsession. Obsessive thoughts are trickier because there is usually a self-flagellating story about what a bad person you are to be having the thoughts. Nonsense. The only thing to do when your eyes are glued to the ground of obsession is to raise your head. Don't get down on your hands and knees and grovel in the thoughts. Notice them but pay them no mind. Starve them of your attention and they will subside.

The hard truth is that life includes pain, sadness, loss, suffering, and death. But all of this can be happening and you can be entirely free within it if you simply feel it all in its entirety. Feel it down to your bones, and it will pass!

The additional suffering occurs when you resist what is happening because you have some story, belief, expectation, or judgment about the way it should be. If you are obsessively contracted around the original cause of the pain, in this case the loss of love, you are in agony instead of acceptance. The pain is natural, but most of the suffering is extra.

Rather than resist, sit with the pain and keep love as your meditation partner. Sit with love right in the middle of all the madness. Use any challenge, in the arena of love or otherwise, as an opportunity for self-reflection and growth.

The only alternative is to feed the obsession by focusing your attention on the other person, at which point it becomes impossible to grow and learn and change.

The stories of my mind sometimes just disappear. But they do so on their own, not because I did anything. If my happiness depended upon there not being any story, then I'd be miserable. Sometimes I still realize at the end of the day that I had a low-grade nattering story going on. It was happening all day long and I *wasn't even aware of it*. This isn't denial or being unconscious; it's just that it was nipping at my heels but not biting my head off.

But other times my awareness is so blasted with drenched, direct experience—*now swimming in the lake, now hiking the mountain, now eating delicious vegetarian food, now writing these words in front of a crackling fire*—that the neurotic mind can't get a toehold.

Take a moment right now as you are reading this book and fully relax. Feel your weight in the chair, your breath moving in and out of you. Just rest fully in your beingness and you'll notice that any thoughts that come up are not dragging your eyes down into the dirt. They are eclipsed by the now consciousness waving at you in the form of a chair, a plant, a window, another human being. Your world becomes drenched in this rich way of seeing, and the thoughts simply recede.

This is the way in which now supercedes obsessive thinking. There's nothing else to do. It is the ultimate acceptance of what is regarding the objects of your love.

Finally, know that it's important to treat the end of any relationship with great care, integrity, and communication. A lot of the pain caused by the end of a relationship is because the person ending it didn't take the time to explain it gently but firmly. Don't just bolt. Don't lie. Don't become a missing person. Don't send an e-mail. That's just cowardly and doesn't honor what it was that you had in the first place.

Honestly tell the other person what is going on, and do it in person. Give the person the opportunity to work through his or her feelings. You might be surprised at the result. In being deeply honest, you might create an opportunity for the relationship that didn't before exist. But even if it doesn't work out, taking care will go a long way toward diminishing the pain of obsession in the other person and, surprisingly, in yourself.

AWAKEN TO LOVE

Love sought is good, but given unsought, is better.
—WILLIAM SHAKESPEARE

As Steve Marvel, a dharma friend of mine, says during his comedy routine as the famous sage Nisarforgottalotta: "Enlightenment is being happy whether you like it or not."

The same could be said about love. You don't need to seek it, for you are it. It will get you if you give it half a chance, because *you are the source and heart of all the love you feel*.

With this realization will come great love, which is not choice or predilection or attachment, but a power that makes all things loveworthy and lovable.

So why save your's love for that one special person? Why wait until you are partnered or with your family to give and receive love?

The idea that romantic love is necessary for happiness, that you need a partner to be complete, is a belief system that is limiting and obscures the truth, which is that you are already love and can look on the world and even total strangers as love itself.

Awaken to this fact.

And do as the Red Hot Chili Peppers exhort: "Give it away, give it away, give it away now . . ."

THE END

Death and Belief and Fairy Tales

No one here gets out alive.
—JIM MORRISON

The doorbell rang. Dead asleep, I buried my head in the pillow, willing it to cease. It didn't. I opened my eyes a slit to see Omar, my cat, looking at me crankily, as if to say, "Get the door!" I sighed and got up.

As I stumbled downstairs I could see the gray light of dawn outside my window. I opened the door a crack.

"Yeah? Who is it?" (I'm not good in the morning.)

"Jerry," came the reply, followed by his trademark deep and rattling cough.

It was Jerry. Jerry . . . Dachau thin, with skin the color of a manila envelope. Jerry's strung-out smile revealed a few rotting teeth as he leaned against the doorjamb and took a long drag off his ubiquitous cigarette.

"Arthur . . . I really need a loan. . . ."

"Jerry, it's five in the morning!"

Jerry lived in a room under the stairs and acted as the "manager" of the apartment building, a gift the owner had bestowed on him. Jerry knew me as a soft touch, as I had given him the odd $20 "loan" here and there, which he had always drunk or injected in his arm. This morning I was not feeling charitable.

"Jerry. I'm going back to bed. I'm not giving you any more money."

"Okay then, let me use your phone, I gotta call somebody." He coughed again, and it sounded like there were marbles in his lungs.

I could smell the liquor on his breath. Jerry was always a friendly presence, teetering around town on an old bicycle with what would have been a ready grin, except he was missing both front teeth. Normally we had an amiable relationship, but right now I just stared, completely out of patience, crankier than my cat.

"No, Jerry. You can't use my phone. I'm going back to bed." I shut the door.

"Thanks a lot for nothing," Jerry called through the door.

"Right," I muttered, crawling up the stairs and under the covers, falling instantly asleep.

This was my last conversation with Jerry, who died three days later. It wasn't an overdose or anything really specific. It was some kind of kidney failure from years of self-abuse.

His death hit me harder than I thought it would; I felt his absence in many ways, from the cigarette smoke trailing up the stairs to his cough to his tipsy wave as he tried to maneuver the bike with a belly full of booze. Jerry was an old-school addict, living from fix to fix.

I felt terrible about our last interaction. I had always taken a minute or two to talk to Jerry when we saw each other. I had assumed I would see him again, maybe lecture him about ringing the doorbell so early in the morning and apologize for being short with him.

But now he was gone, just like that. The opportunity to make things right was gone as well.

And in a weird way, I missed him.

LIVE WITH THE AMBIGUITY

If you were going to die soon and had only one phone call to make, who would you call and what would you say? And why are you waiting?

—STEPHEN LEVINE

Death happens every second on the planet. When we say goodbye to a friend on the phone or a family member at home or goodnight to a lover before bed, there is no guarantee that we will see them alive again. This is just a truism. And it can happen in the most ordinary circumstances. Two blocks from my apartment, at a farmer's market I attend regularly, the car of an old man careened out of control, killing ten people and injuring forty. You couldn't feel safer than at this neighborhood market, where people meet and greet and shop. And yet massive death was visited upon this peaceful scene, right out of nowhere.

You'd think the capriciousness of death would inform our lives; you'd think we'd be more generous, less acrimonious, and more loving because we know any of our lives could end at any moment.

But it doesn't really work that way. We are on the planet with full awareness of our eventual death, and yet our entire lives are about avoiding this fact. We live in noisy denial, trying our best to chase away any thoughts of death with the proverbial sex, drugs, and rock and roll. We also like to throw in a lot of work, materialism, and noise—anything that can give us some semblance of control over the uncontrollable fact that we are going to die. In fact, every previous chapter in this book is about a topic in which death, or fear of it, plays an unseen role.

But death is a positive aspect of life because it gives life meaning. Without the punctuation of death, life would be one long run-on sentence. The fact that we don't know when it's going to arrive, today, tomorrow, or in thirty years, is an invitation to live with the ambiguity of our lives. If we can learn to live with the not knowing, we become more flexible people.

Humankind has a tendency to go in the opposite direction, into the realm of belief, superstition, and control. When we do think about death at all, it is through religions that were created to give us an explanation of why we are here and what happens after we die. We look to religion to provide answers, but are asked to swallow all sorts of visions based on beliefs formed when the people creating them thought the world was flat.

Religion, in attempting to provide concrete answers, often

makes us miss the point. Once we think we know, we somehow lose sight of the fragile beauty of human life and too often get caught up in the dogma.

In the meantime, we deal out death to each other on this planet in an incredibly casual way. People will kill each other over anything—a slice of pizza, an argument over a parking spot, a $5 bill (all in the recent news). The governments of the world are busy killing their citizens to teach them that killing people is wrong, in spite of overwhelming proof that capital punishment doesn't prevent murder.

The world also has deadly squabbles about belief systems, which we cling to whether they are religious beliefs or superstitions or New Age thinking or simply views of the world based on psychological conditioning. We all have our goggles on, viewing reality based on our own subjective experience. Our time on this planet is incredibly short, yet we can't seem to remember what is important. If it weren't so tragic, it would be funny.

But belief, in all its permutations, is not necessary to having a direct experience with the mystical. In fact, it is possible to have such an experience with no beliefs in an external deity whatsoever.

NO HANDRAILS

Nothing is more dangerous than active ignorance.

—GOETHE

We are at a point in human evolution when religious belief systems no longer serve, even if they are not as blatantly dangerous as the ones held by terrorists who kill people for their religious values. The radical truth is that all religious belief needs to be put under a microscope, including the ones that underpin the mutually incompatible doctrines of Islam, Buddhism, Christianity and Judaism.

As Sam Harris writes in his book *The End of Faith*, "Our situation is this: most of the people in this world believe that the Creator of the universe has written a book. We have the misfortune of having many such books on hand, each making an exclusive claim as to its infallibility."

If all the major religions have a different book, written by a different God, each with a different immutable and infallible "truth" that is enforced by different cosmic systems of rewards and punishments, is it any wonder our world is riddled with religious violence?

As the nondual sage Nisargadatta Maharaj wrote in *I am That:*

> Having never left the house you are asking for the way home. Get rid of wrong ideas, that is all. Collecting right ideas also will take you nowhere. . . . Don't rely on your mind for liberation. It is the mind that brought you into bondage. Go beyond it altogether.

But the human mind has created incredibly byzantine and arcane visions of what they think is going on here on planet Earth. And even more about what happens when we die.

Billions of people believe in karma and past lives, heaven and hell, the second coming, the first coming, and so on. But these beliefs are a product of the mind and not necessarily, as Nisargadatta said, the means to liberation.

The real truth is that nobody knows what happens after we die.

And to those who say they do know because they had a near-death experience, or NDE—they died and came back—I would say that they didn't really die. Even those with EEGs that were flat, for EEGs measure only gross surface effects—they do not measure brain activity below the cortical surface. Being dead is like being pregnant; you either are or you are not. Gerd H. Hövelmann's thesis, "Evidence for Survival from Near-Death Experiences? A Critical Appraisal," is a definitive critical review of the NDE literature, and includes the observation that the interpretation of NDE's is "structured by and largely dependent on cultural expectations" and physiological reactions.

My purpose isn't to get into a repudiation of all the individual beliefs around death—that would take an entire book in itself. Suffice it to say that death is a great mystery, along with the reason we exist in the first place. Why is that so hard to accept?

Our consciousness of this mystery is the price of being human, and one that I am willing to live with. We can either relax into the great mystery called life or we can try to assert control over our reality by claiming to know how everything works. As Donald Rumsfeld famously once said: "There are no knowns. There are things that we know we know. There are known unknowns—that is to say, there are things that we now know we don't know, but there are also unknown unknowns. These are the things we do not know we don't know." Death belongs in the group of unknowns. We know we are going to die, but we don't know what happens after that point.

By saying that certain people will go to heaven and others will go to hell (to choose one example), religious belief attempts to authoritatively answer questions about the unknowable. Much of this belief is a halfhearted attempt at putting our minds at ease and saving us from anxious uncertainty. As Friedrich Nietzsche harshly wrote:

> If the Christian dogmas of a revengeful God, universal sinfulness, election by divine grace and the danger of eternal damnation were true, it would be a sign of weak-mindedness and lack of character not to become a priest, apostle or hermit and, in fear and trembling, to work solely on one's own salvation; it would be senseless to lose sight of one's eternal advantage for the sake of temporal comfort. If we may assume that these things are at any rate believed true, then the everyday Christian cuts a miserable figure; he is a man who really cannot count to three, and who precisely on account of his spiritual imbecility does not deserve to be punished so harshly as Christianity promises to punish him.

While you don't have to go as far as Nietzsche's condemnation of a very human foible, even seemingly harmless beliefs can be dangerous because they feed the *dynamic* of belief—they open a Pandora's box of irrationality.

When the Jim Carrey movie *Bruce Almighty* was released, the producers used the number 776-2323 as the phone number for God instead of the usual movie phone number (which begins with a 555 and leads to an information line). All over the country people with the 776-2323 phone number began to get calls from people who sincerely wanted to talk to God. These were not crank calls. They saw a number and wanted to talk to God, because He was out there somewhere, and in the dualistic nature of many people's belief, why shouldn't communicating with God be as easy as picking up the phone? They would rather look outward to a phone number in a movie than inside to themselves to find a connection with God.

This is a naive belief that's not without its humor, but other beliefs are much more chilling. I remember a circulated e-mail that said we didn't need to worry about the suicide bombers involved with September 11. As their punishment, they were going to hell and God was going to subject them to being "blown up in buildings over and over again for all of eternity." There was no need to do anything because their punishment was already complete.

Now, aside from believing in a God that is less compassionate than the average person, is this belief any less crazy than the belief of the suicide bombers that they were going to sit with Allah and seventy-two virgins as a reward for murdering innocent people? Is it ultimately any less dangerous than the belief that the best way to get to heaven is to kill as many people as possible who don't believe in your particular God?

You can paddle full steam, with wholeheartedness and intent, but you will never get to your destination if you are heading in the wrong direction. In the same way, you don't *wake up* by earnestly believing in something, whether it is the literal effect of ritual, crystals, or the afterlife. It is better to sit still with *not knowing* because when you have a harmless but irrational belief, it opens the door to other beliefs that may not be so innocent. And because belief is so individual—there are billions of individual cosmologies in the world—they will naturally clash.

CONVICTION

In religion and politics, people's beliefs and convictions are in almost every case gotten at second hand, and without examination.

MARK TWAIN

Living in the realm of belief engenders a lack of vigilance, intellectual rigor, and clarity. As Carl Sagan wrote: "Skeptical scrutiny is the means, in both science and religion, by which deep thoughts can be winnowed from deep nonsense." Beliefs in concepts such as heaven and hell, or the immutability of the written words in a text such as the Koran, have an impact on people's actions. Just ask Salman Rushdie, who lived under a *fatwa* against his life for "blaspheming" against the Koran in his book *The Satanic Verses*.

When you forgo skepticism for belief, you enter the land of superstition and irrationality. All bets are off, because people will believe anything. They will believe a healer can cure them with a snap of a finger. They will believe aliens are riding in on the trail of a comet, and kill themselves for that belief. They will believe that one race is superior to the next. They will believe that the world will end on a certain day or that a psychic can read their minds or that the world was created in six days five thousand years ago. People take religious texts and instead of reading them as metaphors read them as literally as a phone book. They are then ready to go on a crusade, armed with the "facts" of their different cosmologies.

By succumbing to blind belief, the part of the brain that involves critical thinking—crucial in discerning the lies of politicians, demagogues, charlatans, and theocrats—atrophies. By blindly believing in one arena, we are more easily manipulated and controlled in other arenas; we lose our precious skepticism, which can lead to tragedy. We are told our beliefs are so important—so much more *right* than those around us—that others will burn in hell for theirs or, worse yet, we should eliminate or kill anybody who disagrees with us.

Violence in the name of dogma has been happening since the Crusades. Just in the past ten years millions have died as the dark side of religious belief made itself heard from the Middle East (Judaism versus Islam) to India (Muslims versus Hindus) to Northern Ireland (Protestants versus Catholics). The partners in crime, the enforcers of rabid belief—namely, genocide and ethnic cleansing—are always waiting in the wings to do the dirty work. In this way an external hell on earth is created based on the religious conditioning of people who, if they were born in a different family with a different religious faith, would have an entirely different set of beliefs they were willing to die for.

DON'T KNOW

Better is one day in this life than all eternity in the next.

—TALMUD

Religious beliefs postpone true happiness for after we die, when we can experience heaven or hell or nirvana, depending upon how we live our lives—as if this world were all just a staging ground for some postmortem payoff. Religion gilds the lily of direct experience. It is a bureaucratization of spirituality, imposing a place (church, synagogue, temple) where we worship and people (priests, rabbis, mullahs) who act as go-betweens between us and the divine.

Of course, great good has come out of religion as well. People have been motivated to acts of altruism and selflessness. They have absorbed guidelines for behavior. They have been comforted in times of need. Religious organizations have helped the needy, the poor, and the sick.

I'm not denying that this is a complicated issue. What would it be like without the Ten Commandments to keep people from behaving badly? How would people feel without a belief in a supreme being watching their every move? What would happen without religion to hold out the metaphysical carrot and stick to prevent a total breakdown in order?

Is humankind ready for that?

I honestly don't know.

But I find myself asking the question: can it be worse than it is right now?

WAKING UP

For life in the present there is no death. Death is not an event in life. It is not a fact in the world.

—LUDWIG WITTGENSTEIN

Wakefulness can be achieved without belief systems. As people wake up from their own conditioning, fear, and beliefs, they will encounter their true nature, which is loving and compassionate. It is unnecessary to add more beliefs to encounter this nature; in fact, belief systems actually seem to obscure it.

Part of the reason religion doesn't work, doesn't seem to stick in terms of behavior, is that it's not a part of people's direct experiences. The falseness of the explanation, what we are told to believe by those in charge, dilutes whatever truth may be there. If the same authority tells you the earth was created from scratch in six days five thousand years ago *and* that love is the answer, a cognitive dissonance arises. Religion shoots itself in the foot, clinging to myths that make no sense. Not to mention anachronisms such as prohibitions against masturbation or premarital sex, decrees that most people practicing the actual religions ignore.

Whether these religious beliefs reassure or whether they create feelings of identification that historically have led to separation, competition, and war, they are simply unnecessary in order to have a direct experience of God or reality or consciousness. Though I use the word *God,* in no way do I mean an external God watching and judging everything I do. Rather, I mean God as a consciousness or energy that informs everything on the planet.

The dharma asks you to awaken to your direct experience; nothing needs to be taken on faith.

As this book has tried to demonstrate, right now is a life raft on the choppy ocean of thoughts, with its constant demand for more stimulation, its story or belief system or conditioned conflict.

When the mind is finally ignored or even silenced, the wonder of a blade of grass can become indescribable. No belief or any other interpretation of mind is necessary to experience this. When we are fully awake and present in every moment, the world gets as vivid and magical as it does on an acid trip. When the blinders of religious belief, conditioning, and superstition are removed, you have a direct and raw experience of the world, which is inherently wondrous and mystical and filled with God.

For what could be more mystical than a bumblebee landing on a flower? Or a baby's smile? Or tree leaves waving in the breeze? What is more profound than the simple recognition of the connectedness of life in this moment? Why resort to magic or belief systems that are being sold by people with questionable agendas?

Instead, live with the mystery of not knowing. That is truly mystical.

Man's belief systems are akin to doodling on the divine. When Christians ask me what is my idea of heaven or hell, I say, "This planet." We live in heaven and yet feel the need to create another imaginary heaven that we may go to when we die. This relieves us of the responsibility of caring for this precious planet as if it already was heaven.

It is clear to anybody with their eyes open that this planet is heaven. Anybody who has dived in the coral reefs has experienced heaven, floating weightlessly amid the beauty of colorful fish and unexpected creatures. Yet if we continue our current devastation of this beautiful planet, the coral reefs will disappear within thirty years.

Anybody taking a walk in a forest or park after a fresh rain can experience heaven. Yet we think nothing of cutting down trees that are eight hundred years old. In the American Northwest alone, the sequoias, which used to run for five hundred square miles, now exist in an area of only three square miles.

Our children will inherit a world much bleaker than the one we were gifted with. We are denuding, poisoning, drilling, stabbing, burning, and acidifying the heaven we have, hoping for the heaven we might get when we die.

And so we create hell on earth.

This is not to say that all rituals are bad. Just be careful what your intent is. If you enjoy the ritual, then enjoy it for its own sake. Enjoy it because it's relaxing or because it creates closeness with family or because you like making the gesture or reciting the prayer. But don't expect anything from it. Don't get into a relationship with the ritual akin, as the Buddha said, to a beggar begging for money while sitting on a pot of gold. You already have everything you need to wake up.

The real truth is that we have lost sight of this heavenly world, exchanging it for stories about reincarnation, about heaven after death—bedtime stories that were meant to comfort short-lived humans centuries ago. Our technology is in the twenty-first century and our minds, on a good day, are in the sixteenth century. It makes for a deadly combination.

I can hear people saying, "Who is he to say that he has the corner on reality?" Sometimes I am challenged in my dharma conversations by people who say the absence of a belief system is a belief in itself. And they are right. When you don't believe in something, that is still a form of belief, even if it is a nonbelief. But the absence of something is not exactly the same as that thing. The neutral absence of a belief is more liberating than the baggage of a belief itself. To not believe in the power of animal sacrifice, the existence of heaven and hell, or reincarnation creates more freedom and responsibility than adherence to those beliefs.

So while nonbelief may be a belief, it is freer than belief because it enables you to walk the planet with less baggage.

In this way you are more connected to yourself, your emotions, and the people around you because you are not in the identification of *me* and *my* beliefs. You just *are*.

In this way you are less prone to spiritual violence, either perpetrating it or receiving it.

THE EMPEROR IS BUCK NAKED

Everybody wants to go to heaven, but nobody wants to die.
—DUNGEON FAMILY

Ironically, the need to pay attention to one's emotions is particularly keen in spiritual circles, the very place where detachment or faith, depending on the religion, is prized. Many are drawn to a spiritual path out of deep emotional or physical pain and deprivation, giving them a heightened sensitivity and a desire to look for answers that will ease their suffering.

This is particularly true of spiritual teachers, who are often on a heavy ego or power trip. They can involve you in some messy, unresolved psychological dynamic, whether they are a Catholic priest molesting young boys, the local yoga teacher womanizing his students, or a terrorist recruiting for his religious cause. These days, as ever, religion is just as good a source of violence and the perversion of spirituality as the secular world.

As P. T. Barnum used to say, "There's a sucker born every minute," and nowhere is this truer than when a person is selling salvation to somebody who really needs to believe. Modern-day Tartuffes abound, peddling their beliefs with their eye on the money.

The entire self-help movement is based on two principles: you are not fine the way you are, and you can do something to fix or control it. But there is no need to control everything to be free. In fact, the opposite is true: the fewer belief systems, the more freedom; the less control, the more freedom. So you might want to take a long look at somebody trying to make you believe that you're not fine the way you are. Such a person is operating on the level of personality, which can be constantly fiddled with. On the level of awareness, nothing is wrong, nothing needs to be changed.

Your true nature, your birthright, as H. W. L. Poonja said, as experienced right now in this moment without belief, is just fine.

Often, when the mind wants to believe, then the emotions are ignored. But it is the emotions, sometimes the barest flitter in the corner of your awareness, that will lead to the deeper truth of a situation, whether it is to warn you of a man who will kill you or help you discover that often the people selling salvation are just as broken, and unconscious as yourself.

Nowhere is this truer than when death gets doled out in the name of spirituality.

JUDGEMENT VERSUS DISCERNMENT

In Deborah Layton's book, *Seductive Poison: A Jonestown Survivor's Story of Life and Death in the People's Temple*, she tells her harrowing story of indoctrination and subsequent escape from the cult shortly before the nine hundred members were convinced/coerced into drinking cyanide-laced Kool-Aid. Jim Jones, the charismatic charlatan, started out by selling spirituality to needy, idealistic people who wanted to make a difference in the world. Because he initially did some good deeds and made political friends by supporting their campaigns, he was given a lot of attention and accolades from the political and social establishment, which then reinforced his status and made it easier to recruit more devotees.

It wasn't long before cult tactics were used. The sleep deprivation, the "us or them" mentality, the paranoid "if anybody leaves, they're fair game" doctrine of hassling ex-members, the long and humiliating harangues of anybody who didn't toe the line—they were all established fairly quickly. If the members of the church had been able to listen with their hearts rather than believing with their minds, they would probably have identified many ways, both large and small, that the reality being painted was not loving.

When you are in any situation, whether it be with your local yoga teacher or a massive gathering with a spiritual leader, pay close attention to how you feel. Do not shove any feelings in a box while trying to be spiritual. When confronted with a person who is working some hidden agenda, you will know it by the slightly queasy feeling in your stomach. Not quite nausea, its most common symptom is anxiety, perhaps just on the edge of your awareness. When that is present, it is the alarm telling you that there is some dissonance that your mind is not picking up or that your mind is rationalizing.

And equally as important, if your heart has run away from you and is caught up in emotion, projection, and ecstasy, pay attention to your mind. The heart can be easily deluded, so both mind and heart must be honored equally. They must work in balance to discern whether the emperor has no clothes.

In any organization, one of the first things you will be accused of if you question groupthink is that you are too judgmental. Any skepticism (disbelief of religious doctrine) will be incorrectly labeled as cynicism (sneering belief in the worst of people). You will be accused of not getting it or not being sensitive or ready for the truth. This is all a way to get you to abandon your reason and logic while accepting anything because it comes wrapped in the veneer of spirituality. You can lose your money, your mental health, and even your life.

But there is a difference between *discernment*, which is perceiving clearly with the senses in the moment, and *judgment*, which is applying preordained ideas and values to a situation. Discernment helps you determine what is true or not. Judgment, separates the world into "us" and "them," "good" and "bad." But it is possible to discern that something is untrue, without necessarily judging it.

But to do so requires being tuned in rather than tuned out.

THE DANGER OF SNAKE OIL

There are so many fraudulent teachers because there are so many seekers who don't want the awesome responsibility of their own wakefulness. People look around for somebody, anybody, to take it off their hands. And there are those in the world, healers, channelers, shamans, psychics, teachers, and sages, who will gladly step up and, with the razzle-dazzle of some slight of hand, sell you a bunch of belief systems for a pretty penny. It *is* very appealing to be instantly "healed" by somebody who snaps their fingers at you or does an extraction or employs any number of bogus techniques. In our "pop a pill and feel better" culture, easy solutions are very seductive.

To be truly free, we must evolve out of the paternalistic need to have an authority figure take care of us, either emotionally or spiritually. This means forgoing the dependency trap and finding the path ourselves.

One of the most important signs that a person is not a spiritual teacher is if he or she is in any way peddling the idea that your wakefulness depends upon him or her. It is not true. A real spiritual teacher will constantly reflect it back to you. Just you. Not you in relationship with them, or some external (literal or symbolic) God. A real spiritual teacher will gently but persistently say, "This beingness is your true nature." Echoes of this are found in the Christian tradition: "The kingdom of God is within you."

If a teacher is not saying this, then he or she is selling snake oil and is not a teacher. If you don't want to take responsibility for your spiritual life, the charlatans will spring up to take your money and assuage your pain with a Band-Aid of belief. But because they breed dependency and because it's based on a lie, what they are doing is ultimately harmful because it infantilizes the disciples. It takes advantage of their neediness, feeding like a vulture on their desperation as they swallow belief after belief, until they can no longer discern the reality because the muscle of discernment is so atrophied that it doesn't work.

You can compare this phenomenon to a new pilot who enters his first fog bank. He can't see anything and has to rely on his instruments. But he doesn't trust his instruments, and like a person who adds one belief after another, the pilot keeps making adjustments—a little more and a little more, until when he flies out of the fog, he is completely upside down. The pilot can sometimes right himself; otherwise he crashes. The spiritual equivalent of this is getting so lost that you cannot discern reality anymore.

The people perpetrating this dependency, whether deluding themselves because they believe it or cynically lying, are sorely misguided.

TOSS YOUR CRYSTAL

The world needs more rationality and more heart, not less of both.

I have a friend who used to have a lot of New Age "you create your own reality" beliefs passed on through a channeler. No matter how many times I would joke with her, saying, "Schizophrenics create their own reality," she used to get angry at the idea that she might give up her belief systems. And yet she wasn't happy; there was a kind of desperation and attachment to her beliefs that didn't cultivate freedom. We would have long discussions about it until I realized that she *needed* those beliefs. They were her way of exerting control over an inherently uncontrollable universe. I, in turn, gave up on trying to control her beliefs. I was powerless to do so. She would change when she was ready.

Science, although merely an understanding of the universe as we comprehend it in this moment, is getting better and better at explaining so-called miracles. Science can actually, as Carl Sagan said, light a candle in the darkness. Science is simply the application of the scientific method to any claim. Can outrageous claims of pseudoscience or antiscience be replicated in a controlled environment? If they can't, then exercise your skepticism.

For instance, I have met several New Age believers who swear they have out-of-body experiences and guided journeys. They call these miracles and take them as a sign that they are special or in contact with supernatural beings or aliens. But scientists have recently found a less celestial source of these journeys: the right angular gyrus of the brain. The new thinking is the result of the case of a woman, age forty-three, who was undergoing treatment for epilepsy originating in her brain's right hemisphere. A team of researchers at the university hospitals of Geneva and Lausanne implanted electrodes in the suspect region to record seizures. They then used a weak electrical current to map the brain. The doctors—and the patient—then got a surprise.

When the current was applied to a particular spot, the woman experienced a sense of lightness, as if she were floating above herself. More remarkably, she seemed to see part of her body as if she were viewing it from the ceiling. When the doctors asked her to move her limbs, she experienced other illusions: one arm seemed shorter than the other; her legs seemed to fly toward her face; if she closed her eyes, her upper body felt as if it were flying toward her legs.

The doctors believe her sensations were caused by a failure of the brain to integrate tactile sensations and balance. Transient out-of-body experiences can occur in anyone, but a glance around is usually all it takes to ground the brain in reality again.

The right angular gyrus, however, sits quite near the vestibular cortex, the seat of balance. Jolting the Swiss patient's gyrus apparently threw the delicate feedback system out of sync, creating a state of neural chaos that was exacerbated when she moved her eyes and body.

So, far from being a magical event, this state of being is a result of physiological stimulation or abnormality. This same area is being looked at as the cause for near-death experiences.

Humankind, in its search for something beyond or something to explain the great mystery of the world or simply to feel special, asks such questions as "Why am I here?" and "What is my purpose?" and "What happens after we die?" We want to *know*, because not knowing can be painful and even terrifying. And so our answers come in the form of constantly grasping at metaphysical straws. At the core of this is a kind of spiritual danger, one that prevents you from actual happiness in the now.

There is nothing to learn. And nothing to unlearn. Simply drop ideas such as "Follow me and I will show you the way." Or "If you change this about yourself or believe in this or become more pious, then you will be happy."

It is not true.

Release the superstition and the magical thinking.

Relax into the simplicity of the moment.

Sit comfortably and shut your eyes.

In silence.

Breathe.

Witness the mind. Don't go for the ride.

You already have everything you need for your freedom and happiness.

Just as you already have everything you need to be human.

WHAT TO DO

> Self-surrender is the surrender of all self-concern. It cannot be done, it happens when you realize your true nature. . . . The first steps in self-acceptance are not at all pleasant, for what one sees is not a happy sight. One needs all the courage to go further. What helps is silence. Look at yourself in total silence, do not describe yourself.
>
> —NISARGADATTA MAHARAJ

So how does one avoid getting in a battle with intractable belief systems around the world? Simply avoid the power struggle of arguing with people about their beliefs, which is like stepping in front of an on coming bus. Don't try to deprogram them—they won't like it and will get immediately defensive.

The world teeters on the edge of meltdown as people cling to their beliefs with more and more fervency. Don't become a proselytizer or a missionary in your own right, which, aside from being simply exhausting, can be destructive in unintended ways.

When you are talking to people about their beliefs, it is best to simply say, "That has not been my experience." To try to replace one set of belief systems with another, or even with none, is pure hubris. It is as if I were to drop this book down your chimney without your permission, like the Christian missionaries who drop transistor radios with only one Station on indigenous tribes around the world. Don't be a missionary in your daily life! It destroys your freedom and assaults the complicated psychological needs of the believer. You will make an enemy, not a friend.

Toni Morrison said: "The function of freedom is to free someone else . . . and if you are no longer wracked or in bondage to a person or a way of life, tell your story." It is one thing to tell your story and direct experience and another to take on other people's bondage and try to change it by proselytizing. Stay in your own freedom when encountering all beliefs, whether that of the born-again Christian saying you are damned for your lack of faith or the New Ager who insists on the latest and amazing astrologer/healer that she's found.

Stay loose; don't get caught in the stickiness.

Besides, in terms of seeing people's desperate attachments, haven't we all been there? Haven't we all had them at one point or another?

As Albert Einstein said: "A man should look for what is, and not what he thinks should be." What we think should be is usually just an attempt to heal some old wound. As I've said before, it is like cleaning your eyeglasses with a greasy rag, a never-ending process of personality wiping personality that simply results in further obscurations.

See and accept what is and thus avoid the suffering of trying to change another person, place, or experience into something it is not.

That is freedom.

The same is true in a global sense. While I feel a world without strong belief systems would make for a much freer populace much more able to live without violence and war, others feel the world would be denuded without the religious beliefs that are the backbone of various cultures. *Vive la différence.*

DEATH

I'm not afraid to die, I just don't want to be there when it happens.
—WOODY ALLEN

My cat just walked into my office and meowed. He'd been outside all morning in the small garden separating my apartment from the street.

"Yeah, yeah, Omar," I said to him. "What else is new?"

I glanced down as Omar meowed again and a tiny little bird dropped out of his mouth. It was as surprising as a magic trick. The bird fluttered around but couldn't really fly. Omar immediately pounced, and I grabbed him just in time.

I took Omar out and locked him in the bedroom. Then I chased the tiny bird around the office and finally captured it. I could feel the bird's heart vibrating against my palm. I had no idea what to do, as I'd never been able to keep a baby bird alive. I took it out in the garden and placed it underneath the tree where I thought its nest was.

As I sat there watching, I was filled with mixed feelings. I was afraid and filled with concern for the bird. I didn't want the bird to die a horrible death. I wanted to save it but was powerless. I decided the best thing I could do was leave it and hope its mother found it.

A half hour later, when I checked, it was gone.

I have no idea what happened to the bird. I could tell myself a nice story, a happy ending, but quite simply, I'm not sure.

In so many ways this encompasses our relationship with death. We don't want to die, we fear death, we avoid it, we want to stop it and save ourselves and other people from it. But finally we must just accept death as the event that gives life meaning. It is our destiny, the final adventure. When we are not caught up in imagination or stories, it can ultimately be looked at with more curiosity than fear.

What is going to happen? We don't know. Ain't it a hoot?

Death, boiled down to its essence, can simply make us glad for the incredible privilege of life.

Miguel de Unamuno y Jugo wrote, "Science says: 'We must live,' and seeks the means of prolonging, increasing, facilitating and amplifying life, of making it tolerable and acceptable. Wisdom says: 'We must die,' and seeks how to make us die well."

What happens as we live our life, how attached we are, how much baggage we cling to, what our beliefs are—all of these things will have an effect on how we die. This is one of the side effects of living a spiritual life versus living a strictly material life. Everything that happens is here for our learning. Everything. Including death.

Consciousness, of which we are an intrinsic part, is almost devilish in its ability to serve up exactly the right lesson to dissolve the ego at exactly the right time, whether that lesson is a person or an experience. This is true no matter what we may think about it at the time or how bad it may seem. In fact, we may think it's the worst thing in the world as we go through it, and then afterward realize that life was pushing us in a direction we already needed to go, teaching us a spiritual truth we needed to learn. The relationship that broke our heart has taught us compassion. The lost job has loosened our identification with what we do. The failure has helped dissolve our ego.

Death is no different.

Embrace it all; see it all with a sense of humor.

For how we live will have an impact on how we die.

So how do we die well?

We start by living well.

We start by living moment by moment . . .
Aware that any moment could be our last.
Awake, we don't believe any stories about death.
Awake, we don't believe any stories about life.
So we simply witness any fear that arises in the moment of death.
The fear is a part of our biological program.
We greet death the way we greet life, breath by breath.
Awake and in the moment.
Just like life.
Until there is no more breath.
We don't know what comes next.
We don't hang on to what has passed.
Just like life.
Until the experience of life ends.
Suddenly.
Unexpectedly.
Just like this book.
Right now.

ABOUT THE AUTHOR

Arthur Jeon received his B.A. in humanities from Harvard University in 1985. After graduation he worked for a management consulting firm that specialized in applying systems theory to Fortune 500 companies managing change. Seeking more creative work, he eventually became the marketing director of an ad agency in Boston, Massachusetts. This work reignited his passion in writing and led him back to school to get his MFA at USC film school. For the past ten years he has been living in Los Angeles and working in the film industry as a screenwriter.

As a longtime yoga practitioner (he now teaches yoga in Los Angeles), Arthur began his journey as a spiritual seeker in the early nineties. Gradually he became steeped in the tradition of the nondual teachings of Advaita Vedanta, the mystical Vedic teachings of India that propose simply a recognition of indwelling presence as our true nature. He began to hold dharma conversations in 2001. It was out of these that the idea for the book *City Dharma* was born.

Visit the book's website at *www.citydharma.org* to check on Arthur's speaking and retreat schedule.